WILLIAM MAKEPEACE THACKERAY

The Paris Sketch Book (1840)
'The History of the Next French Revolution' (1844)
Various essays in *Punch* (1849)

HENRY JAMES

The American (1877)

Four Meetings (1878)

Madame de Mauves (1879)

A Bundle of Letters (1880)

Portraits of Places (1883)

The Siege of London (1883)

The Reverberator (1888)

The Tragic Muse (1890)

Parisian Sketches (1898)

The Ambassadors (1903)

A Small Boy and Others (1913)

Notes on Novelists (1914)

Within the Rim (1918)

WALTER PATER

Renaissance Studies (1873)
Moore: *A Modern Lover* (1883)
Imaginary Portraits (1887)
Appreciations (1889)
Gaston de Latour (1889)
Essays from the "Guardian" (1890)

THE NINETIES

Moore: *Confessions of a Young Man* (1888)
du Maurier: *Trilby* (1894)
Pater: *Miscellaneous Studies* (1895)
The Yellow Book (1895)
The Savoy (1896)
Crackanthorpe: *Vignettes* (1896)
Harland: *Comedies and Errors* (1898)
Symons: *Poems* (1898)
Symons: *Studies in Seven Arts* (1906)
Moore: *Memoirs of my dead life* (1906)
Moore: *Ave* (1911)
Moore: *Salve* (1912)
Moore: *Vale* (1914)
Symons: *   *Paris* (1918)

*   *(1921)

*   *y Street* (1924)

*   *(1921)

THE VIEW OF FRANCE
From Arnold to Bloomsbury

THE VIEW
OF FRANCE

From Arnold to Bloomsbury

CHRISTOPHE CAMPOS

LONDON
OXFORD UNIVERSITY PRESS
NEW YORK   TORONTO
1965

Oxford University Press, Amen House, London E.C.4

GLASGOW NEW YORK TORONTO MELBOURNE WELLINGTON
BOMBAY CALCUTTA MADRAS KARACHI LAHORE DACCA
CAPE TOWN SALISBURY NAIROBI IBADAN ACCRA
KUALA LUMPUR HONG KONG

*Printed in Great Britain by
The Camelot Press Ltd., London and Southampton*

CONTENTS

ILLUSTRATIONS

The illustrations on pages 27, 31, 51, 52, 75, and 169 are reproduced
by kind permission of *Punch*.

· 1 ·

A WAXEN IMAGE

Discoveries respecting the application of steam to
the purposes of travelling have facilitated the intercourse between different countries, and thus aided
in destroying that ignorant contempt which one
nation is apt to feel for another. Thus, for instance,
the miserable and impudent falsehoods which a
large class of English writers formerly directed
against the morals and private character of the
French, and, to their shame be it said, even against
the chastity of French women, tended not a little
to embitter the angry feelings then existing
between the two first countries of Europe; irritating
the English against French vices, irritating the French
against English calumnies. In the same way, there
was a time when every honest Englishman firmly
believed that he could beat ten Frenchmen; a class of
beings whom he held in sovereign contempt, as a
lean and stunted race, who drank claret instead of
brandy, who lived entirely off frogs.

HENRY BUCKLE (1857)

IN Western Europe and a few other relatively civilized areas
of the earth, the idea of 'nationality' is fast becoming a paradox. The countries that used it to obtain their independence
in the wake of the American and French revolutions are the first
to realize that it is in a state of transition. Most people pay lip-
service to international ideals. And yet patriotism survives,
fostered mainly by newspapermen or the followers of professional
sport at moments of national crisis. The Janus politician combines
in the same platform the interest of 'humanity' or the United
Nations, and a feudal conception of local honour. An Englishman
may have a German *au pair* girl in his house, and yet if pressed

reveal a deep-set hatred for all the Germans he does not know personally. We seem to have acquired enough critical sense to realize that most patriotic claims are partial and political, yet we are vaguely and uneasily conscious that there may still be some truth in the distinctions between nations with which the nineteenth century imbued us, and that surge up fiercely when we least expect them. The matter is not without importance: if there should really be such things as national characteristics, if the English should be by nature moral, and the French frivolous, how can the two ever expect to agree on any principle overriding their private interests, let alone take part in a form of European or World government?

In trying to define national features, we are of course more lucid where other countries are concerned. We think ourselves quite natural; it is the others who have peculiar traits. This little illusion is confirmed on a quite serious level: the foreign historian often sees more clearly than the native one. Thus the French can still read Carlyle on the French Revolution with some profit, and they have provided England with one of the most lucid observers of her nineteenth-century social history in Halévy. Tocqueville, narrow and partial when he wrote on French internal politics, helped to reveal American democracy to itself, and the same might have been said a century later of André Siegfried. The judgements of others on our nation are thus liable to enrich us. What, after all, is a country but what its neighbours think of it? An individual only exists fully in the light of someone else's opinion: in the same way, if we disregard the constant and universal claims of political integrity and military superiority, a nation can only be properly defined if some attention is given to the opinions of the foreigners who love or hate it. Though he may be highly critical about what he discovers, a Frenchman can learn a great deal about France by examining the ideas of the English. It was with this in mind that I undertook this study.

Yet even in the judgements of foreigners we can find surprisingly little clear thinking. During my youth, when I lived alternately in England and France, I had to answer many exasperating questions. In France I was asked, 'How do the English behave?', and in England, 'What are the French like?' as if differences of this sort could be expressed in a few sentences. I was then expected to approve or disapprove of ridiculous statements such as 'the French are talkative' or 'the English are hypocrites'. The old story about the French sailor who, having spent half an hour on shore at Dover and met two women with their hair dyed red, told everyone on his return that all Englishwomen had red hair, seemed sadly to the point. Its moral could be applied to many books. A few years ago it was still fashionable to write solemn and detailed comparisons between people of various countries. These studies, however genuinely wise their authors may have been, are based on pseudo-psychology and their conclusions are frankly woolly. André Siegfried and Salvador de Madariaga were undoubtedly amongst the most learned men of their time: yet how can we accept Siegfried's theory (in *The Character of Peoples*) that France is the land of *individuals*, or Madariaga's idea (in *Englishmen, Frenchmen, Spaniards*) that it is the home of *thought*? Who has not heard and seen for himself that a certain category of Englishmen, too, pride themselves on their individualism (known as eccentricity) and that the French are also subject to thoughtless passions? Surely, no quality is purely French and France cannot be characterized by any single abstraction. Such ideas, once detached from the web of the book that bore them, are easily dismissed.

Others, however, vague and latent in society, retain a threadbare currency because no one examines them with care. Prudent people use them in unguarded moments because they assimilated them in their youth. Incensed by an unfortunate speech made in Paris criticizing English foreign policy, many an Englishman who drives through France every summer and enjoys it will suddenly find himself condemning the frog-eaters and their unchaste women in terms borrowed as far back as Dickens and Carlyle. Henry Buckle, who in 1857 thought all this was coming to an end, would be sadly disappointed. It is this set of latent ideas that I intend to investigate. Madariaga or Siegfried, who merely applied organized thought to these traditional impressions, will then need no further commentary.

At this point it might well be said in return that the popular image of France, though providing endless material for music-hall numbers, is not taken very seriously. Two great wars have tossed peoples about all over Europe and should have begun to produce more open minds. But this is unfortunately not the case. We shall see that living in French trenches during the First World War did not teach the English much about their allies that they did not already suspect; it merely gave them an opportunity of visiting 'Gay Paree' to confirm what they had read about it. International tourism does not help much either, since it operates in a circuit of its own, removed from direct contacts with the people. Englishmen visiting France in the summer are mainly concerned with the weather, the schedule for the return journey, the prices of accommodation, and the immoral tactics of German and Belgian drivers; the French exist only as a kind of picturesque background to the holiday resorts. Most tourists are therefore content to refer to the French in terms of suspicions they already had about them; in other words, to use what has been handed down in the English tradition.

These latent ideas that make up an image of France somewhere in the British national subconscious have a definite origin; the very fact that they consist of catch-words and set phrases such as 'French morals' or 'gallic wit' suggests that this origin is connected with literature. Indeed, the average Englishman's view of France is conditioned by the ideas of literary men of two or three generations ago, and to judge it thoroughly it is necessary to return to these literary sources. Few people, when they remark that they found the French middle classes difficult to approach, realize that they are quoting directly from Arnold Bennett. They are still influenced by him if they say that the middle classes were quite hospitable after all, because had it not been for Bennett's personality and his very peculiar approach to France this rather silly idea would never have been expressed in the first place. Some of these latent ideas may be quite correct, others out-dated, others wildly mistaken. I hope to be able to judge them with reference both to France itself and to the circumstances of their birth.

I can foresee other objectors claiming that information about France is gleaned, not from English authors, but from French literature itself. There are always those who take pride in being in touch with the latest French books. Our century as a whole believes it has attained an international culture of sorts. Critics such as Huxley (in *Critical Essays*), R.-M. Albérès (in *L'aventure intellectuelle du XXᵉ siècle*) or Colin Wilson (in *The Outsider*) may hint at a breakdown of cultural frontiers by showing that literary and sometimes philosophical movements have become linked. They may be convincing when they take care to choose countries that are closely connected economically or politically in any case. But in fact literature, now as at the end of the last century, is a painfully national affair. In the very few cases where language, the epitome of nationalism, does not restrict the reading public unduly, cultural interests and levels of learning differ sufficiently in various countries to prevent books from circulating. Since the intellectual life of Britain and the United States began to drift apart, few works have been popular here and there at the same time: Faulkner, highly rated in America and idolized in France because he appeals to current trends in the French novel, is not so well known in England. The English, usually enthusiastic over French literary movements after they have passed, have only recently firmly adopted Camus, Sartre, and the existentialists, to whom the French have given little thought during the last ten years. Translations may become part of the literary atmosphere of a period: between 1880 and 1910 Balzac and Flaubert, Zola and Maupassant, Tolstoy and Turgenev, were widely read in London; today Mallarmé, T. S. Eliot, Proust, Thomas Mann are European figures. But authors such as these are rarely eloquent about their home country: they are usually popular because of the very universality of their appeal, or because they are innocuous to national pride or prejudice.

Even in exceptional cases such as that of Zola, where the author does not take the French setting for granted but gives document-ary information about it, readers usually look to the manner rather than to the matter. Here, literary cosmopolitanism bears exclusively on technique. Balzac is internationally accepted as the great painter of society, Maupassant as the ingenious story-teller, Zola as the inimitable realist: but the world of fiction is sealed off from everyday use, and Balzac and Zola only influence the Englishman's mental picture of France occasionally and at second remove—when an English author such as Henry James or Arnold Bennett happens to note that Balzac's country priests or Zola's Paris streets are true to life. The English learnt far less about France from all the works of Flaubert and Zola than from George Moore's slender *Confessions of a Young Man*. This is even more striking if we turn to less realistic fields: T. S. Eliot's verse was conceived in Paris and inspired by Mallarmé and Laforgue, but of the three poets only Laforgue could occasionally give an outsider any idea of what Paris is like. Eliot's readers, though they know that poetry is now cosmopolitan, would still define France as a very foreign country.

Literary influence has only a very indirect bearing on the image of a nation: the latter is formed, not when the leaders of thought read foreign books, but when they travel to another country with the more or less direct intention of criticizing their own. The characters they depict in their own books are a proof of this. Though by now most of us have travelled across at least one frontier, the literature of the last fifty years cannot boast of more than half a dozen foreign heroes. Henry James is continually praised for having invented the 'international novel'; yet, except in five of his works, he is content to make his Americans meet and talk with other Americans in front of varying backcloths. Fortunately, a few native characters in fiction have been given leave to visit Paris or Rome and compare these cities with those at home. This reveals the desire of the public to trust its own men of letters rather than alien authors. It is an understandable reaction: not only do these reliable men possess a more critical eye, but they translate in terms of the national interests of the time the knowledge they have gained from travels, tradition, or hearsay. Matthew Arnold's mission to France to report on the *lycées* when English education was about to be reorganized is a striking instance. The literary image of France thus made up becomes a standard reference; like a photograph that is passed around, it may only reflect the point of view of a single person or group but develop none the less into a stereotype. Its influence extends to later travellers, since they in their turn will look for the slightest trace of the features they were led to expect.

This mental picture, though it can depend at times on the whim of a travelling novelist, thus usually changes very slowly. Authors such as Somerset Maugham, who are commonly said to have revealed France to their contemporaries, have really done nothing of the sort: at the most they can make a slight adjustment in the focus of an image made up of age-old prejudices. Small distant countries such as Sweden or Malaya may be suddenly revealed to Londoners when some native film director becomes famous and does not emigrate to Hollywood, or when an Englishman happens to write a book of short stories about them; but at no time has the English reader felt ignorant of France, the foreign country closest to his own both in distance and in thought. Prejudice is self-sufficient. Six centuries of military and economic rivalry combined with a religious schism do not help prevent catchwords and epithets from flying back and forth across the Channel. Though not always taken in earnest these are never felt to be quite inadequate, and English and French have always known themselves to be close, if spiteful, acquaintances.

Their information about each other, however, varies a great deal in accuracy. On the one hand, most of the accusations are reciprocal: French wit is said in England to conceal shallowness, but it is well known on the other side of the Channel that English reserve disguises emptiness; the French are a nation of *petits-bourgeois*, the English a nation of shopkeepers; puritanic disgust at the blatant viciousness of Parisian life is equalled only by the horror of a Taine at the sordid streets of London. On the other hand, huge injustices grow at times out of a mere lack of active interest. Calais periodically achieves a reputation for being the gateway to a picturesque and exotic existence, which assuredly it is not; Paris is called a province of the devil, which on the whole is unfair; whilst certain French culinary delicacies have been a constant source of misapprehension and mockery. Sheer ignorance appears at times: in 1859 *The Illustrated London News*

published a large wood engraving of Delacroix' 'Dante crossing
the Styx' and attributed it to Ary Scheffer. Roger Fry, who
noticed this, remarked in *Characteristics of French Art* that forty
years later the same periodical would 'blush to confuse MM.
Vuillard and Bonnard'.

English ideas on France vary, not between ignorance and
knowledge so much as between what we may call a live interest
and an ossified one. Nations, like individuals, lose and rediscover
one another, and go through periods of attraction and repulsion.
Often the forerunners of popular thought, feeling the need to
renew their culture or some traits of their life, turn outwards in
what Herbert Spencer calls 'anti-patriotism'. Their work then
lies open, for a short while, to infection or inoculation through
the image of a foreign country for which there appears a live
interest, and which is made to stand for something relevant to the
national preoccupations of the time. A people, like an individual,
reveals its ideals through what it seeks in others. As long as the
foreign country remains an active influence, knowledge of it is
corrected and refined; later, though the image may retain currency it becomes set. Periods such as these have appeared alternately in France and England since the Renaissance: during the
first twenty years or so of the English Restoration a narrow but
influential section of the ruling class thought only of French art
and manners; the French eighteenth century from the publication
of the *Lettres Philosophiques* to the ministry of Turgot swore by
all things English; the current was again reversed during the
decline of the age of Victoria from the second Reform Bill to
the First World War.

This last period of intense interest still determines the view of
France in England today, and it will provide the material for this
study. We might for instance imagine a young man making his
first visit to France immediately after the First World War.
He will be a rather exceptional being, for we will suppose that
he is interested neither in jazz nor in the post-war economic crisis,
but in the literature of the previous half-century. A discriminating
advisor will have helped him to choose the books said to be of
interest as far back as Thackeray, and we will also suppose

(slightly unhistorically) that he has read Clive Bell's *Civilization*. With the seriousness of youth, he has noted down the opinions of his favourite authors on the country he is about to visit. Let us also give him a French companion to provide occasionally some more expert knowledge while leaving him the critical detachment of the foreigner; and he may be able to answer three questions: What image of France could one derive from the recognized men of letters of the time? How and why did the elements of this image come into being? How much of it is, or was, true to life?

During the long sea route to Dieppe, one of the literary fashions of the period, we shall have time to reflect on the abundance of material. During the third quarter of the nineteenth century the perfect conditions for a period of live interest had been created. According to Cazamian's *History of English Literature*, from 1875 onwards '. . . the Victorian spirit obscurely loses its self-confidence and meanwhile, the need of a spiritual renovation appears and forces itself upon the national consciousness.' Novels such as those of Grant Allen up to 1895 show how the intellectual youth of the country, thirsting for new ideas and horizons, was seduced by the social, scientific, and religious doctrines of Darwin, Matthew Arnold, Stuart Mill, and Huxley. Europe as a whole was uneasily exploring the flaws in the industrial system it found itself committed to, and losing some of its faith in the unlimited power of knowledge. The age of Schopenhauer and of anarchism, labelled '*fin de siècle*' and 'decadent' by its own contemporaries, was one of emotional unrest, when it was easy to think that other countries had perhaps found better answers to the current problems. As a result the main currents of English literature changed their course in a diffuse quest for a new morality, and flowed for a time through France. At the same time, as the result of a literary influence that has been well explored from a technical point of view,[1] the main British authors tried to model their position in society and the atmosphere of their profession on those of the French: hence the schools and groups—New English, Camden

---

[1] For instance by Madeleine Cazamian (*Le Roman et les Idées en Angleterre*) and by Ruth Z. Temple (*The Critic's Alchemy*).

Town, *Yellow Book*, Bloomsbury—that characterize the artistic
history of the period.

Serious analyses of the French as a people were also encouraged
by the contemporary racial theories. Racial characteristics,
exploited poetically by the very first Romantics, could by the
middle of the century be used in argument by serious-minded
historians such as Taine and Gobineau; Matthew Arnold and
Renan could create categories such as 'Gallic', 'Celtic', or 'Latin',
in which it was fashionable to place a host of bizarre traits.

France: the content of that magic word was still influenced by
Revolutionary romanticism in the works of mid-Victorians such
as Swinburne and Meredith. Widened by Matthew Arnold, who
used his idea of the 'intellectual Frenchman' as a model for the
reform of England, it had a major place in the novels of Henry
James and George Moore and was closely linked through
Thackeray and Pater with the whole of the aesthetic nineties.
Artistic and moral freedom were the main preoccupations of
this group, when they visited Paris, and they constantly had to
face the apparent necessity of linking the two. Around 1910 the
live period was drawing to an end: the generation of Galsworthy,
Wells, Belloc, though steeped in a French atmosphere, no longer
found it necessary to describe France. Arnold Bennett conscientiously imitated Zola and exploited the moral issues raised by the
francophiles of the previous generation; the Bloomsbury group
continued to pay frequent visits across the Channel, but from this
point of view it was only a kind of extension of the previous
generation, because its contemporaries could rely on purely
insular thinkers such as Shaw, Chesterton and Kipling. By the
end of the First World War the image had begun to crystallize
again. This does not mean that the English lost sight of France.
In the twenties Paris was known to be the place in Europe where
life was best. But the people of the time did not discover anything new about it, and in this sense their interest was no longer a
live one. Curiously enough, it was only then that popular opinion
accepted France as Britain's closest neighbour: on the whole the
francophiles had, over the previous fifty years, been thought the
disreputable exceptions. Carlyle, Froude, Kingsley, George

Eliot, Queen Victoria's advisors, had all helped to establish an admiration for things German. Carlyle even contrived to make a hero out of Frederick the Great. England and Germany stood alone in Europe against Napoleon III. Even in the nineties France had mainly a *succès de scandale*: serious people preferred teutonic culture. German metaphysics were taught in the universities; there had been two professors of German in Cambridge for a long time, when the first chair of French was created in 1919. Even after the war, E. M. Forster's intellectuals and Huxley's intelligent young men preferred Strauss and Wagner to Debussy and Ravel.

Literature is an art of repetition: in a study such as this it is too easy to be over-meticulous. Since there is no lack of material concerning the image of France during this period, I shall interpret 'literature' in its narrowest meaning. Books by specialists[2] without any didactic or artistic pretensions cannot be considered. I have assumed that any documentary study of France must have been inspired by some previous work of literary interest, and I have preferred to look for the latter rather than to give an account of the former. The question to be asked is 'How did the most influential authors consider France?' rather than 'Which Englishmen knew France best?' The obvious answer to the second question would have been: the most obscure ones, the expatriates and the foreign correspondents, those who were practically merged with the French anyway. Literary criticism will also be dismissed as 'technical' since it contributes little to the image I am seeking. Henry James's interesting essays on French novelists must remain neglected, whilst it is worth while dwelling on George Moore, a shallow critic, but one who spread the impression that the Parisian seminaries of poetry and painting were typical of the nation. On the other hand, while James's remarks on French landscapes throw a searching light on his moral appraisal of the people, the shelves of musty travel books after Baedeker would be too tiresome to consider. The best criterion is that there should be comparisons: beyond the stalwart colonies of expatriate tea-drinkers, or the long-haired artists trying to hide

---

[2] The best are probably P. G. Hamerton: *French and English* (1889) and J. E. C. Bodley: *France* (1898); or, in a lighter vein, R. C. Sherrard's books on Paris.

their Anglo-Saxon origin, there were some who turned to
France because there was some English moral to be drawn—they
are the only creators.

I have saved our young man, now stepping ashore at Dieppe,
from a tiresome catalogue by letting him consider only works of
recognized intrinsic value. As I had already, not without pre-
sumption, granted this imaginary critic some discrimination and
a literary turn of mind, let us suffer him occasionally to use his
voyage of study as an excuse for some thought on literary matters
and an occasional theory on the books concerned. Having started
off on a search for France in English literature, he will inevitably
be drawn into judgements on his fellow countrymen. The light
from France will pick out for us some features of England.

· 2 ·

AN INTELLIGENT SOCIETY

Matthew Arnold

But if thy nation Arts refuse
And if they scorn the immortal Muse
France shall the arts of Peace restore
And save thee from the ungrateful shore.
                                    BLAKE

For an Englishman the word 'French' denotes a nebulous, inscrutable essence viewed through personal reminiscences; if examined with some care these are seen to arise as often as not from stereotyped opposites. It conjures up pictures of refined fairy books, courtly and sweet, and of vivid realistic novels that one's daughter should not be allowed to read. It brings to mind honour and chivalry and a life of duelling and romance, combined somehow with a set of exquisite social manners wistfully attributed to the eighteenth century. It suggests a gay, carefree artistic life in Montmartre attics and yet at the same time a highly centralized system of government, often on the verge of being a police state; 'France' possesses the self-conscious rationalism of Corneille's heroes, but also the sparkling shallowness of champagne. It includes a certain *douceur de vivre*, of the sort said by Talleyrand to have been known only to people who had lived in Paris before 1789 and impressed on the English by the French *emigré* aristocrats; but it also stands for bloody revolutions and the struggle for freedom against established order.

These features are now imprinted on the English mind, but the literature of the last century shows that they were only discovered progressively. The events of 1848 lent new vigour to the English conviction, retained ever since 1815, that France stood for an anarchical political system and a set of dangerous revolutionary ideas: exactly as today our scrutiny of communism tends to efface for us the features of the Russian people. The early Victorians lived under the shadow of the French Revolution and in fear of similar events in England. Their apprehensions were, indeed, not ungrounded, since as late as 1870 the Commune sparked off socialist demonstrations in London. The strong Tory reaction made thought on France two-dimensional. Shelley, Blake, and Wordsworth had praised the home of political liberty, but Carlyle's aspersions were sustained by England's apparent national interests: '. . . the French Nation distinguishes itself among Nations by the characteristic of Excitability.' In spite of their brilliant Restoration the French continued to practise periodic riots, and were obviously not to be trusted. Suspicion was predominant, and the national anti-Napoleonic heroes, Wellington, Nelson, and Pitt, remained very much in the English mind. The last violent campaign against France in the Press was during the crisis of 1840, but even in 1832, at the end of two particularly friendly years, the young Disraeli saw fit to write a strong pamphlet denouncing 'Ministerial Gallomania' as unnatural.

Artists rarely shine where politics are a burning concern: literature was as colourless on the subject as the Press. Dickens, writing with the authority of a national institution, looked on French public life with superciliousness. Though his letters show how he came to appreciate the brilliant luxurious Paris of the Second Empire, the impressive theatrical spirit of *A Tale of Two Cities* shows us little more than small people struggling against their oppressors, a typically Dickensian theme with a new Parisian backcloth.

After 1850 thought on France progressed slowly from political to moral ideas. Apparently tamed by Napoleon III, the cradle of the Revolution began to appear more sober to the minds of English liberals. France was governed rather too autocratically for their liking, but at least it was no longer a hotbed of socialism. The political cartoons of the period show John Bull or Britannia dealing, not with loose, red-capped Marianne, but with a rather formal, crowned, vacant-eyed 'Madame France'. Admittedly, there was a Napoleon on the throne, but the first Bonaparte's brigandage and bloodshed were half-forgotten because his name-sake was such a crackpot diplomatist. Besides, by the time of the second Reform Bill England could admit timidly that even Republicanism was not wholly wicked. The removal of this barrier, coinciding with what Cazamian called 'an obscure loss of self-confidence', opened the eyes of the English to the organiza-tion of society and the arts on the other side of the Channel. As it happened, the seriousness and intellectual vigour of the later French Romantics were to allow at about the same time a reassess-ment of the legendary French shallowness.

Matthew Arnold may be made to represent this change of attitude; indeed he played no mean part in bringing it about. His approach as a poet is strongly coloured by the traditional Roman-tic enthusiasm for the Revolution; but, linked with the themes of early romanticism by trade rather than by temperament, he soon allowed this to dwindle to a literary admiration for certain French authors. Between the first and second series of *Essays in Criticism* we can see his thought turning towards concepts of intellectual and social progress adapted to the needs of England, but he continues to base it on French ideas and ideals, faithful to the principle that the critic who only knows his own country does not know it well. When he writes, in 'The Function of Criticism at the Present Time', that the English critic of literature and society must dwell on foreign thought, he is thinking mainly of France. At the end of his life he rallied to middle-class feelings and condemned France on moral grounds, but he had by then contributed much to what Disraeli would have called the 'gallomania' of the period that followed. He is thus a kind of sober link between two groups of francophiles who were perhaps equally clumsy in proclaiming their allegiance: the contempor-aries of Wordsworth amongst whom he was brought up, and those of George Moore who were to deny Arnold, forgetting that he had been like them in his youth.

The support he gave to France before 1870 was more important than his successors thought: he was the first 'serious' author, apart from Carlyle to have expressed interest in France since the Revolution. His admiration could not, like that of the early Romantics, be attributed to the innocent extravagance the public allows poets. Furthermore, the very nature of his prose was to bring his view of France before everybody's mind: he considered it his job not so much to invent ideas as to disseminate them. He repeated his formulae endlessly until they reached their goal, and in the end it was impossible after him not to think in terms of his ideas. We shall see that the Bloomsbury group, who poked so much fun at Arnold, yet found it difficult not to begin from his premises: Frenchmen are intellectual, well-educated, socially minded, but immoral.

I. INTELLECTUAL LIGHT

Arnold's interest in France was mainly due to two men, who crop up time and again in his essays, Sainte-Beuve and Renan. Around them there is clearly a little group of critics and poets, whose main link is perhaps the *Revue des Deux Mondes*, and who for Arnold represented France. His essays are always inspired by something they have written, which he wants to pass on to the English.

Sainte-Beuve was his first model. Arnold must have read him at Oxford, and he met him in Paris in 1849. He defended him, later on, from attacks by the *Quarterly Review*, and Sainte-Beuve wrote to him gratefully that he had passed through French life and letters 'by a deep inner line, which confers initiation'. He also described Arnold, in a mood of rather flippant generosity, as '*un français et un romantique égaré là-bas*'. Arnold found himself in a position very similar to Sainte-Beuve's: he marked a passage in his copy of *Portraits Contemporains* which says that an indifferent but intelligent poet can become a good critic. Both began as poets at a time when the star of poetry had begun to decline, and were lucid enough to realize that the poetic manner they were not powerful enough to reform was no longer adapted to what they wanted to express.

Arnold met Renan in 1859, on his second visit to France, and a few months later he wrote to Mrs. Forster of

a Frenchman whom I saw in Paris, Ernest Renan, between whose line
of endeavour and my own I imagine there is considerable resembl-
ance . . . with respect both to morality and intelligence, I think we are
singularly at one in our ideas.

Renan seems in particular to have inspired Arnold's interest in
Celtic literature, the French Academy, contemporary Italy, some
aspects of French higher education, St. Paul, as well as the
problem of State control and individualism. For a time Arnold
was also influenced by George Sand: the admiration he expresses
in *Mixed Essays* shows how her idyllic socialism must have
impressed him.

These literary figures, together with the two studies he made of
French education, represent the horizons of Arnold's France. His
knowledge is gained mainly at second hand, and altogether he did
not spend more than a few weeks across the Channel. Some
critics persist in believing that Arnold's youthful affair with a girl
called Marguerite in Switzerland had something to do with this
influence of France on him. First, there is no evidence that
Marguerite was French at all; secondly, I think the whole adventure too Wordsworthian to have been lived in anything except
the spirit of imitation.

For Arnold's early interest in France was cultivated. At Oxford,
with no more than the knowledge of French given to any young
English gentleman, and in memory of the Romantic poets, he
affected a liking for France forty years before Pater's aesthetic
young men. It well befitted his early conceit to admire the French
actress Rachel so passionately that he followed her to Paris. The
city must have impressed him as in a later poem he imagines it
did Heine:

> Paris drawing rooms, and lamps
> Blazing, and brilliant crowds,
> Starr'd and jewell'd, of men
> Famous, of women the queens
> Of dazzling converse. . . .

On his return Clough wrote:

Matt is full of Parisianism; theatres in general, and Rachel in special:

he enters the room with a chanson of Béranger's on his lips—for the sake of French words almost conscious of tune; his carriage shows him in fancy parading the Rue de Rivoli; and his hair is guiltless of English scissors.

He had acquitted himself of the verse he owed to Rachel, but also contrived to take French lessons and meet Sainte-Beuve. In 1859 he returned to France as an inspector of the educational system, and appears to have had more mature conversations with Sainte-Beuve and Renan. Immediately on his return he began the campaign for the improvement of the British public that took up most of his life.

The *Essays in Criticism* reproduce this rapid progress from youthful romanticism and republicanism to an interest in the intellectual life of Paris. The essays on Maurice and Eugénie de Guérin belong to the former mood. Many readers have wondered why Arnold should have made this strange choice of authors to study. The Guérins are and were practically unknown in France. There seem to be a variety of possible reasons. The Guérins, together with Sénancour and George Sand, formed a vague subliminary group linked by mutual admiration.[1] There was also an understandable desire, unfortunately misplaced in this case, to be associated with a literary discovery; but above all the Guérins are a perfect illustration of a certain tradition about poets, which we shall meet again in Pater's imaginary portraits. Curiously enough, the image of the Romantic artist was becoming associated with France, probably because all the English Romantics, who were of a slightly earlier generation and tended to die young, had disappeared from the scene. This was a recent idea, because until the 1830's the French poets had all striven to imitate their English predecessors (as Vigny's *Chatterton* shows). Amongst other poetic qualities such as their powers in naturalistic interpretation, Arnold stresses in the Guérins their intense, semireligious enthusiasm for the beauties of a simple life nearer to the lessons of Nature:

[1] Sainte-Beuve had written about them all. George Sand wrote a preface to a book of Guérin's, and Arnold may have heard of the Guérins through Lacordaire when he visited the school in Sorèze described in *A French Eton*: Lacordaire knew Lamennais, whose disciple Guérin had been for a time.

Religion had clearly possessed itself of this force of character and reinforced it: in the shadow of the Cévennes, in the sharp and tonic nature of Southern France, which has seen the Albigensians, which has seen the Camisards, Catholicism too is fervent and intense.

Both the Guérins practised 'confessions' in the best romantic manner. Eugénie's are all the more interesting for having been intended only for her brother. Add to this the usual lack of emotional attachment:

Maurice resists being riveted and held stationary by any single impression, but would be borne for ever down an enchanted stream. He goes into religion and out of religion, into society and out of society, not from the motives which impel men in general, but to feel what it is all like.

He almost attains Wordsworth's state of 'wise passiveness'. The picture is completed by death at the fashionable early age of twenty-eight.

Except in these two early essays, Arnold's main interest in France is social and political. His ideas on the Revolution, also inherited from one of Wordsworth's early passions, first appear in a poem written in 1848 to a 'republican friend', probably Clough. Arnold does not separate the literary revolution from the political one, which seems to him more worthy of interest. He agrees with the ideal if it is

to prize

> Those virtues, prized and practised by too few,
> But prized, but loved, but eminent in you,
> Man's fundamental life; if to despise

> The barren optimistic sophistries
> Of comfortable moles, whom what they do
> Teaches the limit of the just and true.

But a second sonnet, printed opposite this one, expresses his fear lest this proud ideal be too ambitious for man's vicious nature. Admittedly, the crowds seemed to be taking part in a constructive movement based on genuine intellectual reasoning. What Arnold had read in George Sand seemed to confirm that the education of the masses by the first Revolution had not been lost, and had become a feature of French life. Arnold introduced this idea in 'The Function of Criticism at the Present Time':

That a whole nation should have been penetrated with an enthusiasm for pure reason, and with an ardent zeal for making its prescriptions triumph, is a very remarkable thing, when we consider how little of mind, or anything so worthy and quickening of mind, comes into the motives which alone, in general, impel great masses of men. . . . As no sincere passion for the things of the mind, even though it turn out in many respects an unfortunate passion, is ever quite thrown away and quite barren of good, France has reaped from hers one fruit—the natural and legitimate fruit, though not precisely the grand fruit she expected: she is the country in Europe where *the people* is most alive.[2]

But on the other hand this glorious rush to put principles into practice might fail to leave the ideas time to mature and adapt themselves to circumstances. Seventy years later Arnold would have supported Trotsky, seventy years earlier he would have sided with Burke. The 1789 revolution left no time for self-examination: the masses can carry their newly found ideas too far; they should be conscious of the issues involved but not necessarily in charge of affairs. Arnold wrote in 1848 in a letter to Mrs. Forster that the 'idea-moved masses of France' are politically

as far superior to the *insensible masses* of England as to the Russian serfs, and at the same time they do not threaten the educated world with the intolerable laideur of the well-fed American masses, so deeply antipathetic to continental Europe. . . . But I do not say that these people in France have much dreamed of the deepest wants of man, or are likely to enlighten the world much on the subject, and I do not wonder at Guizot, who is an austerely serious man, rather despising them.

In 1848 men of letters and ideas played at least as prominent a part as in 1789; also their influence was less hidden to the English

[2] George Eliot, who to some extent shares Arnold's perceptiveness over the important trends of the time, has a similar reaction. She writes to John Sibree in March 1848:

I should have no hope of good from any imitative movement at home. Our working classes are eminently inferior to the mass of the French people. In France the *mind* of the people is highly electrified—they are full of ideas on social subjects—they really desire social *reform*—not merely an acting out of Sancho Panza's favourite proverb: 'Yesterday for you, today for me.'

than it had been by the shock of the Terror and by the shadow of the Napoleonic wars. A great deal was made of Lamartine's election to the Assemblée Législative.

It was true, as Arnold points out in 'The Function of Criticism at the Present Time', that the French revolutionary spirit asked of things 'Is it rational?', instead of 'Is it according to conscience?' as the English revolution of 1642 had done. But in spite of the evident influence of George Sand, Arnold's conclusions are little different from those of any Victorian Radical: the people should be kept in touch with events but helped to make the decisions. Here, he says, is the function of criticism. As it was left to Burke, and not to Pitt, to draw the moral of the first revolution in France, so the poet or critic must be the prophet of the masses, helping them to apply theories or interpret useful foreign trends. Arnold thus contrives to practise and to preach at the same time.

The other essays develop this idea. 'The Literary Influence of Academies' explains how an organized consciousness of what is rational and what is not can affect the literary scene:

A Frenchman has, to a considerable degree, what one may call a conscience in intellectual matters; he has an active belief that there is a right and a wrong in them, that he is bound to honour and obey the right, that he is disgraced by cleaving to the wrong. All the world has, or professes to have, this conscience in moral matters.

The idea is borrowed directly from Sainte-Beuve, who had said that the critic should investigate not whether he liked or was moved, but whether he was right in liking or in being moved. A conscious, ethically minded *élite* will improve the morals of society by a kind of diffusion: in the same way the general respect for intelligence will be increased if men of letters set the example, as they do in France. There the Academy, a literary tribunal designed to give the world of letters a high tone, lays down and maintains standards of reference that are generally accepted. Because of this, says Arnold, England, still a country of intellectual eccentricity, has developed its lyrical poetry, whereas French literature, standardized and academic, can only produce artificial verse. On the other hand, French prose is the result of intelligent thought emended by the recognized principles of good taste and urbanity. I must add immediately that, where French poetry is concerned, Arnold's absurd application of a reasonably acceptable idea has since become unfortunately encrusted in English criticism. We may accept Arnold's premiss that France is a more intellectually-minded nation than England, but it is surely difficult to deduce from this that the French cannot be poetic. The two faculties are not and never have been exclusive. One wonders in which category Arnold would have put himself. But he had an unfortunate tendency to fall for these easy contrasts.

Two things can be said in his defence. First, this idea, which he was to develop later on in *Irish Essays*, was not his own. Dryden had written in his Dedication to the *Ænead*: 'Impartially speaking, the French are as much better critics than the English as they are worse poets.' Coleridge, de Quincey, Sainte-Beuve himself, had accused the French of being prosaic. Secondly, the French poetry Arnold (and Dryden) knew was in fact prosaic. None of the French Romantics equalled the freshness and inventiveness of Keats and Shelley, and in spite of their widely advertised spirit of revolt against the rules, the technical means they used were notoriously unimaginative. In 1864, when Arnold wrote this essay, the Parnassian movement had reached the height of its crystalline artificiality. But it was far too easy to shoot down Victor Hugo in the way Arnold chose to use in his essay on Heine. He merely quoted two bad lines from *Hernani*, which no one would dream of using in illustration of Hugo, and compared them with two of the best lines in Shakespeare. In a lecture at London University in 1911 Emile Legouis, defending French poetry from attacks in the Arnoldian strain, reversed this type of argument neatly by choosing two good lines from Hugo and two frightful lines from 'The Rape of Lucrece'.

Besides, Arnold should have known better than to condemn the whole of French poetry on the strength of what he had read. Baudelaire had published *Les Fleurs du Mal* six years before, and at the time Verlaine was already sending contributions to the literary magazines. Sainte-Beuve himself had done a great deal for the rediscovery of the French poetry of the sixteenth century, which is anything but prosaic. Unfortunately, English critics always had suspected that their own language was the only really poetic one. Foreign verse is more difficult to appreciate than one's own, but for complex reasons stemming originally from the Norman conquest no English critic will ever admit that he is not proficient in French.

Let us return to Arnold's 'intellectual conscience'. He chooses Joubert as a double illustration of his ideas. Villagers made Joubert a Justice of the Peace while he was away and without his knowing, such was their respect for him as a local sage. Later, because of his reputation amongst intellectuals and on the advice of the academic Fontanes, Napoleon made him a governing councillor of the University. Both acts of confidence were successful: Joubert turned out to be an honest if reluctant judge, and a good councillor. Also, in his philosophical works he sheds light on metaphysical problems left obscure by men of a more inventive genius, purely by submitting them to firm intellectual principles and expressing them in the clear logic of his mother tongue: indeed French is 'in itself so favourable a vehicle for such sayings, that the making them in it has the less merit.'

Throughout *Essays in Criticism* there are references to Amiel, Montesquieu, Schérer, Renan, Sainte-Beuve, and Michelet, to remind us that France is a nation of scholars and refined thinkers with intellectual standards. At this point the comparison with Germany favours France, because there is beauty in intellectual good taste. Arnold quotes Amiel:

The notion of a thing's *jarring of the taste* is wanting to German aesthetics. Their elegance knows nothing of grace; they have no sense of the enormous distance between distinction (gentlemanly, ladylike) and their stiff Vornehmlichkeit. . . . A short article by Sainte-Beuve, Schérer, Renan, Victor Cherbulioz, gives one more pleasure, and makes one ponder and reflect more, than a thousand of these German pages crammed to the margin and showing the work itself rather than its result. The Germans heap the faggots for the pile, the French bring the fire.[3]

---

[3] Henry James reached a similar conclusion on the French in his literary criticism:
When we others of the Anglo-Saxon race are vulgar we are, handsomely and with

These essays are of course designed to justify Arnold's own position. We must not exaggerate his admiration for all things French (particularly in view of what he wrote later on), and it should be remembered that he was using the French example to establish himself in England. What he really meant was that since poets were no longer the leaders of the age, since he had taken Sainte-Beuve's advice and become a critic, he should be given the same consideration as his French counterparts. Also, he was not the only man of his time to recognize the value of French criticism. But it is important to us that he gave a French pedigree to the idea that intellectualism seeps down from the sages to the people, and advertised France, against the Carlylean tradition, as an intelligent society.

There is a good deal of truth in Arnold's picture of the French scene: if the colours are slightly too rosy it is no doubt because of his personal interest in the matter. He introduced a debate that still continues when the 'highbrow' is compared to the French *intellectuel*: the latter is described nowadays as more *engagé*—the French word springs to mind today because the idea still has so many French connections, exactly as the French word *culture* came naturally to Arnold's pen when he tried to describe the forming of the intellectual conscience amongst the French *élite*.[4]

the best conscience in the world, vulgar all through, too vulgar to be in any degree literary, and too much so therefore to be critically reckoned with at all. The French are different—they separate their sympathies, multiply their possibilities, observe their shades, remain more or less outside of their worst disasters. They mostly contrive to get the *idea*, in however dead a faint, down into the lifeboat. They may lose sight of the stars, but they save in some fashion as that their intellectual souls. (*Notes on Novelists*: 'Emile Zola'.) J. S. Mill also echoed these ideas in his *Autobiography*.

[4] In *Culture and Society* Raymond Williams holds that Arnold borrowed the word from Newman, who had first used it in a similar meaning in 1852, twelve years before. This is possible, but it would seem that Arnold was far more absorbed in French literature at the time. Before writing 'The Literary Influence of Academies', which was a review of Pellisson and d'Olivet's *Histoire de l'Académie Française*, re-edited in 1858, Arnold must have read Sainte-Beuve's review of it, published in 1858 and collected in Volume 14 of the *Causeries du Lundi*, and Renan's review in the *Journal des Débats* in January 1859, collected in *Essais de Morale et de Critique*. In these reviews Sainte-Beuve mentioned *des essais nombreux de perfectionnement et de culture pour la langue*, and Renan wrote of *une forme de culture intellectuelle qui s'impose à tous*. Sainte-Beuve had already used the word in this meaning in his essay on the death of M. Vinet (first published in 1847); besides, the word was commonly accepted in French in this sense: the first reference in *Littré* dates back to Voltaire.

The *intellectuel* does have a greater influence on public life in France: intelligence is on the whole rated higher, and can be openly praised without superciliousness. Dr. Arnold had said that he tried to give his pupils, first, religious and moral principles; secondly, gentlemanly conduct; and thirdly, intellectual ability. This order still prevails in much of England outside a few academic strongholds—to say of some one that he is intelligent will usually scare people out of electing him to a society or a committee. It is not always in good taste to bring real ideas to bear on public issues: Arnold himself was accused in his lifetime of saturating politics with thought. In France men of letters, unashamed of their intellect, are effectively involved in matters that go beyond the boundaries of literature. They act as the organ of all. There is no danger of their being sneered at, as a novelist is in England even today who dabbles in social and economic theory, not because he does it badly so much as because he has the effrontery to try. The famous debate between Camus and Mauriac in 1945 is a case in point: a decision of principle had to be reached on whether to treat the former 'collaborators' to the Vichy régime as criminals in their own right. The country was swayed by the articles of these two novelists, trusting to a literary dispute to bring out the right and wrong principles. Ideas and ideologies are constantly reassessed in France, sometimes wholly rebuilt: the succession of French constitutions and re-publics is a manifestation of this. Even newspapers contain far more argument and rhetoric. Arnold's observation was sound, and his idea, widespread in England and popularized in the nasty expression 'Gallic logic', is true. But he did, perhaps in the interest of his own campaign, over-emphasize the final effect of all this on the masses: the *intellectuels* often seem to debate in a vacuum, and the argumentative newspapers have a smaller circulation than any of the English press. The French may love reasoning for its own sake, they may admire *un bel argument* or *un beau paradoxe*, and yet be unwilling to act for it. The year 1848 had been a turning-point. The people who fought in the revolution realized that they had been led astray by their intellectual leaders; and from then on, except in a few crises such as the Dreyfus affair, the

c

nation, without despising the intellectual, has not taken him as an oracle. To appear in the right light, Arnold's 'sage' should perhaps be placed side by side with the Logician from Ionesco's *Rhinocéros*.

II. EDUCATION AND METHOD

Arnold's journey to France in 1859 to report on elementary schools also produced two interesting works on secondary education: a short essay entitled *A French Eton* and a detailed report, 'Schools and Universities on the Continent'. Another essay published in 1868, 'Higher Schools and Universities in France', merely added some technical detail to the latter, the introduction to which was reprinted later as 'Democracy'. Were we to compile a survey of views of France according to subject matter, *A French Eton* would fill the chapter on education. The topic is not normally in the minds of visitors to France who write about their experiences; the press usually approaches it from a purely political angle.

Arnold's report immediately took on absolute value. France as a place of education was not new to English minds: it had long been customary for gentlemen to go there to complete their schooling, either, like Tristram Shandy, with experience of 'Life', or, like J. S. Mill, with academic experience in the universities of Paris or Montpellier. Arnold adjusted this reputation to the level of the middle classes. The subject was eminently topical: Arnold was sent by the British Government, which had been debating educational reform since 1857, so that the problem was ripe for him. There had been a Royal Commission to investigate the public schools, Eton in particular. When the foundations of State education in Britain were eventually laid down in 1870 and 1902 by the Bryce commission and the Forster and Balfour Acts, most authors interested in the reform mentioned the virtues or the defects of the French system, of which Arnold had provided the definite picture.

Yet the source is surprisingly slender: *A French Eton* takes up 120 pages, with roughly twenty on France. Arnold describes the *lycée* he visited at Toulouse and compares it briefly with Lacordaire's private school at Sorèze, where the same standards are enforced by State inspectors. He is struck mainly by the cleanliness and scrupulous organization of school life. Though sports seem neglected (still a truism in England, even though the emphasis has in fact changed somewhat), the dormitories and dining halls are of exemplary neatness and cleanliness. Order and good sense rule the curriculum; it includes some of the rudiments of science, and therefore develops an interest for a useful subject that English schoolboys are encouraged to stifle; and it does not neglect the native literature, whereas in England only Greek and Latin are considered worthy of being taught. The education at Toulouse is cheap, because of course State schools are not profit-making, and this brings Arnold to the root of all the honesty and efficiency he observed: only the State can provide real guarantees by choosing teachers on their impersonal academic ability and organizing

INTERNATIONAL COMPARISONS.

Henri Dubois (who can speak English) to his friend 'Arry Smith (who can't). " PARDON ME, MON AMI ! YOU ARE VERY PRETTY BOY, YOU DRESS IN ZE MOST PERFECT 'CHIC'; BUT VY DO YOU SPEAK YOUR OWN LANGUAGE SO UNGRAMMATICALLZ ? "

'Arry. " WHY DO I SPEAK MY HOWN LANGWIDGE SO HUNGRAMMATICAL? 'ANG IT, YER DOWN'T SUP-POWSE AS I WERE HEDGERKITED AT HETON OR 'ARROW LIKE A BLOOMIN' SWELL, DO YER ? "

Henri. " VOYEZ DONC ÇA ! NOW IN FRANCE ZERE IS NO ETON, NO HARROW : ALL ZE PUBLIC SCHOOLS ARE ZE SAME, AND ZE BUTCHER AND BAKER'S LITTLE BOYS GO ZERE, AND ZE LITTLE CANDLESTICK-MAKERS, AND ZE LITTLE BOYS OF ZE MERCHANTS OF CHEESE LIKE YOU AND ME ! "

'Arry. " COME, I S'Y, WALKER, YER KNOW ! AND WHERE DO THEIR CUSTOMERS' LITTLE BOYS GO ? "

Henri. " PARBLEU ! ZEY GO ZERE TOO ! ! "

['*Arry, suddenly conscious of his deficiencies, feels bitterly towards his country.*

the programme of education instead of leaving it to the initiative
of individuals.

Repeated insidiously, these ideas imprinted themselves on the
late Victorian mind. Arnold's easily-remembered formulae made
it a commonplace that in France thought in general and education
in particular were not only based on established intellectual
authority, but were State-run. This was part of a wider campaign
of his: he realized that the trend in Europe was towards more
centralized States and he advised his countrymen to follow the
example of France in this field too. He wrote in *Democracy*:

> The power of France in Europe is at this day mainly owing to the
> completeness with which she has organized democratic institutions.
> The action of the French State is excessive; but it is too little under-
> stood in England. . . . The ideas of 1789 were working everywhere in
> the eighteenth century; but it was because in France the State adopted
> them that the French Revolution became an historic epoch for the
> world, and France the lode-star of Continental democracy. Her air of
> superiority and her overweening pretensions come from her sense of
> the power which she derives from this cause. . . . I think it is more
> profitable for a Frenchman to consider the part of delusion contained
> in it; for an Englishman, the part of truth.

Later, whether Arnold was campaigning for better schooling or
for a national theatre, he never forgot to mention how a French
Minister of Education had boasted that he knew exactly what all
the schoolboys in the country were studying at any given moment,
thus intending to show how much better it was to submit to a
central authority. Those interested in French literature might link
this with the strength of the classical tradition, based on Reason
and imitation. Exaggerate this image slightly, and it will be clear
why, for a long time after, the Frenchman was made to appear in
England as a former pupil of a *lycée*, with a certain line of opinion
on everything and no personal thoughts. We shall see how Clive
Bell took up and developed the same view.

The French State is more centralized; French education is
intellectually more rigid. Both ideas were and still are true. But
Arnold put them forward in a very brittle way. Where education
is concerned, the French and English approaches were and are

different. It is not so much that the French system relies entirely
on tradition and authority: it tries to put forward the historically
orthodox views on a subject, and to teach a method before
encouraging personal judgement. Arnold mentioned the way the
syllabus was organized: there are many other instances. French
students are made to write dissertations in which they must show
a balanced view of the different sides to a problem before they are
allowed to give their own answers. It is heartbreaking to apply
these norms to British students, as I have often tried to do, since
they have been carefully taught at school to look down on anything that may have been said already. They would like to prove
their worth not by width and lucidity of outlook but by brilliant
improvisation. Needless to say, the gift for this is not given to all.
Where Frenchmen are set a subject, the English student is asked
to write around a topic: the terminology is telling. No doubt the
English feel that the essay reproduces their search for a personality
—but this form, of which so many admirable examples are found
in English literature, has, I believe, questionable value as a method
of teaching. It is too easily misunderstood. The careful thought
that must have led up to its apparently casual opinions is forgotten. Pupils at an art school cannot draw before learning the
laws of perspective. They also sketch in pencil diagrams that may
disappear in the finished picture but are none the less necessary.

Method and organization are also more apparent in French
civic life, as Arnold repeatedly pointed out. His ideas on the
Comédie Française, which have only recently borne fruit, and his
plea for an English Academy, still unsuccessful, spring from a
similar belief. He might have mentioned other fields: for instance,
the French train their high civil servants in a special establishment,
the *Ecole d'Administration*, where they learn very advanced econo-
mical and political theory—whilst the English genuinely believe
that three years spent in the ferment of Oxbridge society, plus a
good family background and an aptitude for lusty team sports,
are sufficient qualifications for the civil service. Personality still
prevails over Method.

Arnold's exhortations, however, were often accused of
encouraging intolerance and dogmatism. Unfortunately the case,

as he puts it, touches the innate English liberalism to the quick. 'How about individual feeling, initiative, tolerance?' it would ask. As with the idea of the intellectual conscience perhaps, Arnold tried to shock rather than to convince. What he may not have sufficiently grasped and certainly did not emphasize was that the French respect for authority and method is a rational platform from which one can try to reach a different level of tolerance and feeling. One may respect reason and orthodoxy, but there can be several orthodoxies and various ways of applying reason in any matter. The student may say what he likes in the conclusion to his dissertation if he has given plausible reasons beforehand: his opinion merely stands less chance of appearing fatuous.

The value of the two approaches to this very vague field is of course still open to question. But it must be said that though Arnold clearly saw the advantages of a 'high conscience' and of Method in intellectual matters, and made laudable attempts at the kind of general criticism this implies, he did not apply the tolerance that should go with it. He tried to impose on the English his own conception of sweetness and light with the dogmatism of the self-made man (for he was, in a sense, a self-made cosmopolitan) and did not see the contradiction this entailed. It is easy to understand the violent reaction of such essentially English, that is to say individualist and liberal, minds as that of Lytton Strachey to the unfortunate example concerning the Minister of Education. In their eyes Arnold's is an attempt to force upon them a crude system that they instinctively despise; for this same reason we smile today at some of the soap-box speeches in his later essays. It is easy to object to Arnold, as Strachey did (' "The State shall be my governors but not my critics" wrote a greater-than Arnold'), that a State theatre would ruin free appreciation of talent. One could also think that a French Eton in every English town would make for a regrettably standardized generation of schoolboys. Nowhere is it more apparent how difficult it can be to plead for a foreign way of life, to praise it sufficiently while taking care not to offend one's readers by dogmatism. Arnold did manage to create a current of opinion that agreed, partly out of intellectual snobbishness, with his advice; but, in the long run, it was not he who was responsible for what changes there have been in England. For when Arnold was moderate and impartial, only the concessions he made to his countrymen were accepted. He was not the only observer of his time to recommend French centralization to England, and his remarks had no more effect than those of other politicians or economists. When he became dogmatic, in his later essays, he was suspected of being a dangerous infiltrator. And his literary reputation helped surprisingly little. Those who were prepared to consider his ideas because he was a professor of poetry, and an established, if self-appointed, national critic, only did so as a concession to his conception of culture.

A caricature of Arnold in 1881. *Punch* thought the Sweet and Light must have come from Champagne.

It has long been accepted by the intelligentsia in England that it would perhaps be better to have an Academy and a National Theatre, and an organized syllabus for schools—but as a fashionable, rather than a workable idea. Those who continue to hand it down can or will do precious little to put it into effect. Arnold's 'culture' has an unfortunate self-sterilizing quality about it. In this particular case, it may have been that he was not French enough, in spite of what Sainte-Beuve could say, to appreciate or at least to explain to his readers the ultimate value of 'intellectual standards'; but in becoming so he would perhaps have stepped a shade too far away from the English, so that they would have been able to listen with an easy smile and shrug him off as a foreigner. Such, unhappily, is the spirit of nations.

III. EQUALITY

We are following more or less the chronological development of Arnold's thought on France. The French respect for intelligence had struck him first, and he noted as part of the 'intellectual conscience' their habits of method and centralization. In commenting on the organization of French social and political life, Arnold inevitably touches upon the republican ideal. This leads him, in *Mixed Essays*, to assess the respect for equality on the other side of the Channel and to search for its origins. The instances he notes, in 'Equality', 'Numbers', and '*Porro unum est necessarium*' are true enough. But instead of pointing out, as he might have done, that equality is merely one of the intellectual principles that the French mind is so eager to put into practice, Arnold tries to explain it by an elaborate theory of races, and it is difficult to understand how anyone can have believed it.

The principle of equality is illustrated for instance by the French laws of bequest. Compulsory division of estate sometimes leads to fragmentation, but it also provides a just distribution of wealth.

There is a general equality in a humane kind of life. This is the secret of the passionate attachment with which France inspires all Frenchmen, in spite of her fearful troubles, her checked prosperity, her disconnected units, and the rest of it. There is so much of the goodness and the agreeableness of life there, and for so many.

As a result the lower classes have achieved self-respect, which is even more important than material well-being. The common people have become the soundest part of the nation. Arnold describes French peasants seen through eyes worthy of George Sand: they are ignorant, but

at the same time full of intelligence; their manners are excellent, they have delicate perceptions, they have tact, they have a certain refinement which a brutalized peasantry could not possibly have.[5]

[5] Here Arnold is quoting from P. G. Hamerton's *The Intellectual Life* (1873). Hamerton was a typical 'artistic gentleman' of the nineteenth century, an artist of sorts who

In Italy Arnold finds the French soldiers virile and energetic by contrast with the Italians; thanks to their education in equality, one does not feel that they are inferiors. There is only a short step, which Arnold does not hesitate to take, between this and the idea that the French peasant classes are more cultured than the English. This is a fallacy. Even George Sand was content to praise their unruffled attitude and did not try to make out that they were educated. French education was certainly more developed at the time, and since the lower middle class had always been more predominant, with less of a cleavage than in England, it reached further down in society. But it did not transform the peasants and the soldiers to the degree he suggests. It is too easy to go to a country with the idea that people there are more (or, usually, less) cultured and intelligent than at home, and to read this into strange faces and customs.[6]

A second, and perhaps less clear, instance of the French genius for equality was related to the much-discussed Irish question. France had persuaded Alsace, a foreign province, to feel at one with the rest of the country simply by treating its inhabitants as equals.

> The French government may discourage the German language in Alsace and prohibit Eisteddfods in Brittany; but the *Journal des Débats* never treats German music and poetry as mischievous lumber, nor tells the Bretons that the sooner all Breton specialities disappear from the face of the earth the better. Accordingly, the Bretons and Alsatians have come to feel themselves a part of France, and to feel pride in bearing the French name; while the Welsh and Irish obstinately refuse to amalgamate with us.

Arnold's report on French equality is correct so far. He is dealing with what he had observed himself, which was simply

published essays and travel sketches. He owed literary allegiance to Arnold (he admired Sainte-Beuve, Joubert, Sénancour, George Sand) and shared Arnold's later belief that France was entering a moral decline. He married a Frenchwoman and lived near Paris, at Autun. His *French and English* (1889) is a good report on the France of the time.

[6] Henry James makes a similar mistake (see below, p. 119). Richard Le Gallienne, who can usually be relied on to catch hold of an idea just before it reaches the ground, goes into ecstasies in *From a Paris Garret* (1946) when two removers recognize *Les Trois Mousquetaires* among his books: 'It is wonderful how that old yarn has reached all classes.'

the legacy of the Revolution, still apparent even in the less liberal régime of Napoleon III. The mistake comes when Arnold tries to systematize his remarks by suggesting that this is not only a modern political ideal, but stems from a general feature of the French race. He brings up Voltaire to support him: the remarkable legacy of the French seventeenth century is similar to the one bestowed on mankind by the age of Pericles. It is:

l'esprit de société, the spirit of society, the social spirit. And another French writer, looking for the good points in the old French nobility, remarks that this at any rate is to be said in their favour: they establised a high and charming ideal of social intercourse and manners, for a nation formed to profit by such an ideal.[7]

The fallacy lies in the last few words: *a nation formed to profit by such an ideal*. Arnold dives headlong into it on the next page, with the word *congenital*:

From the first moment when the French people, with its congenital sense for the power of social intercourse and manners, came into existence, it was on the road to equality. . . . It was not the spirit of philanthropy which mainly impelled the French to that Revolution, neither was it the spirit of envy, neither was it the love of abstract ideas, though all these did something towards it; but what did most was the spirit of society.

There are two blunders here. First, a group of people whose ideal is social intercourse will, naturally, be brought to recognize each other's rights to personal opinions and belongings. But they will not necessarily apply the same rules to human beings of a different caste. The aristocrats of Louis XIV's court made a vague but very real distinction between what we would call the top and bottom of society (they would probably have said 'society and other people'). Arnold seems to forget that a revolution was, after all, necessary to bring about what he considers, eighty years later, as natural.

The second mistake lies in Arnold's pushing the 'spirit of

---

[7] Voltaire makes this point in *Le siècle de Louis XIV*. But he is writing in the middle of the eighteenth century, and merely explaining how the influence of court life made philanthropy possible. The 'other French writer' Arnold mentions is Renan (*Dialogues Philosophiques*, 1874).

society' or the 'genius for equality' back into the mysterious
gestation of the French people. If the French have always possessed
it, one might ask, why did it only appear after 1789? Arnold tries
to account for this in 'Numbers', by a long dissertation on racial
history.

The first inhabitant of France, he writes, was the Gaul,

gay, sociable, quick of sentiment, quick of perception; apt, however,
very apt, to be presumptuous and puffed up. Then came the Roman
conquest, and from this we get a new personage, the Gallo-Latin,
with the Gaulish qualities for a basis, but with Latin order, reason,
lucidity, added, and also Latin sensuality. Finally, we have the Frankish
conquest and the Frenchman. The Frenchman proper is the Gallo-
Latin, with Frankish or Germanic qualities added and infused.

The three features of the new 'race' thus created, Gaulish gaiety,
Latin rationality, and German seriousness, were mingled and
held in check by a system of moral values, the medieval catholic
faith. However, when this began to fail and other European
countries felt the need of a Reformation to preserve the check on
popular instincts, France somehow let the Gaul in her get the
upper hand. He, in his 'gaiety' and 'rationality' forgetting
Germanic 'seriousness', refused to acknowledge the Reformation.
This explains why the last full flowering of French literature was
at the Renaissance but before the Reformation when the three
qualities were still to be found together.[8] The French art of the
seventeenth and eighteenth centuries only appears great because
of the relative 'decadence of European institutions'. Meanwhile:

[in the Frenchman] the chief source of seriousness and of moral ideas
is failing and drying up, and what remains are the sources of Gaulish
salt, and quickness, and sentiment, and sociability, and sensuality, and
rationality. And, of course, the play and working of these qualities is
altered by their being no longer in combination with a dose of German
seriousness, but left to work by themselves. Left to work by themselves, they give us what we call the *homme sensuel moyen*, the average
sensual man.

'German seriousness', in Arnold's terminology, means morality: here France is vigorously condemned by the protestant

[8] This essay was first published in 1885. Pater's *Renaissance Studies* appeared in 1868.

moralist. In *Literature and Dogma* Arnold crushes the French idea of equality, which he had seen fit to praise when he was talking about politics, and expounds the dangers of a morality made to the measure of man:

> We all have in us this *homme sensuel*, the man of the 'wishes of the flesh and of the current thoughts'; but we develop him under checks and doubts, and unsystematically and often grossly. France, on the other hand, develops him confidently and harmoniously. She makes the most of him, because she knows what she is about and keeps in a mean, as her climate is in a mean, and her situation. . . . And from her ideal of the average sensual man France has deduced her famous gospel on the Rights of Man, which she preaches with such an infinite crowing and self-admiration. France takes 'the wishes of the flesh and of the current thoughts' for a man's *rights*; and human happiness, and the perfection of society, she places in everybody's being enabled to gratify these wishes.[9]

Arnold's investigation of the sources of equality thus ends in a condemnation of the French race. His ideas about race history seem to have been generally accepted in Britain: since his day, Gallic and Latin have been commonly used as synonyms for French. His explanations are ingenious, and no more. It should be said immediately that he is not solely responsible for them. Taine and Renan influenced him, and he had probably read Michelet's poetic flights on the origins of France. But their effect on English thought has been so widespread that he must be put on trial for them. This is not the place to discuss the existence of Arnold's sentimental invention, the Celt, but the rest of his race-chemistry does concern us.

In fact, had nineteenth-century historians not been walled in by the climate of national-romanticism, they would have realized that the English have the same racial constitution as the French. Both are formed from an original population (which may as well be called Celtic) and Germanic invaders—Franks and Anglo-Saxons. Both were influenced by a Roman occupation of a few hundred years. If we accept, as Arnold and his school do, that the inhabitants of Brittany and those of Wales are related, let us not

---

[9] Again, in 'her climate is in a mean' note the influence of Pater.

believe childishly that a 'racial invasion' sweeps through on horse-back and pushes the older inhabitants into mountainous regions. Obviously, it merely dominates them politically and perhaps linguistically, and there must have been Celts left in England. Even after the Germanic invasions, the English and the French were as closely related as people must be who were born some thirty miles apart. Political influences may, of course, have shaped them differently: today two Germans from either side of the Iron Curtain may well be found to have entirely opposite opinions on many things. But this will have nothing to do with racial features, which is what Arnold supposes. It would be ridiculous to say that the East Germans have acquired the characteristics of Slavs.

But Arnold's theory was attractive because, for historical reasons, the English prefer to think of their ancestors as Anglo-Saxons whilst the French are proud to be the descendants of the Gauls. This because of fortuitous ideas that have nothing to do with racial characteristics if such things exist. First, the Franks found a stronger adherence to the Latin language in Gaul than the Anglo-Saxons did in England: the Roman administration had had five centuries to impose it. Their German tongue was obscured by Gallo-Latin, whereas the Anglo-Saxons at least made a pretence of using theirs, even if large parts of the West of England retained their own dialects. Thus the English, looking back at their early literature transcribed in the official language of the time, find words descending directly from German stock, whereas the French documents of the same period are written in Latin.

Secondly, because a Roman general dabbling in politics wrote up his war-memoirs as an election pamphlet and happened to enjoy momentary political success, the Gauls have gone down in French history as the instigators of the first patriotic resistance to invasion: the siege of Alesia, where Vercingetorix had the support of widespread tribes, naturally appealed to French historians after the Revolution. They were imbued with the right of peoples to independence, which revolutionary France had proclaimed, and were tempted, as Arnold was, to transfer this into the past. For

them the Franks were invaders, therefore not attached to the
national soil: when they finally set up the Merovingian kingdom,
of which one might be proud in retrospect, it was so large as not
to correspond clearly to modern France. Though Charlemagne
is a picturesque figure in popular French history, it is as a colourful
personality rather than as the head of a 'mother race'. The Gauls
were probably not natives of France at all (there is some evidence
that they were themselves invaders from northern Germany—
and they were in fact blond), but they are given the credit, and
French history books for children—even in Africa—used to begin
with the well-known phrase 'Our ancestors the Gauls . . .'.

In England on the other hand, most of the periodic invasions
spread vaguely over most of the island, starting from the estu-
aries. There was no organized resistance to the Romans, and in
any case English historians have never been particularly keen on
claiming for their ancestors the authorship of the revolutionary
principle that had been the excuse for Napoleon's conquests. If
they remember any invasion at all as part of the national history
it is that of William the Conqueror, which was resisted (much less
picturesquely and heroically) by a force of Anglo-Saxon rulers.
So the ancient Britons are felt to have been less nationalistic than
their successors: they have been degraded in popular feeling to
the rank of Celts and relegated to the western and northern
peninsulae, where the original language did indeed survive
longer.

Add to this the fact that for French historians and social
thinkers of Arnold's time, Germany was an enemy, and could not
be recognized as the mother of the race. England on the other
hand was going through a strong pro-German phase. Finally,
nineteenth-century historians, especially in France, were very
impressed by romantic views on what ancestors should have
looked like to be acceptable: the picturesque blond moustaches
of the Gauls were in their favour—though the Franks had had
interesting possibilities, exploited by most medieval historians,
since they were apparently well known for their courage in war.
Indeed, it is striking that interest in the Gauls disappeared from
literature from the fourth to the nineteenth century. Traditional

French literary thought before the Revolution always related France to the Franks. Ronsard called his epic poem the *Franciade* and traced the genealogy of the nation back to Priam through the Frankish kings. The Franks, says Arnold, suddenly lost control at the time of the Reformation; yet no sixteenth-century source gives us any evidence of blond moustaches having returned to fashion.

Races cannot be defined by one characteristic, even if they do exist. Arnold tries to describe them in a painfully simple way. Unfortunately, it is because of their childishness that his labels have stuck in the popular mind. He might admittedly argue that such was his aim, since by this time he was mainly trying to impress on his readers that the French, in their passion for equality, had lost their morality; yet the smallest amount of thought would show that apart from being absurd historically his racial traits are in any case relative. It is a fact that as one travels south in western Europe one seems to meet people who are more and more energetic, dark, and excitable—but England and Germany are not an absolute North. As Meredith puts it: 'With Germans we are supercilious Celts; with Frenchmen we are sneering Teutons.' In mixing his racial ingredients Arnold might well have taken note of the theory of his contemporary Henry Buckle, which was far more reasonable.[10]

In fact Arnold proceeds rather like the compiler of a crossword puzzle: planning as answers the racial configurations suggested by the contemporary French historians, he gives as clues the racial features necessary to lead to the conclusion he has in mind. We could maliciously retrace his footsteps. Since we have decided that modern France is not too moral and that the Gauls have stifled the Franks, let us call the former talkative and the latter moral: this arrangement turns out to be even more convenient for a British author, since he can lay claim to German descent and can therefore conclude with relief that his countrymen are more virtuous after all. In the same way, given a modern word and certain recognized philological laws one can work backwards

[10] *A History of Civilization in England* (1857–61). The features of peoples are formed by their surroundings; but after a certain degree of civilization the moral and educational climate takes over, and, though it began as a product, becomes itself an influence.

to an Indo-European root that will suit it perfectly and impress the layman. No matter if it is not to be found in any text; just add a modest asterisk in front of it. Arnold did not remember to put in the asterisk.[11]

Given the weakness of his racial theory, it would however be as well to recognize the root of Arnold's feeling. France undoubtedly gives many visitors an impression of gaiety and sociability that is not to be found in England: a puritan conscience such as Arnold's will naturally contrast this sooner or later with 'moral seriousness'. But the difference, such as it is, would seem to be due to the climate more than to anything else. In the south of France there are more opportunities to meet and talk and be sociable simply because it rains less. 'Racial features' only push the reasoning back a few generations, without explaining anything. If Western Europe was populated from a single source they have no reason to exist; if not, there has been sufficient intermingling on all sides to obliterate them. In any case the difference here between the French and the English has been grossly exaggerated, as any one who knows both countries will realize. The gay, talkative, frivolous Frenchman with the 'spirit of society' is a product of Paris and the warm, fertile southern plains and seaports. In large areas of France people are surly and uncommunicative, even bluntly melancholy, and might well answer the common description of the Englishman; whilst in England the 'spirit of society' could be found amongst Cockneys or in the Lowlands of Scotland, or indeed in any youth club.

IV. THE AVERAGE SENSUAL MAN

In the second (1874) edition of *Schools and Universities on the Continent*, Arnold omitted the part dealing with France, originally the mainstay of the work. He said in a preface that the examples of education in Germany could be used to better purpose. By 1882 he had completely reversed his former ideas on the French Eton. He wrote that year in *The Fortnightly Review*:

---

[11] The only possible historical source that I can discover for his theory on the morality of the Franks is that they were noted for being easily impressed by ceremony and superstition: this is not quite the same thing.

a modern French schoolboy, Voltairian and emancipated, reading *La Fille Elisa* and *Nana*, making it his pastime to play tricks on his chaplain, to mock and flout him and his teaching—the production of a race of lucid schoolboys of this kind is a dangerous privilege.

This new attitude, which appeared mainly in *Literature and Dogma* and in the second series of *Essays in Criticism*, and found justification in his theory of races, led him to condemn Latin nations as a whole:

everywhere, among these nations, you see the old indigenous type of city disappearing, and the type of modern Paris, the city of *l'homme sensuel moyen*, replacing it. *La Bohême* [sic], the ideal, free, pleasurable life of Paris, is a kind of Paradise of Ishmaels.

Arnold's reasons were both literary and political. His literary idols were tumbling down. As early as 1853 he had written to Clough that he could no longer read *Valentine* with so much pleasure; in 1859, he did not repeat the pilgrimage he had made to George Sand at Nohant in 1849 because, as he wrote to his wife: 'All Sainte-Beuve told me of her present proceedings made me less care about seeing her.' Her 'proceedings' with Musset, as well as those she had had with Chopin, had been common knowledge for at least ten years. Perhaps Arnold had not believed the rumours. At any rate, in 1859 she had just published a transposed account of them in *Elle et Lui*.

But 1870 is the real turning-point. Within the last few years many of the generation of Frenchmen Arnold had known had died: Vigny, Lamartine, Sainte-Beuve, Mérimée, Dumas. Renan had turned to German culture, and Sainte-Beuve before dying had condemned the new realist movement in art: '*L'idéal a cessé, le lyrique a tari*'. Arnold remaining faithful to his image of idealistic France (already apparent, as we have seen, in his early qualified praise of the Revolution) echoed Sainte-Beuve by disapproving of any sacrifice of the ideal to the real or of imagination to observation in literature:

The spirit of observation and the touch of hardness (let us retain these mild and inoffensive terms) have since been carried in the French novel very far. So far have they been carried, indeed, that in spite of the

D

advantage which the French language, familiar to the cultivated classes everywhere, confers on the French novel, this novel has lost much of its attraction for those classes. [*Essays in Criticism II*]

Now is the hour of the naturalists and realists, of the great work, as it is called, and solid art of Balzac, which Monsieur Daudet and other disciples are continuing; not the work of humanitarians and idealists like George Sand and her master Rousseau. [*Irish Essays*]

Arnold feels that the new fashion lessens the prestige of art and the influence of the critic in society. At this point his condemnation leaves the field of literature: in his letters to the *Pall Mall Gazette* and in 'The French Play in London', he suggests that realism in the novel and on the stage is due to a contemporary moral decline in France. As interest in the theatre began to increase again in London in the second half of the century, companies had returned to the age-old habit of adapting light and sometimes frivolous French comedies into English. The *Comédie Française* also came to London for a tremendously successful season. This met with Arnold's stern reprobation. *Impulse*, one of the adaptations fashionable in 1883, loses much of its interest for him because the moral principles of London are different from those of Paris. In this play a married woman had a transient lover; but there is no such thing, according to Arnold, in England:

Where he exists, where he is an institution, matters may well enough pass as they pass in the genuine French play; logic and experience are in favour of their so passing. Where he is an exotic, nothing can make him tolerable.

But the producers had had to change the plot in England, and punish the lover, making the story ridiculous; in spite of this the audience seemed to appreciate it.

Why should cool-headed people hide their conviction that this sort of drama is detestable, even though the journals of 'society' call to one another, deep to deep, 'Edmund' to 'Henry', that it is very good?

On this point Arnold was probably right, but by 1883 it was difficult to check the francophily of fashionable London; and it was arguable whether the very interest in such situations on the stage did not indicate a change in the moral attitude at home. The hard moralist of *Literature and Dogma* condemned all modern French writers. The 'average sensual Frenchman' in the frivolous plays and the yellow-coloured novels no longer resembled the intellectually conscious middle class or the republican peasantry that he still remembered at times: 'their modern drama, like their lighter newspapers, their novels, and their art in general, is a worshipper of the great goddess Lubricity.' Paris was no longer the centre of light, but the capital of pleasure, and Arnold saw an awful symbol in the fact that a Frenchman was free to call his child Lucifer Satan Vercingetorix.

The first of Zola's 'immoral' novels, *La Fortune des Rougon*, had fittingly been published in the year of the Commune: political events seemed to Arnold to confirm the progress of Evil in France. His attitude towards the Commune changed during the first few months of 1871. In 1859 he had been struck by the order and prosperity of the countryside in the south of France and by the rebuilding of Paris and the splendid pageantry organized by Napoleon III. As political freedom began to disappear towards 1865 he became less enthusiastic, but the first few weeks of the Commune could easily be interpreted within the framework of his social idealism as

an explosion of that fixed resolve of the working-class to count for something and *live*, which is destined to make itself so much felt. . . . It is the French working man's clearly putting his resolve before himself and acting upon it, while the working man elsewhere is in a haze about it, that makes France such a focus for the revolutionists of all Europe.

But though the working class should be conscious of political issues, it should not go as far as taking charge of them with a Commune. Arnold, a middle-aged man who frequented the drawing rooms of the ruling class, had become evasive about the Revolution: he was affected by the agitation amongst the English workers that followed the 1866 Reform Bill. In a letter to his mother (April 1871) his attitude is very conservative:

there is no way by which France can make the rest of Europe so alarmed and uneasy as by a socialist and red republic. It is a perpetual flag to the proletaire class everywhere—the class which makes all governments uneasy.

In a letter to M. de Fontanès he deprecates Burke's praise for the Revolution, and the following years show him building up a new system to explain this sudden decline of French public life.

He finds the key in the very loss of morality that seemed to him to be affecting French literature: the working class may burst out with righteous indignation, but the French, since they have let the Gauls take over from the Franks, lack the virtue to make anything lasting out of this. Whereas in 1859 Arnold had predicted that the French army could beat the combined forces of Austria and Prussia thanks to its self-respect and good organization, in 1870 he considers Napoleon's defeat as a kind of divine retribution for the moral wrongs of France (not an uncommon idea in England at the time). The fall is

mainly due to that want of a serious conception of righteousness and the need of it, the consequences of which so often show themselves in the world's history, and in regard to the Graeco-Latin nations more particularly. The fall of Greece, the fall of Rome, the fall of the brilliant Italy of the fifteenth century, and now the fall of France, are all examples.

Parts of the second series of *Essays in Criticism* are worthy of an avenging prophet:

whatever political combinations may be tried, and whether France gets colonies or not, and whether she allies herself with this nation or with that, things will only go from bad to worse with her; she will more and more lose her powers of soul and spirit, her intellectual productiveness, her skill in counsel, her might for war, her formidableness as a foe, her value as an ally, and the life of that famous State will be more and more impaired, until it perish.

And yet, with touching faith in the French peasant, Arnold tries to find fault rather with the intellectuals. Writing about George Sand again after her death in 1871, he calls her one of the greatest figures of the century *in spite of* 'her faults and Frenchism'. He regrets that she should not have condemned more strongly the blindness of the leading thinkers:

the furies, the follies, the self-deceptions of secularist and revolutionist fanatics filled her with dismay. They are indeed the great danger of France, and it is amongst the educated and articulate classes of France that they prevail. If the educated and articulate classes in France were as sound in their way as the inarticulate peasant is in his, France would present a different spectacle.

The essay on 'Equality', in many ways a summary of Arnold's ideas, gives what appears to be the final verdict: France lacks a 'sense of conduct', and this has spoilt her gift for social inter-course and her respect for method and intelligence.

We shall try to make out later whether France really could be convicted of immorality. Meanwhile, Arnold's condemnation is obviously too drastic: even to a romantic idealist (and he was, in theory, more experienced than that), Zola and the Commune should have appeared as accidental evils. It should have been sufficient to say that the realistic novels were boring and that the political disasters were the result of a weakness in the system. Instead, he helped to foster an opinion of French public life that became traditional. Unfortunately, during the following thirty years the events that reached the notice of Londoners tended only too often to prove this point. The Grévy, the Panama, the Dreyfus scandals could easily give an impression of corruption; and it was also at that time that the English began to think that the instability of governments in Paris reflected oscillations of the whole country, when it was in fact merely a feature resulting from the new Constitution. Well-disposed observers could easily have noted, instead of the corruption, the healthy reactions of the public in the Panama and the Dreyfus affairs. Arnold himself, had he been more tolerant, might have realized that the incessant adventures of the French in search of the ideal State are the result of a feature he had been prepared to admire in his youth; the willingness to apply intellectual principles directly to the realm of fact.

But Arnold was growing old: as his moral principles became more stern he imagined those of the French were weakening. His political ideas had swung to the right, as do those of so many youthful progressists. There was also a general trend, in the course of the nineteenth century, to become more and more suspicious of republicanism: the middle classes used it to gain power, but rejected it when the working classes adopted it in turn as a stepping stone. In a way Arnold's over-violent attacks can be explained by the same reason as his early enthusiasm—by a didactic intention. The younger generation had perhaps learnt his lessons too assiduously because all those who objected, whether lucidly or not, to English 'philistinism' were looking towards Paris. He may have felt that their admiration was too uncritical and accordingly exaggerated his own position. In 'The French Play in London', a plea against the enthusiasm for the *Comédie Française*, he confesses to having been guilty of a similar infatuation for Rachel in his youth, and warns his countrymen against it, as Wordsworth had in 1802 after the Peace of Amiens ('Shame on you, feebled heads, to slavery prone'):

> There is a new generation growing up amongst us,—and to this young and stirring generation who of us would not gladly belong, even at the price of having to catch some of its illusions and to pass through them?—a new generation which takes French poetry and drama as seriously as Greek, and for which M. Victor Hugo is a great poet of the race and lineage of Shakespeare.

He had in fact always made reservations on the value of French poetry. But to the iconoclastic young men of the 1880's, venturing to Paris in search of the pernicious moral influences they had been warned against, Arnold the romantic poet, the social idealist, the educator of the middle class, could well appear old-fashioned.

At the back of Arnold's mind there is always the idea that the image of France must be put to some use: as George Watson has pointed out, all his remarks are intended to be exemplary or cautionary:

> What makes me look at France and the French with such inexhaustible curiosity and indulgence is this,—their faults are not ours,

so we are not likely to catch them; their merits are not ours, so we are not likely to become idle and self-sufficient from studying them. . . . I no longer dance, nor look well when dressed up as the angel Gabriel, so what should I now do in Paris?—but I find such interest and instruction in considering a city so near London, and yet so unlike it! . . . I do not wish them [my countrymen] to be the café-haunting, dominoes-playing Frenchmen, but rather some third thing . . .

Though exemplary tales about foreign countries may sometimes have this effect, to say what one wishes is in this case the worst way to set about obtaining it. Arnold recommends order, measure, and elegance to the English, but if we examine the various facets of his view of France we find it exaggerated first one way and then the other because he is trying to convince; his overrating French intellectuals and his underestimating French morals are defensible in a way. But seen as a whole his interest in France is too tempered to be convincing, because in the middle of his career he took to expressing his scorn for French morals each time he praised French intellectuals. We may affect to scorn the blindness of a lover, but we are more readily convinced of his mistress's qualities if he compares her with the sky than if he says he has his eyes open and makes the compromise for us. In his criticism of England, Arnold pandered too much to English pride.[12] He merely played 'Rule Britannia' in a minor key. He encouraged a complacent form of self-depreciation that is still at large. His progressive ideas on education were restrained by too much conservatism for him to be taken seriously by a generation that also included disciples of Owen or William Morris:

[12] Arnold's successors illustrate this. Two critics, George Saintsbury and Edward Dowden, both very much under his influence, water down his ideas on France considerably. Saintsbury, in his book on Arnold (1899), mentions the Panama and Dreyfus scandals and criticizes Arnold for having been too lenient to French morality! He also says, rather obviously, that the French Academy has only been beneficial 'because the French spirit is academic', and that Arnold should have realized that the French Eton was French but not at all Eton. Dowden, in an article on Schérer (1889), says that he had a similar moral vigour to Arnold's: *though* a Parisian he had been born in Geneva of Protestant stock. The title of Dowden's Taylorian lecture for 1889, *Literary Criticism in France*, is also Arnoldian. But his admiration has been narrowed down to Sainte-Beuve. The other critics, he says, are *too French*: to be a critic one should not be too systematic (i.e. too un-English). Sainte-Beuve is for him an exceptional case. Finally, William Lecky follows a similar path in *Democracy and Liberty* (1896), where he regrets the passing of Lamartine and George Sand.

culture is not, as he occasionally appears to make out, a painless cure to save the middle classes. In the same way he would like to take a few hints from France so that England may remain as English as ever. The compromise he makes over the introduction of an Academy is a good illustration, and one of many. Ruth Temple has already made this point in *The Critic's Alchemy:*

> His counsels of perfection were proffered with so much deference to the *status quo*, his adverse criticism of his readers was cushioned with so many compliments of just the sort they would take to themselves with smug satisfaction, that one questions his effectiveness as a propagandist. The English public would so much rather be thought good than clever that it can scarcely have been disconcerted to be so described. . . . [It had long thought] the French nation artificial and frivolous if not actually immoral. May not Arnold's exhortations have confirmed, instead of shattering, these hoary prejudices?

Arnold's contribution to the image of France was not immediately apparent, except in the realm of education: his latter warnings, as those of J. S. Mill, William Lecky, and George Saintsbury, were disregarded by a young generation more interested in the superficial side of Parisian life. But the *lycée*-educated Frenchman with a gift for society had become one of the accepted ideas of the English. In uncritical minds Arnold's racial theories still hold fast.

· 3 ·

THE REPUBLIC

Swinburne and Meredith

She, likewise half corrupt of sin,
Angel and Wanton! Can it be?
MEREDITH

IN 1870 insular English opinion needed little encouragement to
return either to wholesale censure of France and her crackpot
dictators, or to the vague poetic faith in republicanism to
which Arnold had been sensitive in his youth. There was general
sympathy for Germany, and British interests obviously lay in the
creation of a second continental power capable of counteracting
France. Also, Bismarck's part in forcing the war upon his king
and upon the French ambassador was not known until after his
death in 1898. It was presumed at the time that France had started
the hostilities, as usual. A few weeks later, when Germany had
won a few battles, it was not felt, as it suits some historians to
believe now, that there was anything particularly wicked in
Germany doing in 1870 what France had done to her 'quiet
inoffensive' neighbour many times before. Carlyle, who had just
finished his *Life of Frederick II*, wrote a letter to the *Weimar
Gazette*, extracts of which were published in *The Times*, and
where he condemned

that ill-disposed France which has inflicted on it [Germany] such
interminable mischief during the last 400 years—wars heaped upon
wars without real cause except insatiable French ambition.

In January 1871 even *The Fortnightly Review*, under the intelligent liberal editor John Morley, published articles by Germans condemning French ambition. Not until May did it throw any light on the miserable state of France after the collapse of the Empire.[1] In this it followed the main trend of liberal opinion in England. George Eliot's correspondence gives a similar account of English sympathies: writing to a German friend she says that until Sedan her sympathies and those of all England were with the Prussians. A letter to a French friend in August 1870 takes an Arnoldian stand:

> I am very sorry for the sufferings of the French nation, but I think these sufferings are better for the moral welfare of the people than victory would have been. The war has been drawn down on them by an iniquitous Government, but in a great proportion of the French people there has been nourished a wicked glorification of selfish pride, which like all other conceit is a sort of stupidity. . . . Whatever charm we may see in the southern Latin races, this ought not to blind us to the great contributions which the German energies have made in all sorts of ways to the common treasure of mankind.

Her moral horror of the war is great, and she does not want to write much about it because it is 'too much with her'. In April 1871, however, her sympathies have changed in the opposite direction to those of Arnold:

> I love the French and am grateful to them for what they have contributed to the mind of Europe, feeling that the Good outweighs the Evil. The sad prospect of calamities yet to be heaped on what they have already endured makes the reading of the news and correspondence in the journals a daily grief.

And although the war awoke old suspicions, it also brought back a tradition of poetic defence of France: in the early months of 1871 Swinburne and Meredith, taking up the poetic rôle abandoned by Arnold, published odes in which they made France a symbol of Freedom.

I. ANGEL OR WANTON?

On the face of it Swinburne would have seemed the better placed

---

[1] In an article by Frederick Harrison, an active disciple of Comte, President of the London Positivist Committee.

A DUEL TO THE DEATH.

FRANCE. "PRAY STAND BACK, MADAM. YOU MEAN WELL; BUT THIS IS AN OLD FAMILY QUARREL, AND WE MUST *FIGHT IT OUT!*"

FRANCE, SEPT. 4, 1870.

"AUX ARMES, CITOYENS;
FORMEZ VOS BATAILLONS!"
The "Marseillaise."

A WORD TO THE WISE.

"'DESCENDED FROM THE GODS! ULYSSES, CEASE;
OFFEND NOT JOVE: OBEY, AND GIVE THE PEACE.'
SO PALLAS SPOKE."—*Odyssey Book xxiv.*

Some of Sir John Tenniel's comments on the Franco-Prussian War; his attitude changed towards the middle of September 1870. Notice the slow transformation of William I from an elderly gentleman being forced into a duel by a scoundrel, to a Hun chieftain. The image of a poor suffering France appears in November (see overleaf).

THE "NIOBE OF NATIONS."

"GAUL TO THE NEW CÆSAR.

"DEFIANCE, EMPEROR, WHILE I HAVE STRENGTH TO HURL IT!"

"CALL OFF THE DOGS!"

of the two to appreciate France. He cherished a sentimental connexion with Bordeaux, where ancestors of his were said to have lived in exile on two occasions: in his 'Song of the Centenary of W. S. Landor' he mentions

> Mine own twice-banished fathers' harbour land
> Their nursing-mother, France, the well-beloved.

This explains, according to a letter to Norman McColl, why he wrote his 'Ballad against the Enemies of France' in answer to Carlyle. With Swinburne as with Arnold, the impact of France is obviously becoming mainly literary. Swinburne was popularly supposed to be under French influence and he enjoyed playing to this reputation. His 1909 insertion in *Who's Who* lists '*Educ.* France, Oxford'. He visited Manet's studio in 1863 and met Whistler and the artistic society of Paris through Fantin-Latour and Legros, the Slade professor. He corresponded with Hugo and Mallarmé and contributed poems in French to the *Tombeau de Théophile Gautier* and to the review *La République des Lettres*; he mentions the latter with studied casualness in letters to Morley and Lord Houghton: 'I, as a French poet of the day, have been solicited to help in setting it on foot, together with Leconte de Lisle.' He transposed French verse forms into English, translated Villon, imitated the Pléiade poets very convincingly in *Chastelard*, wrote *A Year's Letters* after the manner of Laclos, and was commonly believed to have practised Baudelairian perversity in *Poems and Ballads*. He showed more discrimination with French poetry than Arnold (he recognized Baudelaire as early as 1861) and in return his wild manners were highly appreciated by the young self-conscious Parisian artists. A youthful article on 'Church Imperialism' for the Oxford *Undergraduate Papers*, on the other hand, shows a good knowledge of French political life: Swinburne is able to distinguish clearly between the various trends in the catholic party, a minor issue of the day.

And yet with all this, Swinburne's attitude to France was never more than 'literary' in the worst sense of the word. He did not spend more than a few weeks there, and he assumed the knowledgeable pose of the English aristocrat on the subject. There are

two main attitudes to France in his work: a lifelong, indiscrimin-
ating admiration for Victor Hugo, and a republicanism applied
indifferently to France or to Italy. Napoleon III, who had
oppressed the French and Italian nations and exiled Victor Hugo,
he consequently hated with personal spite. Thus:

The reputation for contempt of danger which he earns by calculated
parade of physical hardihood, is nullified by an exhibition of the most
abject moral cowardice. A tyrant of clearer insight might have used
to far other profit his escape from the unjustifiable attempt of
Orsini . . .

Swinburne discovered Victor Hugo through *Les Châtiments:* his
early poem-pamphlets attack Napoleon, Hugo's Aunt Sally, gaily
and irresponsibly; one is tempted to trace all his political thought
back to Hugo, not a very reliable source. 'A Song in Time of
Order' for instance, might well be attributed to a patriotic
provincial newspaper during a national disaster:

> When the devil's riddle is mastered
> And the Galley-Bench creaks with a Pope,
> We shall see Buonaparte the bastard
> Kick heels with his throat in a rope.

Political poetry at its best does not survive long; even in Swinburne's day these were second-hand vociferations.

The Third Republic, not really republican until 1880, also had
its share of abuse from his pen. By the late 1880's he had become
actively interested in the affairs of England, so that any political
quarrel, such as the Franco-Russian treaty or a controversy in
English and French periodicals over the value of the system of
Common Law, was a pretext for more angry verse with as its
theme the title of second-rate leading articles: 'Falsehood, thy
name is France!' At the time of the *Rondeaux Parisiens* Swinburne
exclaims in apology that Hugo's death has set him free from
former obligations to restraint: one can but wonder which.[2]
With this in mind, it is difficult to treat his cries of joy at the

---

[2] Lafourcade, an excellent French critic of Swinburne, points out maliciously that the
Rondeaux are too violent to be taken seriously: they could therefore be interpreted as
ironic counter-criticism of England. Fortunately, Watts-Dunton eventually published
them at a time when no one could take them seriously: in 1917.

proclamation of the Republic seriously; any revolution would probably have received the same support. Nevertheless, as Lafourcade remarks, 'it was from this quarter that came the single confirmation of all the vain prophecies which Swinburne's Muse poured upon an unheeding world'. Swinburne wrote to Rossetti that 'on hearing the fall of the Empire' an ode had literally burst out of him.

Four months later *The Fortnightly Review* published another ode, this time from an unexpected source. Its author, Meredith, had not dealt with political subjects before and his ties with France were as slender as Swinburne's were numerous. He had crossed the Channel twice without paying attention to very much apart from the food. His education was completed at a time when it was fashionable to round off one's studies in a German university. Much as French critics like to claim *The Egoist* for their classical tradition, or *The Shaving of Shagpat* as Voltairian, he does not seem to have been more widely read in French than any moderately cultured Englishman of his time. His second wife, though he later chose to consider her as a reflection of a country he had come to like, was not French but of a Swiss family long established in England. At most, his stay with her in Normandy prompted the loving descriptions we find in *Beauchamp's Career*.

Meredith, too, criticized Napoleon in verse: the fashion started by Hugo died hard. A sonnet entitled '*Il y a cent ans*' is a disgusted commemoration of the rise of Napoleon I; some patriotic poems on the centenary of Trafalgar savour of Kipling. The last of his series of four odes on France published in 1898 deplores the fact that Napoleon should have become the patron saint of France instead of Joan of Arc. The conversations from *The Graphic* collected under the title *Up to Midnight* analyse Napoleon's failure quite lucidly and in any case less passionately than Swinburne had done:

To perpetuate a dynasty requires a clean hand, or a strong one, not a surpassingly flashing one at legerdemain, that hatches an egg in a pocket-handkerchief, an eagle out of a chestnut. Work well for the day; leave a dynasty to take care of itself. A dynasty in France is the lid on a pot. There's nothing for it to take root in. . . . Of all men he should have been alertest, for when he gained his throne he agreed to supply the place of Providence to the French people, to labour for them, to think for them, to fatten them, and to give them glory cheap.

He thinks that the Napoleonides were at odds with the traditional genius of France because they were confidence tricksters rather than great lucid men:

The Monarchist Thiers, the Republican Béranger, and all the French song-writers, assisted to sow the Napoleonic legend. By their aid the French have been fed on falsified history for fifty years.

Finally, Meredith judges once and for all French militarism, which led the country into error under Napoleon as under MacMahon a few years later. His opinion might well apply in our own day.

Her philosophers said one thing, but military glory stuck to the passions of her people. And many of her philosophers allowed themselves to be hoodwinked by the idea that France should be dominant 'for the good of mankind', instead of seeking to make her dominant by virtue and a bright example. She trusted to the sword without even testing the steel. She is down, I grieve for her; I detest the severities practised upon her. But I cannot forget that she appealed to the droit du plus fort.

During the war Meredith, without being germanophile, had not approved of the French position. The news made it difficult for anyone not to condemn France for warmongering. Meredith wrote to his friend Maxse (said to have been the model for Beauchamp), that France was in need of a bitter lesson. For his was not a casual interest, any more than was Swinburne's. France was the preoccupation of the day. Swinburne's attacks are those of a disgusted lover, Meredith's coolness is that of a puzzled friend: neither wished to condemn France absolutely.

Both Swinburne and Meredith were, in fact, in a cleft stick; divided between patriotism and idealism, they lived through the same dilemma as Wordsworth had in 1793 when war was declared. The age demanded of poets that they proclaim their patriotism (an attitude still illustrated for instance by Hardy's film-script, *The Dynasts*). As a result, they could only serve a republican cause if it were not directly contrary to British interests. Many poets were interested in Italian unity in the 1850's, and England did not have a great interest in its outcome; yet Elizabeth Browning still had to apologize, in the preface to *Poems before Congress*, for not always showing 'a patriotic respect to the English sense of things', and could only permit herself mild criticism of 'Little Pedlingtonism'.[3]

There was a second problem: for Swinburne and Meredith, Napoleon III was obviously evil, and yet on the other hand both felt more or less obscurely that France stood for a kind of intellectual freedom. They faced a dilemma that began when Napoleon I was crowned and has lasted to the present day: how to reconcile esteem for the self-appointed home of Reason and Freedom with the scorn that Englishmen in particular must also feel for a country that goes through a fit of shameless militarism or gives itself a king stork every forty years or so. The notoriety of France as a trouble-maker in Europe, especially in the last century, worried the admirers of her letters: the 1870 war is brought up against her in a book of literary criticism as late as 1907.[4] Progressive intellectuals were in a position similar to that of communists in Western Europe today: they were constantly being accused of placing their faith in a dangerous neighbour, and they were perhaps not as experienced as we are in the failures of political idealism. Little can be said in defence of France on this score: as Meredith wrote, her philosophers at least are not always absorbed by the general feelings—but this is true of philosophers anywhere. English observers, we should perhaps add, commonly disregard the fact that French government is much more centralized than their own: it must therefore be appreciably stronger,

[3] She, like Swinburne, swung with the vane of events in the course of *Poems before Congress*, starting with praise for France:
> Happy are all free peoples, too strong to be dispossessed
> But blessed are those among nations who dare to be strong for the rest.
Then turning against Napoleon when he drew back from his commitments in Italy:
> Napoleon—as strong as ten armies,
> Corrupt as seven devils.

[4] J. C. Bailey: *The Claims of French Poetry* (p. 182). This book is also one of the most rabid instances of the theory according to which poetry is uncongenial to the French language (see above p. 22-23). Its greatest merit is that it provoked Lytton Strachey into writing his well-known essay on Racine in reply.

and this need has not been properly met by either the third or the fourth Republic.

Swinburne's and Meredith's odes are both attempts to solve this dilemma at the time of the 1870 crisis, through a medium that was common amongst poets and historian-philosophers of the last century—grandiose allegory. Adhering to a tradition of fervent Napoleonic or anti-Napoleonic verse started by Wordsworth, Coleridge, Scott, Southey, and Byron, they both imagined France as a woman representing Freedom but 'waited on by dread and doom.' The problem is twofold: how can Freedom have allowed herself to be plundered by the Bonaparte family? And how can one reconcile her virtues with the crimes she must have committed in order to be punished by a divine hand, as she is at present? If the odes are stripped of the heroic war-imagery they have in common, they hinge on these two questions.

Meredith's ode, as finally published, is the third of a sequence of four. He has already answered the first question in his ode on the 1789 revolution: France weds the revolutionary principles and True Liberty when she meets them in the shape of a heavenly bridegroom half-way from the sky. When faithful to him she is a splendid woman:

> The brilliant eyes to kindle bliss,
> The shrewd quick lips to laugh and kiss,
> Breasts that a sighing would inspire,
> And laughter-dimpled countenance.

Unfortunately, she is also wanton; she deserts her gentle lover, first for the Terror, then to become a slave to the young Titan she has fostered—Napoleon. He in his turn deserts her, preferring Fame.

Swinburne's allegory, which appears in his antistrophes, is somewhat more entangled: France has a soul, Liberty, and when united they are

> The voice whereat the thunders stood astounded
> As at a new sound of God unknown.

But they have somehow parted during the events leading up to the second Empire: France has 'done ill against her soul'. It is this soul that we see, rising ghoulishly from the ashes of the civil war at the beginning of the poem. It brings a robe that France will wear as a bride once the two are reunited. Here too the husband will descend from the sky, but for Swinburne he is a vaguer divinity, called

> Light of light, name of names, . . .
> Life, spirit, blood and breath . . .
> Lord of the lives of lands,
> Spirit of man

and later the

> . . . kingless people's king,
> Called by thy name of thanksgiving
> Freedom, and by thy name of might
> Justice, and by thy secret name
> Love . . .

In fact he somehow becomes a second symbol of Freedom.

In the image that closes his poem Swinburne really evades the second question. He suggests that the sun has merely been misted over for a time, that this is the September of France's glory, which will eventually lead to another spring. We feel the poet thinking that now Napoleon is gone it will be possible to blame him for all the sins of the country he misled. Meredith, on the other hand, is more ambitious for he also asks why France should have let herself be led into such suffering. What is it in her that conspires against her own ideal? He first tries to analyse what makes for the enlightenment of France—this is the main point of interest in his poem for us. The various qualities of which France is 'mother' have been adulterated in the misery of civil war: Pride, Delicacy, Luxury, Heroism represented by a martial youth, Honour, Glory, and finally Reason, have all rotted. The last loss is the greatest: her Reason makes France even more acutely conscious than others of the justice and logic of her degradation; it thus becomes a stabbing conscience and it remembers earlier crimes such as lawless Might or Carnage, whose ghosts rise to feed off her body. Though the mother of Reason, in a supreme desertion of self, tries to appeal to the mercy of the gods (there had been a revival

of superstition in France during the war), she is considered guilty
of supreme ὕβρις for having created nations—this was stealing the
divine fire, and she is punished, as Prometheus was, by vultures.
The events of 1870 are in fact a retribution for her early unfaith-
fulness. The poet advises her to purify herself in her suffering:

> Now is Humanity on trial in thee
> Now may'st thou gather humankind in fee:
> Now prove that Reason is a quenchless scroll;
> Make of calamity thine aureole,
> And bleeding lead us thro' the troubles of the sea.

None of this is outstanding poetry; but I find the last few pages
of Meredith's ode moving, particularly in view of the difficult
problems it attempts to solve. It shows us Meredith in a slightly
different light from the one we are accustomed to associate with
his brilliantly sarcastic novels and his cynical poetry. The lack of
ease here goes with a great deal of earnest feeling. By contrast
Swinburne's effort, in spite of the talent shown in its magnificent
rhythms, is no more than an ecstatic exercise in noble rhetoric.
The profusion of colour and sound leads to nothing but cumula-
tive vagueness.

Meredith seems to have helped himself from his friend's ode,
which contains in germ much of what he says.[5] But there is more
stuff in his poem, even if this philosophizing is not exactly poetry.
It is at least more than circumstantial verse put to martial music.
Meredith's judgement on Napoleon, where he had suggested
that France might be redeemed by her philosophers, is taken
up and developed here. Note the set of Revolutionary virtues of
which France is mother: they are all opposites of Christian virtues
(humility, poverty, valour . . .) and they culminate in Reason, a
contrary to Faith. France is judged by pagan gods through a
pagan idea of Fate for a classical sin (excessive ambition), and she
is condemned to the punishment of Prometheus; this gives full
value to the line 'Now is Humanity on trial in thee'. France is for

---

[5] The image of Prometheus—found first in Byron—is in the first of Swinburne's
antistrophes; also the cry 'O many-wounded mother, redeemed to reign' which gives
Meredith his list of Revolutionary virtues; and the idea of France as a humanist value
('Proclaiming manhood to mankind'). M. E. Mackay gives in the appendix to her
Meredith et la France a convincing list of the images borrowed.

Meredith a civilizing force, even if it has failed temporarily; it is no longer a mere abstract figure of revolt, but is connected with pagan ideals—we shall see how this also reflects a trend in Walter Pater's view of France. Reason is the mother of a kind of humanism, based on a 'quenchless scroll' that is the best in humanity. Few Frenchmen could want higher praise of the aim of the Revolution, nor could many point to a poet who had written of it with such lucid, albeit magnified, enthusiasm.

II. FRIVOLITY

Meredith's novels do not fully develop the ideas suggested in his ode; they reveal instead a curious tension between traditional patterns and attempts at personal theories that are perhaps marred through a loss of real interest. The scattered references to France are linked by the idea that the people there are sharper-witted, a trait that Meredith finds appealing, but unfortunately connects with frivolity.

There is a certain amount of confused thought when, imitating Arnold in one of his more dogmatic moods, he generalizes lightly about racial features. Thus, in *One of our Conquerors* we read that the French

> are the most mixed of any European nation; so they are packed with contrasts: they are full of sentiment, they are sharply logical; free-thinkers, devotees; affectionate, ferocious; frivolous, tenacious; the passion of the season operating like sun or moon on these qualities; and they can reach to ideality out of sensualism. Below your level, they're above it:—a paradox is at home with them!

Meredith thought that people of racially mixed parentage are more sensitive: his Emilia and Diana are instances of this principle, and he extends the quality to the French, supposing quite wrongly that they are more mixed than other European peoples. (They merely appeared to be so at the time because many of the founders of ethnography were French and magnified their home material.) Another theory of his is that the French, and particularly the Normans, are Celts;[6] which also creates some confusion. This idea

[6] He said in an interview: '*La lourde pâte anglo-saxonne fermente grâce au levain de Normandie*' (*Revue de Paris*, 1910). Arnold had written much the same thing in a letter to his

is in the mind of Mrs. Lovell, the sensitive heroine of *Rhoda Fleming*: she had admired Napoleon, and liked in the French

their splendid boyishness, their unequalled devotion, their merciless intellects; the oneness of the nation when the sword is bare and pointing to chivalrous enterprise.

She liked their fine varnish of sentiment, which appears so much on the surface that Englishmen suppose it to have nowhere any depth; as if the outer coating must necessarily exhaust the stock, or as if what is at the source of our being can never be made visible.

Alvan (*The Tragic Comedians*), Matey Weyburn (*Lord Ormont and his Aminta*), and the countess of Saldar (*Evan Harrington*) also praise the capacity of the French for action; but the French are not alone in Meredith's mind, since the same qualities are emphasized in Irishmen in *Celt and Saxon*. He is merely using the 'Celts', French or Irish, as weapons with which to spur the English.

Meredith had shown some poetic enthusiasm for Reason: for most of the intelligent characters in the novels France is the home of clever conversation, which their author naturally admired. In *The Egoist* Mrs. Mountstuart reflects on the dullness of her dinnertable: 'Must we import Frenchmen to give them an example in the art of conversation as their grandfathers brought over marquises to instruct them in salads?' In *The Tragic Comedians* Alvan compares Clotilde with Paris, and symbolizes her qualities by light:

his beloved of cities—the symbolized goddess of the lightning brain that is quick to conceive, eager to realize ideas, impassioned for her hero, but ever putting him to proof, graceful beyond all rhyme, colloquial as never the Muse; light in light hands, yet valiant unto death for a principle; and therefore not light, anything but light in strong hands, very steadfast rather: and oh! constantly entertaining.

Mrs. Mountstuart is obviously meant to be a Celt: 'we' refers to the leaven of English society, and 'them' to the rest of the herd. Alvan's ideas, on the other hand, remind us of Meredith's own lucid remarks on Napoleon's strong government. But there is not only praise for the French mind: its lightness can lead to frivolity.

daughter (1859): 'It is the Norman element in England which has kept her from getting stupid and humdrum too, as the pure Germanic nations tend to become for want of a little effervescing salt with their magnesia.'

One of the talkers in *Up to Midnight* compares the lightness of French conversation with the ponderous seriousness of Germans (see Arnold), and wonders whether the English (Meredith's English) could make the ideal compromise. In terms of piano-playing French conversation is like

> running up the gamut-octaves incessantly and down again, and then bumping the notes and splashing out a tune all to oneself. . . . This it is to be transcendent monologuers, copious, overflowing, possibly brilliant, but it is not to be conversational. A Frenchman sees a dozen things to reply to before you have well begun: a *oui* or a *non* is quite enough to strike a new keynote for another of his symphonies, and he is not to be restrained.

Whereas Meredith's men are mostly British in character, his superlatively sensitive, ideally articulate women are not at home in English society. They are all linked with his intellectual ideal, and the most brilliant are felt to be close to France. We have seen Clotilde compared with Paris; in *Emilia in England* Lady Gosstre says of a society poet who has praised her 'art' that he does not, of course, mean an 'art' similar to his:

> He means another kind of art. The term 'artist', applied to our sex, signifies 'Frenchwoman' with him. He does not allow us to be anything but women. As artists then we are largely privileged, I assure you.

Meredith believed that only frank and perfectly equal relations between men and women could give the interplay of ideas its full scope, and that this was to be found in France. The intelligent woman would have an influence similar to that of the Celt over the rather dull Englishman. Meanwhile Frenchwomen are close to the ideal.

The brilliance and the air of faint mystery surrounding Meredith's women brings to mind the carefully suggested atmosphere created by the Vionnets in James's *The Ambassadors*. Arnold Bennett, too, was to depict it. It does not appear that French women had been seen thus before Meredith. I would suggest that he was extending a feature noted by historians of literature: the influence of the salons, and the great ladies who ran them, on French literature and politics. Walpole had told everyone of

Mme. du Deffand, and observers during the Revolution had noted the importance of Mme. Roland or Mme. de Stael. Sainte-Beuve's *Portraits de Femmes* emphasized the idea in England. However, a remark made by Lord Palmet, a minor comic character in *Beauchamp's Career* who is considered a 'connoisseur in women', launches the author into these thoughts:

Name the two countries which alone have produced the WOMAN, the ideal woman, the woman of art, whose beauty, grace, and wit offer her to our contemplation in an atmosphere above the ordinary conditions of the world: these two countries are France and Greece! None other give you the perfect woman, the woman who conquers time, as she conquers men, by virtue of the divinity in her blood; and she, as little as illustrious heroes, is to be judged by the laws and standards of lesser creatures. In fashioning her, nature and art have worked together: in her, poetry walks the earth. The question of good or bad is entirely to be put aside. . . .

This is enthusiastic praise, and yet the nagging problem of morality lurks behind it: the 'question of good or bad' is to be put aside, and the Frenchwoman is not to be judged by the laws 'of lesser creatures', but the author has had to say it twice, as if to convince himself. As Alvan suggested, he cannot help thinking that there is nothing beneath the varnish.

This passage was inspired by Meredith's one real French-woman: Renée. Her gift of speech is one of the first qualities that impress Beauchamp when he first meets her:

thought flew, tongue followed, and the flash of meaning quivered over them like night-lightning. Or oftener, to speak truth, tongue flew, thought followed: her age was but newly seventeen, and she was French.

At their second meeting she has become more refined:

Renée's gift of speech counted unnumbered strings which she played with a grace that clothed the skill, and was her natural endowment—an art perfected by the education of the world. Who cannot talk! but who can?

The metaphor continues, describing the flight of ideal conversation as that of two birds, in turn circling around and chasing each other. Though it will be appreciated how difficult this is, Meredith manages to sharpen the wings of his dialogue even further during Nevil's stay with Renée in Normandy, thus giving the reader the same sense of sudden depth as at the beginning of one of his books. But there are reservations, which are reflected in the story itself.

Beauchamp's Career begins by trying to assess the French symbolically. The Englishman discovers France but finds difficulty in grasping the spirit of the country completely, and wonders whether to approve of it: Nevil falls in love with a French girl who cannot marry him because of family conventions of her own, and he cannot decide whether to remain faithful to her or not. The pattern was entirely new in the English novel. There had been an attempt at a mixed love affair in *A Tale of Two Cities*, but Dickens only went half way, for he made Charles Darnay partly French. It is difficult to introduce new situations to the novel-reading public: the author who does so runs the risk of being misjudged for twenty years. Even Meredith does not quite dare to upset normal preconceptions, and so he makes Nevil intrude into Renée's family by accident and because of the Crimean War (one of the very few incidents in nineteenth-century history over which the French and English were liable to agree). Later on in the novel, Renée has to struggle in Nevil Beauchamp's mind with the English Cecilia, who perhaps represents his patriotic scruples; unless she is intended to stand for measure against passion as Janet clearly does in *Harry Richmond*, in opposition to the German princess Ottilia.

Beauchamp's Career seems at first to be launching into a studied comparison. There is a parallel between the family spirit in the two countries; Renée shows Nevil how tight her allegiance is to her father's word:

I know my ancestors are bound up in me, by my sentiments to them; and so do you, M. Nevil. We shame them if we fail in courage and honour. Is it not so? If we break a single pledged word we cast shame on them.

Her father is misguidedly but seriously considering the welfare of his children. Meanwhile, Everard Romfrey, when pressed to come to Venice where Nevil, his nephew and closest relation, is seriously ill, laughs at the thought

in hopeless ridicule of a Frenchman's notions of an Englishman's occupations—presumed across the Channel to allow of his breaking loose from shooting engagements at a minute's notice, to rush off to a fetid foreign city notorious for mud and mosquitoes, and commence capering and grimacing, pouring forth a jugful of ready-made extravagances, with *mon fils! mon cher neveu! Dieu!* and similar fiddle-dedee. These were matters for women to do, if they choose: women and Frenchmen were much of a pattern.

So much for Saxon 'seriousness' in this case. The French sense of family honour makes the Englishman's preoccupations appear futile. But this French trait is not developed any further: it merely serves to introduce a mordant bit of criticism of England.

The comparison stops here. Later Renée summons Nevil to Normandy, interrupting his election campaign merely to win a bet with a frivolous aristocrat. This serves to underline the exaggerated seriousness and petty intrigue of English party politics while indicting France with frivolity. Nevil 'stood divided between a sense of the bubbling shallowness of the life about him, and a thought, grave as an eye dwelling on blood, of sinister thoughts below it.' He eventually decides that she is shallow, but when he returns to England he is himself said to have fought a duel—a supreme frivolity. He is convicted in people's minds for hesitancy. It could be an interesting situation, for Nevil by now is in the position of the would-be francophile who has lost his line of retreat into safe patriotism, but is also having doubts on the value of France. Unfortunately, Meredith appears to discontinue the line of thought, for at this point the book turns into a novel of political ideas; Renée, who comes to London melodramatically, is for fortuitous reasons never confronted with Cecilia. Anyway, Nevil chooses neither the French wit nor the English rose, but a serious girl whom he does not love. Renée is cast aside, as was Ottilia in *Harry Richmond*: these two charming creatures are rather sadly wasted—they represented the virtues of their peoples so well and might have danced so prettily opposite their English rivals.

The hero, however, has turned away from France mainly because her wit does not make up for her frivolity. This conclusion contradicts what Alvan said in the quotation from *The Tragic Comedians* about looking underneath the varnish, and therefore also refutes part of Meredith's own feeling. There are two reasons for this. First, though he is attracted to his witty characters and obviously enjoys pulling on their strings, his attitude in the final analysis is deeply English. In each case he prefers to the light, brilliant character, a more profoundly reasonable being, endowed with something very similar to Arnold's 'German seriousness'. The English, says Shaw, think they are moral when they feel uncomfortable: there are traces of this attitude when Meredith strains himself to find a moral always, though he is happier when giving himself to psychological epigram. Renée is not the only one to suffer from her author's pangs of conscience. In *The Egoist* Dr. Middleton is supremely articulate. He proves it by his clever flattening of Sir Willoughby in the coach. But this quality is combined with moral blindness: if it were not for Vernon, the less brilliant but more morally reliable hero, he would give his daughter to the egoist for the sake of his port. Over-subtlety is always punished, and here Meredith is curiously in agreement with his own critics. When Sir Willoughby's sisters try to tell Dr. Middleton that the lord has asked for someone's hand the intellectual depth of the exchange is such that he cannot discover whose hand it is.[7] In the same novel Colonel de Craye, a Norman, is no more than a ladies' jester.

On the other hand the ambitious qualities stressed in the ode of 1871 are such as would make up for the frivolity he seems to discover in the novels. 'Anything but light in strong hands' said Alvan, and Meredith remarks in the *Essay on Comedy*: 'The French lay marked stress on *"mesure et goût"*, and they own how much they owe to Molière for leading them in simple just-ness and taste.' But there is a curious breakdown of these ideas as soon as the background to the English novel is concerned. Compare Alvan's opinion of Paris to the character of the French

---

[7] See also the *quid-pro-quo* that almost spoils the lives of General Ople and Lady Camper. Here too the moral comes right at the end of the story, as if Meredith were atoning for his own sins by an afterthought.

count in *Beauchamp's Career*: the count, shallow, useless, insincere, is merely part of a tradition concerning the French aristocrat, which Meredith takes up without having had any personal experience on the matter, purely because he is a popular figure, known to the readers of the day. He is inherited from Thackeray's moments of more insular thought, or from the scorn of Fielding or Hogarth: Meredith has not seen fit to question his features. This example is very revealing. We can see from it that Meredith has not really renewed the image of France, though he may have touched it and made it sparkle a moment with the wand of his suggestive prose.

The 'bubbling shallowness' of the Frenchman in the minds of the English dates back to the eighteenth century. The Frenchmen who crossed the Channel at that time were actors, valets, dancing and fencing masters, cooks: they shared a reputation for levity and probably deserved it. During the Revolution, England was introduced to the more light-headed members of the French aristocracy: the sensible émigrés returned home under the Directoire or at the beginning of the Empire. Add to this the fact that many Frenchmen are undoubtedly smaller, more agile, and more readily articulate than the average Englishman, and it will not be surprising to see the Frenchman traditionally associated with a prancing puppet. His tongue is as light as the hands that he waves around as he talks. He is carried away by words, impressed by the rhetoric in his poetry, he boxes with his feet and will dance his way into a duel for a trifle. This contrasts strongly with the Englishman's image of himself: strong, sturdy, silent, reliable, the oak as opposed to the willow. But it is no less different from the Frenchman's image of *him*self: for him, the frivolity and paradoxes of witty conversation are superficial. He believes he has, all joking apart, a sense of civic dignity and justice that makes him try more often than the Englishman to adapt fact to ideal: his revolutions should not be taken, therefore, as Carlyle took them, as instances of frivolity. He is conscious that Molière and Montesquieu were Frenchmen too, and that they scorned the mannerisms of *précieuses* and *petits maîtres*. Rational idealism, the love of clear analysis and logical thought he would claim as his own.

· 4 ·

SKETCHES FROM THE OTHER CITY

William Makepeace Thackeray

> What could we do without Paris? There is some-
> thing fatal about the place—a charm about it—a
> wicked one very likely—but it acts on us all; and
> perpetually the old Paris man comes hieing back to
> his quarters again, and is to be found, as usual, sun-
> ning himself in the Rue de la Paix. Painters,
> princes, gourmands, officers on half-pay—serious
> old ladies even acknowledge the attraction of the
> place—are more at ease here than in any other
> place in Europe.
>
> THE PARIS SKETCH BOOK

To appreciate fully the image of the Dancing Frenchman on which Meredith fell back when his own ideas failed, it is necessary to go back a little in history. To pander to an already popularized view of France, Meredith was led to use a set of stereotyped features best represented in the works of Mr. Punch and one of his main originators, Thackeray.

Thackeray thus represents, as it were, a background to our study. During the second empire, Arnold's Intelligent Frenchman had paraded up and down the literary stage, closely followed by the Immoral Gaul; Swinburne and Meredith had then brought the Revolutionary on to the scene, and pleaded for and against him; but Pater and Henry James had not yet founded a new tradition on France, and so Arnold's and Meredith's representations remained spasmodic. As soon as they left the stage the

EXPLANATION OF THE ALLEGORY

Number 1's an ancient Carlist, Number 3 a Paris Artist,
Gloomily there stands between them, Number 2 a Bonapartist ;
In the middle is King Louis-Philip standing at his ease,
Guarded by a loyal Grocer, and a Sergeant of Police ;
4's the people in a passion, 6 a Priest of pious mien,
5 a Gentleman of Fashion, copied from a Magazine.

Frontispiece from *The Paris Sketch Book*

English public must have become conscious once again of the backcloth that Thackeray had painted and Mr. Punch refurbished before a wide audience every week.

It will be useful to see, by comparison with the accepted ideas of their day, how liberal Arnold and Meredith had been. Thackeray represents the most insular approach possible in an intelligent writer, for he did not go to France to draw lessons that would be useful to the English, and therefore does not quite fulfil the criteria I set down for a 'live' interest. But his view must be mentioned because, though most of his remarks are John Bullish and unfair, we also find in his various sketches and essays the first awakening to the French artistic scene.

I. FITZBOODLE AND THE FROGS

Thackeray lived in Paris from 1833 to 1836, and again in 1840 for a little over a year. During his first stay there, he was working intermittently as a journalist, and during the following ten years or so most of the articles he printed in magazines refer to Paris. Apart from those collected in *The Paris Sketch Book* there are about two dozen miscellaneous essays. Thackeray comes to think of himself as an authority on Paris. He talks of the Parisian stage and its minor productions with a familiarity that must have embarrassed his fellow critics. He reviews the works of Eugène Sue (the contemporary Ian Fleming) and distinguishes between the various levels of popular melodrama in a way that shows he was well acquainted with the French literary men and their public. He was in fact even harder on the other Englishmen who ventured to write books on Paris than on the French themselves: he relentlessly exposed their ignorance and the literary tricks they used to make up this kind of book on travel—usually more than half is copied from guide books by people who have not always been to the place they describe. Thackeray, in the spirit of the true newspaper correspondent, regarded France as his field.

Yet we find the same man writing, in *The Paris Sketch Book*, that, as a Frenchman 'might have lived a thousand years in England, and never could have written Pickwick, an Englishman cannot hope to give a good description of the inward thoughts

and ways of his neighbours'. There is a huge difference between
his attitude and some approaches we shall meet in expatriates
later on in the century. Thackeray was in Paris mainly to earn
money as a correspondent and because life was cheaper there
than in London. In his novels we often hear of characters who go
to live in France because they cannot keep up the number of
servants or of carriages they used to have in London. The Anglo-
Indians with whom he was connected and whom he describes
in *The Yellowplush Papers*, are there for this reason. As a result, he
looks on French life with indifference unless it be possible material
for a report to a London journal. He is in a way too intimate
an acquaintance of the French capital to provide the impressions
of an outsider.

It must also be noted that the period Thackeray spent in Paris
coincided with his difficult literary beginnings and the personal
trials he had to endure during the illness of his wife. Ill-luck and
pettishness are often paramount in these first works, which show
his irony developing and practising on fertile French ground.
He insists, hopelessly, on applying English ideas to French ways.
During his first stay there he married the most English girl he
could find. He seems to have whiled away the time in embroider-
ing around the rather obvious extravagances and absurdities of
the French.

Thus in a typical essay, entitled *Foreign Correspondence* and
written in 1833, he says that even in the summer, when nothing
is really happening in either London or Paris, 'the people of
France are always rich enough in absurdities to occupy and amuse
an English looker-on'. But his interest never went much further:
he did not even trouble to make up a consistent view and often
contradicts himself within the space of a few pages. His articles
illustrate how often the French do service for foreigners in general
merely because France is the most convenient place for an exile
to go and live and become conscious of his Englishness. Paris
stands for a certain amount of freedom from English duties, but
any city would have the same part to play if it were at the
same distance from London. Thackeray does not reach the absurdity of the Englishman who said that it was very silly of the French

soldiers to wear blue uniforms; but at times, if we were to take him seriously and not understand that literature is always a form of diversion for him, we might suspect him of this.

The standard introduction by Messrs. Titmarsh, Yellowplush, or Fitzboodle describes the journey from Dover to Calais or Boulogne, the sea-sickness and minor inconveniences of travelling, and the first Frenchmen, who are inevitably profiteers. The author of *The Paris Sketch Book*, fighting against sickness and burdened with an unconscious wife and crying children, is impressed by an amiable Frenchman who offers sympathy and advice during the crossing. The fellow turns out to be merely an agent for a

Fitzboodle sets foot in France

Boulogne hotel. Another story describes how a young and foolish Englishman is caught by an adventuress who 'works' the Boulogne route, and attracts admirers to a gambling trap in Paris. Thackeray used this scheme again in some articles for *Punch* in 1849, and for the rest of the century whenever there was a special event in Paris (the exhibitions of 1867 or 1869, or the various Salons) *Punch* sent an imaginary correspondent who would describe the same kind of journey and adventures amongst the 'Mossoos' in an attempted imitation of Thackeray's style.

One of the first things to be noted was usually the food. When reporting on the change that had come over Paris when he visited

F

it after the 1848 revolution, Thackeray remarked with relief that though the gay fashion shops had disappeared and there were soldiers everywhere, the best restaurants were still, fortunately, well provided. This easy subject has always afforded English observers their worst platitudes and Thackeray is no exception. A long article in *Fraser's Magazine* entitled 'Memorials of Gormandizing', which attempts to give an account of some of the author's meals, is a typical hotchpotch of pretensions. The French eat less, but their food is more pleasantly served; references to various Parisian restaurants seem to show that the author genuinely believed that these things were only properly understood there. But the article presumably did not have to offend its British readers, and so on the next page we have a description of a dinner with some Irish friends in Paris: Thackeray says he ate three times the amount, and suddenly declares that the large spread showed 'Simplicity, Modesty, Hospitality' which the French can only match with

> Waiters with their hair curled
> Pheasants roasted with their tails on
> A dozen spermacetti candles.

Add them up, I say, O candid reader, and answer in the sum of human happiness, which of the two accounts makes the better figure.

Further on he says that the French would do well to eat more beef for it would make them less inclined to brag, more simple and broad in the shoulders, in fact more English. Although he has just praised the French preference for *entrecôte* and ribs rather than surloin, he declares that he would willingly go into battle having eaten English beef; fancy a hundred thousand Frenchmen, who had eaten only soup, turnips, carrots, onions, and gruyère cheese, fighting a hundred thousand Englishmen who had just dined off beef! Of course, the reader is better placed to appreciate beef, since he is at least eleven stone and five feet seven inches whilst Frenchmen are only nine stone and five feet four inches: 'You are a different and superior animal—a French-beating animal (the history of hundreds of years has shown you to be so).' In the same way as the French have no beef, they have no beautiful women:

PUNCH, OR THE LONDON CHARIVARI.—February 11, 1860.

THE NEXT INVASION.
LANDING OF THE FRENCH (*LIGHT WINES*) AND DISCOMFITURE OF OLD GENERAL BEER.

Why do the French have recourse to sauces, stews, and other culinary disguisements?—because their meat is not good. Why do the English content themselves with roast and boiled?—because they need no preparations. And so Beauty like Beef.

These passages were usually written with tongue in cheek. Thackeray is merely using easily recognizable themes and developing them with wit. He is quite liable to add an ironic sting in the tail of a paragraph. In *The Book of Snobs* he has just criticized the French for venturing to believe that they are top-dogs. This is nonsense:

We are better than all the world; we don't question the opinion at all; it's an axiom. And when a Frenchman bellows out 'La France, monsieur, la France est à la tête du monde civilisé!' we laugh good-naturedly at the frantic poor devil. *We* are the first chop of the world.

So we cannot take his criticism of French food and of French pride very seriously; but he was writing for a rather superficial kind of reader who may well have taken this fun for fact. The magazines that employed him were hardly distinguished at the time for their intellectual depth.

It is interesting to see how ideas have changed, in the space of a century, on French food. Since the First World War France has been considered the home of the best food and the best wines; but in 1850 the cooking there was obviously thought to be pretentious and unsubstantial, and the wine light in comparison with English beer and port. Mr. Punch used to point out that French levity came from the light wine they drank. If they had beer and beef they might be men. The cartoon on the previous page uses this idea to illustrate English misgivings at the time of the Anglo-French trade agreement in 1860.

Even though Mr. Titmarsh delighted in sketching the absurdities of the French, it was not always easy to find an excuse for an article; an easy one was to describe one of the public events in Paris that had a topical air about it and into which the author, as an English observer, could easily insert his own personality. This choice of material leads Thackeray to insist on the excitability of the French, a trait obviously more in evidence on days of public rejoicing. At first he is favourably impressed by the atmosphere of expectancy and good humour in the French crowds, and by the colourful splendour of the booths and stands, but he soon comes to agree with Carlyle. Though he had criticized *The French Revolution* strongly, it was mainly on points of style; his descriptions of the people of Paris, with volatility and chauvinism as the keynotes, are very similar:

When a man leaves our dismal, smoky London atmosphere, and breathes, instead of coal-smoke and yellow fog, this bright clear French air, he is quite intoxicated by it at first, and feels a glow in his blood, and a joy in his spirits, which scarcely thrice a year, and then only at a distance from London, he can attain in England. Is the intoxication, I wonder, permanent among the natives? and may we not account for the ten thousand frantic freaks of these people by the peculiar influence of French air and sun? The philosophers are from morning to night drunk, the politicians are drunk, the literary men reel and stagger from one absurdity to another, and how shall we understand their vagaries?

And so we are back with the frivolous Frenchman. The festivals of Shrove Tuesday make Thackeray wonder what makes the French so mad for dancing. It seems to be part of their general intoxication. What power on earth could make Londoners dance madly in pursuit of an ox, as the Parisians do on the last day of Lent? Drums, poles, squibs, and flags seem an essential part of French life: they appear again on St. Philip's day, and English readers must have imagined the Parisians perpetually twirling around and playing at fairs. After the peace of 1871, *Punch* addressed the following verses to France:

> O France, in future, wise as we
> By sore experience grown
> Strive but to keep your own self free,
> Your neighbours leave alone.
>
> Mankind example let us give,
> And woman also France;
> We'll teach the Nations how to live:
> You teach them how to dance.

It is impossible nowadays to imagine the feelings of an early Victorian over dancing, which has become such an accepted part of our civilization that we forget how immoral it was. Dances at court and as country customs, in the form of a group ceremony, were of course admitted, although religious reactionaries still condemned all forms of ceremony not connected with the Church. But dancing with couples in bodily contact, and ballet dancing, were long confined to France, which seems to have fully deserved the reputation Thackeray gives it. As early as the fifteenth century two French kings had to prohibit dancing in an effort to restore public morals.

French levity is not only apparent in their fêtes. It has also made them unfortunately prone to a kind of public claptrap that Thackeray never tired of exposing. A series of three letters to *Punch* in 1840 report on 'The Second Funeral of Napoleon'. The body of Napoleon had been brought back from St. Helena to be buried in state in the *Invalides*. Here Thackeray is well ahead of his time. Napoleon was the historical figure of the century, which lived with Waterloo in the same way as our century lives with

MONUMENT TO NAPOLEON!

On the removal of Napoleon's remains, I prepared the above design for a monument; but it was not sent, because it was not wanted. There is this disadvantage about a design for *his* monument;—it will suit nobody else. This could not, therefore, be converted into a tribute to the memory of the late distinguished philosopher, Muggeridge, head master of the grammar-school at Birchley; nor into an embellishment for the mausoleum of the departed hero Fitz-Hogg, of the Pipeclays. It very often happens, however, that when a monument to a great man turns out to be a misfit, it will, after a while, be found to suit some other great man as well as if his measure had been taken for it. Just add a few grains to the intellectual qualities, subtract a scruple or so from the moral attributes—let out the philanthropy a little and take in the learning a bit—clip the public devotion, and throw an additional handful of virtues into the domestic scale—qualify the squint, in short, or turn the aquiline into a

A page from *George Cruickshank's Omnibus*

Hiroshima. By 1840 the national passions created by the long struggle against Napoleon had begun to subside, and it was possible to see him as a great man and as an indirect factor of England's glory. Thackeray tries to establish this when he says that there is hardly a gentleman's home in England where a print of Napoleon is not to be found. But it was still impossible to praise him openly, because it took even liberal opinion in England fifty years to realize that Waterloo had been fought by the Establishment against the forces of democracy. By 1900 this was accepted: it became the mark of progressive intellectuals to admire Napoleon and write books about him. In 'The Silent People' (1905) Chesterton says that the people of England fought at Waterloo against their own rights. But we have seen that Swinburne and Meredith, even when they felt inclined to admire France, still had to make a vigorous exception for Napoleon. Those venturing to say something in his favour usually added that he was really a Corsican. Thackeray is a welcome exception. He did not profess admiration, but neither did he go through the motions of strong condemnation, and he was accused in some quarters of having given a treasonably long account of this second burial.

But Thackeray, quite rightly, blames French humbug and braggadocio rather than the man who used it to reach power. The formalities and stiffness of the disinterment are amusingly punctured, and they contrast comically with the actual events. The ceremonial necessary to unearth a coffin and carry it a few miles to the *Belle Poule*, a frigate that is to bring it from St. Helena to France, lasts fully three days. During the trip back the ship receives news that a diplomatic crisis has occurred between France and England: its top-heavy staff immediately decide that they must armour it against a possible encounter with a British fleet—they throw their luxurious furniture overboard, and prepare to scuttle their vessel rather than surrender their precious cargo to the hated enemy (who a few days before had received them royally and dined them and given them the body with every possible courtesy!). The journey up the Seine by barge and the march through Paris are equally ridiculed: Thackeray reminds the readers that all the statues put up for the occasion are of cardboard and all the exotic victories inscribed along the route are the names of blood-baths.

For the French are led by their excitability into a sanguine idea of patriotism. Napoleon helped them to establish

a Valhalla idea of a Frenchman's paradise—it was conquest and murder all day. . . . Frenchmen lash themselves into a fury of conceit and blood-thirstiness whenever they hear [the *Marseillaise*], and fancy their brutality patriotism.

The French Deputies swearing allegiance to the Dynasty

The Battle of Reims

It is evident that Louis-Philippe, a peaceful king, does not arouse much enthusiasm at the ceremony. The crowd enjoy singing the *Marseillaise* more than cheering him as he passes. Prudence is not popular in Paris: the French want a Napoleon who will once more 'let them run ahead at a mad gallop'. A few years later the same Joinville who commanded the *Belle Poule* on its bombastic mission incurred Thackeray's wrath. After being courteously shown around some English naval establishments, he wrote a review of French naval power that was a thinly disguised plea for an efficient invasion of England. Though Thackeray may have been temporarily moved by the magnificent ceremonies in Paris, this warmongering disgusted him.

Stage tricks, claptrap, humbug are the matter of French public life, and Thackeray understands why it is so easy to start revolutions over there: 'A Frenchman must have his revolution—it is his nature to break down omnibuses in the street, and across them to fire at troops of the line.' In 1844 he wrote one of the best historical fantasies that has appeared in *Punch*, 'The History of the Next French Revolution'. His ironical forecasts were in part confirmed by the events of 1848; they show a good appreciation of the French political sensitivity of the time, and are also extremely funny. Thackeray imagines that France is suddenly invaded by three pretenders: a madman believing himself to be the son of Louis XVI; the fourteenth cousin of Napoleon claiming that since no one else has claimed to be emperor the right to do so is his; and the duke of Bordeaux, with English support. Louis-Philippe, entrenched in the Tuileries with his money, is content to fortify Paris with a ring of forts with a thousand guns each, and to send out two comical armies consisting mainly of national guards to stop the invaders. The prince of Joinville (Thackeray will not let go of him) goes to Vendée, which has risen in support of the duke of Bordeaux; his national guards, who were very reluctant to continue marching once their pocketfuls of sausages and brandy had been consumed, finally have to be bayonneted into a charge by the troops of the line behind them. They then rush madly and would win the day if it were not for the English and Irish. Meanwhile, the other army entrenches itself in the cellars of Champagne to await the new Napoleon; but he merely waits outside until it is too drunk to fight, and the battle ends in a huge drinking bout, in which Rabelaisian quantities are consumed. The next morning Napoleon suggests that the two armies should advance on the Rhine and conquer Germany, since seltzer water is good after too much drink. The suggestion is so popular that everyone rallies around him and they march on Paris. Here a third of the forts turn themselves over to Napoleon and a third to the duke of Bordeaux, while a third remain loyal, and the 24,000 guns pound each other for three days, whilst Paris continues its normal life: 'The frivolous Parisians were, in the meanwhile, amusing themselves at their theatres and cafés as usual; and a new piece, in which Arnal performed, was the universal talk of the foyers.' Finally, while the forts are destroying each other completely, the mad son of Louis XVI escapes from the lunatic asylum where he has been locked up, and together with the rest of the inmates storms the Tuileries. He is acclaimed as king.

THE HISTORY OF THE NEXT FRENCH REVOLUTION

(FROM A FORTHCOMING HISTORY OF EUROPE)

[February to April, 1844]

A Chapter-heading from *The Paris Sketch Book*

Claptrap is also to be found in French literature. Victor Hugo and Dumas the elder both published books on Rhineland, prompted consciously or not by the interest of the French for a district they felt was theirs by right. Thackeray rapped both on the knuckles immediately: Dumas was prolific with other people's uncertain learning; Hugo, too, borrowed large chunks from guide-books, but critics in Paris had nevertheless been unnecessarily inflated over his work. Hugo professed to have detected somehow the wish of the German population to become French, although he did not understand a word of German himself. Thackeray remarks:

These people are so immensely conceited, that they think the rest of Europe beneath them, and though they have invaded Spain, Italy, Russia, Germany, not one in ten thousand can ask for a piece of bread in the national language of the countries so conquered. . . .

Thackeray's view of Hugo is interesting because it shows how an extremely prosaic person such as he could be completely insensitive to the poetic appeal that enchanted Swinburne. He sees nothing in Hugo but coarseness of detail and swagger of the brush. He condemns 'that strange, grotesque, violent, pompous, noble figure of a poet, with his braggart modesty, and wonderful simplicity of conceit', where Swinburne saw one of the greatest men of his time. What was more, Hugo was particularly suited to the French, who were gullible and deserved to be impressed by his braggadocio. In the interval of a play, hearing that the government had refused to pardon the socialist Barbès, Hugo had written a poem to the king asking for mercy.

In any country, save this, would a poet who chose to write four crack-brained verses, comparing an angel to a dove, and a little boy to a reed, and calling upon the chief-magistrate, in the name of the angel, or dove [the Princess Mary] in her tomb, and the little infant in his cradle, to spare a criminal, have received a 'gracious answer' to his nonsense? . . . Sham liberty, sham monarchy, sham glory, sham justice . . .

Where bombast was concerned, Thackeray was undoubtedly making a valid point, and it is interesting that he should have chosen to criticize the Napoleonic wars in that light, for it was not a wholesale condemnation. Before and after him, to criticize the wars of conquest that had followed the Revolution meant more or less that one had to praise or side with Germany or the forces of reaction in Europe. But although he censures bombast and excitability he does not condemn the feelings or ideas of the French, and we have seen that he does not criticize Napoleon, but the pomp that surrounds his funeral. Thackeray appears to want to correct, rather than reject, the French. His attitude is not far removed from that of Meredith, and he probably laid his finger on one of the main reasons why France 'sinned against her soul'. France does indeed suffer from bombast. Thackeray was in Paris at a particularly sham period in her political history, when few colours amounted to much more than fancy dresses of the moment: Stendhal wrote *Le Rouge et le Noir* partly against the claptrap of 1830, and looking back on the times it is difficult to find any aspect—the poetry, the art, the philosophical thought, the diplomatic intrigues—that was not utterly false. Hugo probably represents the spirit of the time more than anyone. And yet Hugo is still a great national figure, whatever the purists of literature may say against him: he appeals to an innate love of the grandiose, which seems to be a permanent feature in the French. Observe the rounded tones of their political speeches and the inflated style immediately adopted in France by anyone in a position of authority. It is apparent moreover in letter-writing. In England, the more elevated or cultured one's background or position, the more direct and plain one's letters; in France, bombast creeps in and they often become the more stiff and circumlocuted. Whether or not it is a corruption of the legendary politeness of the French in the eighteenth century, it has certainly been a factor in all their most tragic illusions about themselves; it is to this sense that all their most unscrupulous politicians know how to appeal.

II. ART AND MORALITY

This excitability and braggadocio add up in Thackeray's very English mind and in its more ill-tempered moments to what he very quickly calls immorality. This link is already visible in an early description of a Shrove Tuesday fête: he says he is rather scared of joining in the carnival balls at the theatres.

I was so frightened and wonderstricken by the demoniacal frantic yells and antics of the frequenters of the place, as to slink home perfectly dumb and miserable, not without some misgivings lest some real demons from below, with real pitch-forks and tails, should spring out of the trapdoors of the playhouse, as the sham fiends do in *Don Juan*, and drive the dancers and musicians headlong down.

A similar fear of devils is expressed in a *Punch* article in 1849. Thackeray had been visiting some theatres, and was horrified at the destructiveness of the satire that was allowed: religion, chastity, royalty, military glory, even the Republic were laughed at, and the tails of the devils appear again:

Sir, there are certain laws of morality (as believed by us at least) for which these people no more care than so many Otaheitans. They have been joking against marriage since it began; . . . one is puzzled to know what the people respect at all. There is something awful, infernal almost, I was going to say, in the gaiety with which the personages of these satiric dramas were dancing and shrieking about among the tumbled ruins of ever so many ages and traditions. . . . I looked with a vague anxiety up at the theatre roof, to see that it was not falling in, and shall not be surprised to hear that Paris goes the way of certain other cities some day.

It is exactly this feeling that was to be echoed in England twenty years later when the Prussians, and then the Commune, wrecked Paris. What Thackeray had said half-humorously obviously remained and grew in everyone's minds.

The country where shops stayed open on Sundays, where bathing beaches were mixed, where a woman because she was married was allowed to go with her husband to see the grossest of plays; the country of duelling and of marriage bureaux provided Thackeray and all the other Titmarshes with plenty of grounds for insular criticism, when something else had inflamed them. Thackeray for instance sometimes concludes that there are simply different conventions in the two countries; but when he finds that the French have adapted a Dickens play badly and that their critics have condemned Dickens for it, he writes a fiery article the gist of which is that the French cannot judge anything, they are so immoral in every way.

Some of the romantic-sweet stories in *The Paris Sketch Book* further illustrate the immorality of the French. The story of Dambergeac draws a contrast between the wild, extravagant, liberal student, a hater of Jesuits and gendarmes and a great seducer of laundrymaids, and the same man twenty years later: a loyal servant to the king, waiting on the bishop before Mass with gendarmes as his guards. Thackeray had read this in a French book, and it illustrates in his opinion the calm debauchery of the French, because it presents as a surprising fact not that Dambergeac had mistresses when young, but that he has become so religious and moral now:

religion is so uncommon amongst the Parisians, as to awaken the surprise of all candid observers; gallantry is so common as to create no remark, and to be considered as a matter of course. With us at least the converse of the proposition prevails. . . . A French gentleman thinks no more of proclaiming that he has a mistress than that he has a tailor.

At the carnival Thackeray meets Madame Pauline, a *grisette* who has had a perfectly respectable place as governess with an English family, but has wasted her chances (she could have saved up, or angled for a rich marriage while she had the position) and turned down a subsequent offer of a similar job. She chooses to return to Paris to make cheap shirts and, presumably, live not very morally, rather than remain in *cette triste ville de Londres où l'on ne danse pas seulement le dimanche.*

The author is not adamant in the case of Madame Pauline: after all, she seems quite happy in her way of life; and there are thousands like her in Paris, 'cheerful in poverty, careless and prodigal in good fortune, but dreadfully lax in some points of morals in which our own females are praiseworthily severe'. However, further on in the same article he tells the story of a well-to-do young Frenchman who committed the folly of getting married. Instead of making the woman his mistress since there was no hope of a dowry from her, he would insist on making her his wife; he now has to lead a life of hard work to keep his wife, child, and maid. But all this is ironic. Thackeray then points out that the man is happy, sings all day in his *atelier* and does not want to go out to dance on fête days. The moral is made clear.

But Thackeray's disapproval is suspended in a single instance: where art is concerned. The Frenchman who was mad enough (by French standards) to get married was an engraver, and worked all day in a top-floor *atelier*. Since he is the only Parisian character in *The Paris Sketch Book* who does not break moral laws, we may think that he derives a certain innocence from his trade. This impression is confirmed by Thackeray's continual interest in artists and students, who seem to be the one positive element of France in his eyes. His book includes an article on the French school of painting, another on caricatures and lithography in Paris, and short stories ('The Painter's Bargain', for instance) that show us a whole world of artists living apart from the great Babylon. This is the first appearance in English literature of the idea, essential to the nineties, that Paris is the home of art and of the artistic way of life. When French painting became really fashionable at the end of the nineteenth century, many writers were to remember Thackeray and turn back to him for inspiration. The short stories of the nineties are often tailored from *The Paris Sketch Book*.

Amusingly enough, as soon as he is thinking of art and letters and not of morality, Thackeray reverses all the unfavourable judgements he has made on everything else. Thus his violent scorn for the journals that had condemned Dickens without proper knowledge, gives way in another article to admiration for the place given to the man of letters in France. In Paris, journalists are invited individually to attend public events, and the public follows their line of thought, whereas in England only the political position of the newspaper itself is taken into account. Thackeray had satirized the frivolous Parisians who thought only of their theatres, even in time of war, but he was not averse to regular theatre-going himself: he felt at home in a country that did not belittle its dramatic art, and secretly admired Louis Napoleon who when he was imprisoned in Strasbourg had complained of his plight, saying it was inconceivable that he should be a Frenchman and should not have seen Talma act. Drama in England was an amusement and the actor, like the author, was merely a servant of the rich classes. Thackeray tells somewhere that a Warwickshire parson who had published verse was very entertaining at a dinner table; one guest asked another who he was, and on being told that he wrote, exclaimed: 'Good heavens, a literary man! I thought he had been a gentleman.'

This line of thought extends to art in general, but Thackeray is particularly interested in painting. Hugo's plea to the king for the release of a criminal obviously has its ridiculous side, but it does show that the artist is given a better place in society. Society benefits from this:

> In France such matters are far better managed, and the love of art is a thousand times more keen; and (from this feeling surely) how much more superiority is there in French *society* over our own; how much better is social happiness understood; how much more manly equality is there between Frenchman and Frenchman, than between rich and poor in our own country, with all our superior wealth, instruction, and political freedom! There is, amongst the humblest, a gaiety, cheerfulness, politeness, and sobriety, to which, in England, no class can shew a parallel; and these, be it remembered, are not only qualities for holidays, but for working-days too, and add to the enjoyment of human life as much as good clothes, good beef, or good wages.

This curious passage from *The Paris Sketch Book* shows Thackeray as an originator in several respects. In somehow linking art with social happiness he previews much of the aesthetico-social theorizing of the late Victorians. He also suggests Arnold's ideas about equality in France, though Arnold was to attribute it to education rather than to art. The essay on 'Caricatures and Lithography in Paris', which explains why *Punch* was to have a French pedigree, paints a picture of artistic Paris bursting with original talents of all varieties. The demand is equal to the supply over there:

> Humble *cafés* in country towns have their walls covered with pleasing picture papers representing *Les gloires de l'armée française*, the Seasons, the Four Quarters of the World, Cupid and Psyche, or some

other allegory, rudely painted, as papers for walls usually are, but the figures are all tolerably well drawn; and the common taste, which has caused a demand for such things, undeniable. . . . Every one of our readers who has lived in Paris, in any lodging, magnificent or humble, with any family, however poor, may bear witness how profusely the walls of his smart *salon* in the English quarter, or of his little room *au sixième* in the Pays Latin, has been decorated with prints of all kinds. . . . Can there be a more pleasing walk, in the whole world, than a stroll through the Gallery of the Louvre, on a *fête*-day: not to look so much at the pictures as at the lookers-on? Thousands of the poorer classes are there: mechanics in their Sunday clothes, smiling *grisettes*, smart, dapper soldiers of the line, with bronzed wondering faces, marching together in little companies of six or seven, and stopping every now and then at Napoleon or Leonidas, as they appear, in proper vulgar heroics, in the pictures of David or Gros. The taste of these people will hardly be approved by the connoisseur, but they have a taste for art.

Here probably lies the secret of the 'fatal charm' Thackeray confessed he found in Paris. Without it, it would be surprising that he stayed there so long, since he spent a great deal of energy criticizing it. It is certain, looking back, that Thackeray wrote too much, and was at his worst on the subject of France. His novels and his best essays in *Roundabout Papers* do not show much concern for it. But this is probably because his public was not yet interested in what could be learned from France: as his experience grew he found out how to please his readers. This is an unfortunate reflection on his value as a creative writer; but on the other hand most of the authors in this study are indebted to him for the seeds he sowed for them in his youth.

G

· 5 ·

PAGANISM

Walter Pater

OUR study of Meredith has illustrated how a view of France lapsed from a fruitful beginning into age-old suspicions. We have seen one of the recognized literary figures of the day turn away from 'live' impressions and become content with the popular image of the Frenchman. This change, like Matthew Arnold's reversal, occurred shortly after 1871, and the date is significant. French republicanism had finally brought too many disasters on to Europe and France itself to be worth considering or fearing as a serious ideal in England. From 1871 stems the supercilious detachment of the English from French internal politics. As long as Bonapartism did not return, with its state-mongering and international complications, it was felt in London throughout the Third Republic that French politics, essentially unstable, could be disregarded.

But two years after Swinburne's and Meredith's odes had sounded the final blasts of poetic republicanism, and in the year before *Beauchamp's Career* consecrated the collapse of Meredith's active interest in France, there appeared a slender book that was to create, amongst many other feelings, a new sort of francophily: the *Renaissance Studies*. In the work of Walter Pater, French public life is forgotten; we see for the first time an appreciation of France based entirely on the history of art, but given a more general value when personified in his 'imaginary portraits'.

Pater's French culture was very similar to Arnold's. It was

based on Sainte-Beuve, and the references he makes to Obermann, Joubert, and Heine show that he had been impressed by *Essays in Criticism*. It was probably Sainte-Beuve (and Mérimée's *Chronique du Règne de Charles IX*) that led him to a particular interest in the French sixteenth century. His conclusions are similar to those of Arnold, or to the implications of Meredith's ode, for he thinks of France as a pagan country. This, however, is a virtue in his eyes and not, as for Arnold, a reason to flee Paris. We can trace back to Pater the opinion, common in the nineties, that French paganism is a kind of natural morality.

Pater appears to have been an unconscious instigator: his rather diffuse opinions had the quality of prophecies and were turned by others into a rallying-cry. His influence on the 1890's need hardly be shown. Yeats, for instance, writes in *The Tragic Generation*:

If Rossetti was a subconscious influence, and perhaps the most powerful of all, we looked consciously to Pater for our philosophy. . . . Perhaps it was because of Pater's influence that we, with an affectation of learning, claimed the whole past of literature for our authority.

To Pater's mind, the most significant moral path an individual could follow was illustrated in the Renaissance: his disciples were left with the not too difficult task of perceiving the relevance of his teachings to Victorian England. His later works are all variations, or adaptations to fiction or romanticized history, of the scheme of the *Renaissance Studies*: so it is of particular significance that the Renaissance appears to him to begin and end in France. His book opens with studies on mediaeval French authors, and he returns to the poetry of the Pléiade after the chapters on Italy. France comes to symbolize for him an important stage in the quest for a perfect appreciation of Beauty. It is not by chance that such various personalities as those of Watteau, Mérimée, and Montaigne should be the subject of later studies, nor that three of his imaginary portraits should be set in France. There is in each of these works a similar dialectic.

And yet Pater's knowledge of France is almost purely theoretical. He is said to have gone to school with a tendency to value all things German, and his continental background is more

Dutch than anything else. He only progressively discovers the
French and Greek civilizations, which will become his favourite
subjects. The national characteristics of France he describes are
those imagined by a retiring don who would spend holidays
touring the Continent without speaking any language but his
own and who apparently said that all people from abroad gave
him a feeling of vague disgust: one suspects that in France he
looked at cathedrals and landscapes without noticing the human
beings swarming around. The German critic Arthur Beyer suggests that his practical knowledge came from a French History of
Literature and a catalogue of monuments that are known to have
been in his library.[1] France is thus seen through a highly stylized
section of her art, as Nature was seen in Pope's house through
ornate mirrors. Here, as with Pater's other ideas and because of his
bewitching manner, the source is out of all proportion with the
influence. His image of France, based on the haziest of geographical theories and developed with more attention to style than to
truth, passed into the subconscious mind of the nineties.

I. DISCOVERY OF PAGAN FEELING

The *Renaissance Studies* stand on their head in that their unity only
appears clearly in the last chapter: the essay on Winckelmann's
return to classical sources should be read, as it was written and
first published, before the others, for it contains the key to them
all. It clarifies the contrast in Pater's mind between mediaeval
civilization, which neglects feeling in favour of thought, and the
sensual paganism introduced by the Renaissance.

Paganism is normally connected with Greece, commonly
believed to be the last country to have lent at least as much
importance to pleasure and beauty as to Reason. But in modern
times, says Pater, France has taken over this privilege: he gives an
account of the story of Héloïse and Abélard to show how sensualism was revived in mediaeval Paris.[2] Comparable in spirit to the

---

[1] *Walter Paters Beziehungen zur Französischen Literatur* . . . pp. 23 and 107–9. The two
sources, according to Beyer's erudite study, are J. Demogeot: *Histoire de la littérature
française depuis ses origines jusqu'à nos jours* (1862) and E. E. Viollet-le-Duc: *Dictionnaire
raisonné de l'architecture française du XIᵉ au XVIᵉ siècle* (16 volumes).

[2] Rémusat had published a Life of Abélard in 1845.

mild cyrenaicism of Marius the Epicurean at the beginning of his life, it is a rebellion against an ascetic Christian ideal. Abélard belonged to the Middle Ages because he was one of the great scholastic philosophers of the time; but he also composed popular songs and romances in the vernacular. A lodger in the house of Canon Fulbert, he falls in love with Fulbert's niece Héloise, one of the most learned scholars in Paris. The two thus know and represent what is highest in mediaeval culture but are overcome by sensual love. Their adventure can obviously be made symbolic. Pater stresses that as early as the eleventh century Abélard is endowed with the spirit of the Renaissance, unbeknown to his contemporaries, for he is 'the true child of light, the humanist, with reason and heart and senses quick, while theirs were almost dead'. By helping to found prose romance, he brought within reach of popular feeling the praise of human affection instead of religious love.

The first appearance of paganism in literature is in the *fabliaux*: these expressions of intense human sentiment were born in France. At the same time two provençal poets, Pierre Vidal and Bernard de Ventadour, were writing refined, almost exotic verse.[3] In an essay on Romanticism reprinted as an appendix to *Appreciations* Pater defines (after Stendhal) a romantic movement as one that searches for a new type of beauty that will eventually become classic. He uses this Provençal love poetry as an instance:

[here] the very name of *romanticism* is stamped with its true significance: here we have indeed a romantic world, grotesque even, in the strength of its passions, almost insane in its curious expression of them, drawing all things into its sphere, making the birds, nay! lifeless things, its voices and messengers, yet so penetrated with the desire for beauty and sweetness, that it begets a wholly new species of beauty in which the *Renaissance* may be said to begin.

The same spirit appeared a little later in the French prose romances. Pater translates large extracts from *Li Amitiez de Ami et Amile* and *Aucassin et Nicolette* to demonstrate the tone of delightful grace and simplicity with which the new feelings of personal devotion

[3] Pater's study obviously prompted Ezra Pound's interesting translations from these poets.

to a friend or lover are described. Note that though Pater praises this new pagan literature of sentiment, it is a very stylized idea of graceful love: he does not relish anything more coarse, of the kind usually associated with French fiction in the English mind. Rabelais, whom he brings himself to mention, not without disgust, is a different sort of pagan, with 'dubious interests'.

The Renaissance movement will go to Italy to be fertilized, then return to France: Pater thus gives the book a certain symmetry, but appears to lend France a disproportionate place in the first stages of the transformation. He mentions that French authorities show (perhaps not as convincingly as he thinks)

how Saint Francis of Assisi took not his name only, but all those notions of chivalry and romantic love which so deeply penetrated his thoughts, from a French source, how Boccaccio borrowed the outlines of his stories from the old French *fabliaux*, and how Dante himself expressly connects the origin of the art of miniature painting with the city of Paris.

The pattern, however, contributes to the apparent intellectual fullness of the argument: above it the maze of remarks and dense thoughts suggests a richness of meaning, but this is only a superficial impression, like the one given by the entwined leaves of a baroque engraving.

Pagan feeling now becomes fully conscious of itself through the medium of Italian painting: the plastic arts improved on the rudimentary feelings of the *fabliaux*, as Pater suggests in the much-quoted passage that compares a great picture to 'an accidental play of sunlight and shadow for a moment, on the wall or floor'. They obviously had an important part to play in a movement that depended to such an extent on direct sensuous appreciation of the world; yet at the same time the Italian primitives lacked the last quality, which changes sensual imagination into imaginative thought: this was poetry.

What little we do know of Pater's direct impressions of France confirms that he considered it a country of strong primitive sensations. His book on *Gaston de Latour*, which is a kind of biography of the French sixteenth century, stresses the direct forces at work in the countryside and amongst the violent political movements of the time. *Imaginary Portraits* show that he believed there was a fierce 'antinomian' spirit at work underneath the French scene, and emerging at times, for instance in the revolt of the Albigensians. Love poetry, fresh and sweet, is not the only sign of paganism. There is also a strong desire to taste fully of the natural pleasures associated with the Golden Age: 'Apollo in Picardy' and 'Denys l'Auxerrois' illustrate this, for they both describe how a mysterious individual, associated with the pagan gods (Apollo and Bacchus), changes the life of a community for a time. But these resurgences end in an orgy of feeling that culminates in bloodthirsty violence: Denys is torn to pieces by a mad crowd, Apollo causes a child's death. In these scenes, which only occur in Pater's works about France, we can distinguish the far-off echo of the real world. The sudden emergence of 'natural' values followed somehow by bloody events is the tiny reflection in Pater's lens of the revival of French republicanism that led up to the Commune.

II. REFINEMENT

The Renaissance, therefore, sprang from the sensuality of the *fabliaux*. Marius the Epicurean too discovers pagan feeling, in Apuleius; Gaston de Latour finds it in Terence and Virgil. In both the portraits and the historical studies there now comes a calm period during which the first impressions are consciously strengthened and refined, preparing the way for the pleasures of the intellect to graft themselves on to those of the senses.

In the Renaissance this step is shared between France and Italy: Italian finesse is combined with French daintiness to produce a superior delicacy of feeling. 'The old Gaulish desire to be refined, to be mentally enfranchised by the sprightlier genius of Italy' thus brings to the idea of elegance, formed on the other side of the Alps, what Pater calls *'une netteté remarquable d'exécution'*. (This does not explain why the Gauls sacked Rome.) He sees it illustrated in the house of Jacques Cœur in Bourges, or in the work of François Clouet, in cathedrals such as that of Saint Etienne, or in the way the rather coarse *chansons de geste* became refined stories intended for select audiences.

This purely French quality finds its clearest expression in the poetry of the Pléiade, where there is both daintiness and finesse. Du Bellay, who spent a considerable time in Rome before returning home to Angers, symbolizes the artistic trend of the time. In his poem '*D'un vanneur de blé aux vents*' we find

a certain silvery grace of fancy, nearly all the pleasure of which is in the surprise at the happy and dexterous way in which a thing so slight in itself is handled; a moment—and the thing has vanished, because it was pure effect, but it leaves a relish behind it, a longing that the accident may happen again.

These qualities are partly due to the audience for which the poetry was written:

It is poetry not for the people, but for a confined circle, for courtiers, great lords and erudite persons, people who desire to be humoured, to gratify a certain refined voluptuousness they have in them. . . . Like that party of people who tell the tales in Boccaccio's *Decameron*, they form a circle which in an age of great troubles, losses, anxieties, amuses itself with art, poetry, intrigue. But they amuse themselves with wonderful elegance.

Ronsard refines his love for a certain type of Angevine beauty, with her light hair and dark eyes; du Bellay refines his more artificial passion for scholarly questions—correct spelling or the invention of new words. He multiplies the rules governing his verse, a superior refinement that Pater finds doubly attractive. He discovers the same traits in other Frenchmen. Thus, Augustin Filon, in his historical romances, shows 'a delicacy which keeps his large yet minute antiquarian knowledge of that vanished time ever in service to a direct interest in humanity as it is permanently'. When the Duke Carl of Rosenmold, who represents the *Aufklärung* in *Imaginary Portraits*, wishes to enlighten his eighteenth-century state, he naturally travels towards France, the 'new Hellas', even though the period is rather an unfortunate one, and French refinement is only to be found

in the somewhat questionable form of the contemporary French ideal, in matters of art and literature—French plays, French architecture,

French looking-glasses—Apollo in the dandified costume of Lewis the Fourteenth.

The eighteenth century did not agree with Pater's romantic feelings: he remarks sourly in *Greek Studies* that Voltaire was unable to appreciate Dante. But whatever its limitations it was at least the active light of the time 'against the stupidity which is dead to the substance and the vulgarity which is dead to form'.

Mérimée in turn illustrates an exotic, luxurious stage in French fiction. As an antiquarian he appeals to Pater, because he is sensitive to the primitive forces of the ancient pagan world that is so close to the surface of things in his stories about southern France, Spain, or Corsica:

> Mérimée's style, simple and unconcerned, but with the eye ever on its objects, lends itself perfectly to such purpose—to an almost phlegmatic discovery of the facts, in all their crude natural colouring, as if he but held up to view, as a piece of evidence, some harshly dyed oriental carpet from the sumptuous floor of the Kremlin, on which blood had fallen.

The return of paganism is symbolized in Mérimée's story of the *Venus of Ille*, in which a young man, having jokingly put his engagement ring on the finger of a newly unearthed statue of Venus, is unable to remove it and is crushed to death by the statue when it visits him on his wedding night. Mérimée's story obviously impressed Pater, for he uses a similar plot in both 'Denys l'Auxerrois' and 'Apollo in Picardy'.

Refined paganism is only the second stage of Pater's dialectic: it is equivalent to the cyrenaicism of Marius under the influence of Aurelius and before he has discovered in the Christian faith a superior kind of feeling. In the last stage, the part played by France becomes predominant: France carries a southern sentiment into countries of the north, thus, by a kind of geographical contrast, introducing into what was merely refined feeling something that transforms it and that Pater calls pagan sadness.

III. PAGAN SADNESS

In *Renaissance Studies* Pater shows that the poetry of the Pléiade has added to the refined sentiment inspired by Italy a 'sense of intimacy' which he connects with the feelings of the north. For an explanation we may look to *Imaginary Portraits*, where he says that the French town has a specific beauty about it that links the two parts of Europe: 'a beauty cisalpine and northern, yet at the same time quite distinct from the massive German picturesque.' This quality he also claims to have observed in Turner's paintings of the rivers of France.

Du Bellay, he says, illustrates the more quiet and intimate sentiment of the north, by comparing the flamboyant sensations of his stay in Rome with the homeliness of his native Angers. His village scenes have an air of wintry domesticity which adds a languid charm to the more superficial graces of Italy. The other poets of the Pléiade, too,

understand the poetry of winter; for they are not far from the Atlantic, and the west wind which comes up from it, turning the poplars white, spares not this new Italy in France. So the fireside often appears, with the pleasures of the frosty season, about the vast emblazoned chimneys of the time, and with a *bonhomie* as of little children, or old people.

They are therefore 'the naturalisation of Greek beauty in the brown cloud-lands of the north', and France becomes a middle term between two aspects of European sentiment. Its sixteenth-century poetry has the exterior beauty of the Mediterranean without its hardness, for it is mellowed by a depth of meditation only possible in the north.

This is because in the 'cloud-lands' beauty is not so permanent as in Italy: it contrasts with more sombre aspects of Nature and produces in man a melancholy awareness of change. Here are born ennui, nostalgia, sorrow at the passing of the seasons, yet they are expressed in the most becoming of styles because the pagan consciousness of primeval beauty is still there. Pater sees this illustrated in the sadness of the Morvan skies around Vézelay; it is striking in the region of Auxerre where indeed the wine itself, he says, has but a fugitive charm and is liable to go sour soon after it is opened:

A veritable country of the vine, it presents nevertheless an expression peaceful rather than radiant. Perfect type of that happy mean between northern earnestness and the luxury of the south, for which we prize midland France, its physiognomy is not quite happy—attractive in part for its melancholy. Its most characteristic atmosphere is to be seen when the tide of light and distant cloud is travelling quickly over it, when rain is not far off, and every touch of art or of time on its old building is defined in clear grey.

This third stage of feeling is suggested, in one way or another, in most of Pater's portraits and studies: Marius, and the 'child in the house', come to it through a contact with death; Botticelli shows an acute sense of time. But it seems to be native to France. Pater finds it in all the famous buildings he visits (Chambord, Blois, the church of Brou). And it characterizes all his Frenchmen: in particular Gaston de Latour, whose portrait seems to have more immediate appeal than that of Marius, as if Pater were more at home in the French sixteenth century than in the decadence of Rome. Gaston, who had discovered sensual beauty through the poetry of Ronsard, meets him and notices sadness in the 'premature old age' that Pater also attributes elsewhere to du Bellay:

In spite of his pretension to the Epicurean conquest of a kingly indifference of mind, the portrait of twenty years ago betrayed, not less than the living face with its roving, astonished eyes, the haggard soul of a haggard generation. . . . It was but a half-gaiety, in truth, that awoke in the poet even now, with the singing and the good wine, as the notes echoed windily along the passages. On his forty-sixth year the unaffected melancholy of his later life was already gathering. The dead! he was coming to be on their side.

Gaston is now ready to meet Montaigne, who represents the deeper, philosophical, appreciation of this feeling. Pater makes many references showing his sympathy with Montaigne's position.

Watteau, another Frenchman, lived in the eighteenth century but redeems himself by scorning its pleasures. When success comes to him at court, his brilliance never quite surmounts the sadness of his introspective spirit—his native town, Valenciennes, is in the north. The story of his life is told in *Imaginary Portraits* in extracts from the diary of a girl from Valenciennes. She understands the melancholy of his paintings:

Those coquetries, those vain and perishable graces, can be rendered so perfectly, only through an intimate understanding of them. For him, to understand must be to despise them; while (I think I know why) he nevertheless undergoes their fascination. Hence that discontent with himself, which keeps pace with his fame . . . he dignifies, by what in him is neither more nor less than a profound melancholy, the essential insignificance of what he *wills* to touch in all that, transforming its mere prettiness into grace.

As I gaze upon these windless afternoons I find myself always saying to myself involuntarily 'The evening will be a wet one'. The storm is always brooding through the massy splendour of the trees, above those sun-dried glades or lawns, where delicate children may be trusted thinly clad; and the secular trees themselves will hardly out-last another generation.

Melancholy and grace, then, characterize France: they lead one to relish pleasures more consciously and therefore more ardently. Pater explains what he means in the essay on Winckelmann:

This pagan sentiment measures the sadness with which the human mind is filled, whenever its thoughts wander far from what is here, and now. It is beset by notions of irresistible natural powers, for the most part ranged against man, but the secret also of his fortune, making the earth golden and the grape fiery for him.

The feeling existed in Greece, but the Renaissance was necessary for mankind to reach full awareness of it. The portrait of Denys l'Auxerrois shows how a return of Greek paganism would be out of place in modern France, which has achieved a more perfect kind of melancholy. When the people of Auxerre rediscover the unadulterated pleasures of the countryside they are taking a step backwards, which is followed by an inevitable reaction. Denys is destroyed:

With all the regular beauty of a pagan god, he has suffered after a manner of which we must suppose pagan gods incapable. It was as if one of those fair, triumphant beings had cast in his lot with the creatures of an age later than his own, people of larger spiritual capacity and assuredly of a larger capacity for melancholy.

France is thus at a peculiar historical and geographical cross-roads: her art blossomed at the most favourable moment, at the end of the Renaissance, and there was in the country the right proportion of northern to southern spirit to allow a full flowering of pagan sadness. From here to what we now call 'decadence' there is a very little way to go. The Pléiade, according to the following passage, has reached 'a refined and comely decadence':

a thing not vigorous or original, but full of the grace that comes of long study and reiterated refinements, and many steps repeated, and many angles worn down, with an exquisite faintness, *une fadeur exquise*, a certain tenuity and caducity, as for those who can bear nothing vehement or strong; for princes weary of love, like Francis the first, or of pleasure, like Henry the third, or of action, like Henry the fourth. Its merits are those of the old,—grace and finish, perfect in minute detail. For these people are a little jaded, and have a constant desire for a subdued and delicate excitement, to warm their creeping fancy a little.

IV. MELANCHOLY

The luxurious melancholy of Keats's adolescence is still alive in Pater's romanticism; Pater also culls this feeling from the French *art pour l'art* movement: his 'princes weary of love, like Francis the first, or of pleasure like Henry the third, or of action like Henry the fourth', suggest Gautier and Nerval. His view of France underneath all his delicately woven patterns is very simple: it consists of a fresh appreciation of beauty teased by an awareness that it soon passes and sharpened, as by a slight fermentation, with a melancholy and jaded refinement.

Some of Pater's works about French art are excellent. His essays on the poetry of the Pléiade are amongst the rare critical texts that can be read effortlessly and with profit a century later. This is partly because his ideal, in criticism, was to be content with describing the impact of a work on his own mind, without any pretence to dogmatic synthesis. But because of this he does not take enough precautions. As a result, his reader may well, in good faith, mistake the significance of things for him. Thus, if we look more closely, we realize that his ideas on the melancholy of Anjou stem almost entirely from some wooden panels he saw on the chimney of a castle.[4] For Pater's disciples in the nineties this trait, which may be a saving grace in the eyes of the modern reader, was an unfortunate source of error. Like his style and some of the poetry he admired, his view of France is 'all effect'. Such a subtle intellectual construction, rubbed out at the edges and relying on such vague ideas as 'refinement' and 'pagan sentiment', is undoubtedly attractive: one is tempted for a moment to look at things the way he does, lulled by the long, enveloping sentences and sentiments. But he is wrong. He believes in the facile but nonsensical romantic idea that people can be described in the same terms as the scenery in which they live. This may pass with some countries of Western Europe, where the climate and the landscape include a bit of everything—but the Greeks are not necessarily as fiery as their summers, nor the Norwegians as deep as their fjords. Du Bellay may illustrate Pater's system admirably—but Ronsard whose home was in the same province, was no more melancholy than any old man who has had a wild pleasurable youth; Montaigne, whom Pater tends to rank with du Bellay, was not born in 'midland France' but in dusty Perigord; Watteau's paintings may suggest paganism but there is no sadness in them; the typical Angevine beauty Ronsard is supposed to have appreciated, with blond hair and dark eyes, is nowhere to be found either in Ronsard or in Angers where, as in most places, true blondes have light eyes—it merely fitted in well with Pater's ideas on France. Apart from this there lingers the uncomfortable feeling that Pater's knowledge is purely occasional: his choice of subjects owes perhaps more to the chance that brought certain volumes into the library at Brasenose than to his own will. Had the Bibliothèque Elzévirienne not published *Li Amitiez de Ami et Amile*, had a student not left a volume of du Bellay lying in his tutor's room, not only might we have missed Pater's delicate translations and refined essays, but his very ideas might have been different. Had he not chanced on the ten volumes about French

4 See quotation above on p. 98.

architecture, he might have taken his holidays elsewhere and found inspiration in Italian cathedrals instead.

For there was indeed little reason for him to choose France at all, except perhaps that the *art pour l'art* movement led him back in a general way to French art. He could have chosen any foreign country: the moral example he was suggesting is a typical instance of a reform in feelings introduced under the apology of anti-patriotism. But this was not appreciated by those who put it into practice: for them France really became a country of rich hedonism and melancholy. Constant references in the literature of the nineties show that Pater has been taken literally. For instance, here is what Arnold Bennett, in his *Journals*, considers to be typically French:

The vet. seemed a nice quiet dutiful man, younger than his grey hair; he looked as though he had discovered gradually that life must be a compromise after all. He was sad. The captain, aged 50 or so, had the narrow, roughly-gay, and intensely narrow-minded face of an elderly officer who has failed to rise. The whole affair was eminently French and picturesque too. . . . [Next day he sees] a *partie carrée* of two brothers and sisters . . .: they were so human and so French, and so naïve; and the fleeting charm of the girls (neither of them pretty) was so soon to fade, and the men were so soon to become mature and *bête*.

'Sadness', 'fleeting charm': the words recur frequently—in minds prepared to receive them these impressions can arise anywhere. In *The Yellow Book* Stanley Mackower, describing the art of the singer Yvette Guilbert—the Juliette Gréco of the time—finds in her a melancholy typical of her country:

not the morbid melancholy of a creature unable to struggle with the world—but a look borrowed from the whole of nature, something of the look of infinite sadness which shines from the eyes of Botticelli's Prime Vera: and in that look lies a wisdom which makes us wonder.

The reference to Botticelli suggests that Mackower has read Pater: to make his sources quite clear he then quotes from Pater's 'Dionysus' to show that melancholy in general is associated with a move from the country to the town. He goes on:

Such is the look that steals into the eyes of Yvette Guilbert when she leaves the rose gardens of her villa on the Seine, to come and sing in the heart of Paris of the joys and sorrows, the laughter and the tears that are born in the great French city.

There is in Yvette Guilbert's songs—a recording of them was re-engraved recently—the dry pessimism that one associates with most French cabaret artists and *diseuses*. But this is hardly romantic melancholy caused by the contrast between city and country.

Perhaps the most persistent of Pater's ideas, as well as the easiest to refute, is his interpretation of Watteau. The 'northern sadness' of Watteau has become a common feature in most criticism of him since *Imaginary Portraits*. Pater was not the only one to have interpreted him in this way: Verlaine's *Fêtes Galantes* (translated in the nineties by Arthur Symons), suggest that these refined pastoral amusements are only a cover for an essential boredom. Romanticism always did, of course, interpret its predecessors in the light of its own feelings. Yet surely with Watteau this impression is exaggerated. Naturally, a modern utilitarian mind may look on these vain and perishable graces and say they are useless—but the artist may not have approached them in the same way, even though he knew they were not essential to progress or morality. The clouds in Watteau are used to relieve the greens of the forest scenes, and are definitely not meant to suggest approaching thunder: no one can have reflected less than he on the coming Revolution.

Les Champs Elysées, which is in the Wallace Collection, should show how far the imagination has to be stretched to meet Pater's view. The group of ladies in the usual sylvan setting faces the painter, but on the right is a man with his back turned, probably speaking to them. He is some distance from the group, but not far enough away for them to disregard him. There is a description of this picture in the first number of one of the periodicals of the nineties called *The Acorn*. The author, John Todhunter, says this man is probably quoting Herrick to himself:

> Gather ye roses while ye may
> Old Time is still a-flying.

This is of course *possible*, but surely unlikely.

Pater's influence on the period that followed was seminal. He established for a time that France was to be judged according to her art, an idea that will dominate the next three chapters. Strangely enough this view, which conflicts with Arnold's conclusions, is often derived from the same sources. Arnold, for instance, had borrowed from Sainte-Beuve the idea that a critic should seek to establish whether he is justified in being moved, and he had concluded that intellectual principles ruled France. Pater on the other hand, also reading Sainte-Beuve, notes instead a passage that applauds the kind of critics who are content to be *exquis amateurs* and *humanistes distingués*.

From all these hints the men of the nineties, who took Pater's word for gospel and had no time to adjust his views to the real world, gathered that only in Paris could one appreciate to the full that vague and mysterious secret, the artistic way of life. The image of France in Pater is tinged with the exotic and the esoteric; he did not exactly introduce the erotic, but the transition was not difficult to make.

H

· 6 ·

THE GREAT FOREIGN PLACE

Henry James

What happens to France happens to all that part of
ourselves which we are most proud, and most finely
advised, to enlarge and cultivate and consecrate. She
is sole and single in this, that she takes charge of those
of the interests of man which most dispose him to
fraternize with himself, to pervade all his possibilities
and to task all his faculties.

1914

All good Americans, when they die, go to Paris.

LONGFELLOW

THE *Galerie d'Apollon* is a long narrow room in the Louvre,
with no particular significance except that it might well
impress a young visitor. Returning home from it one day
in his boyhood, Henry James was shaken by a vivid dream which
was set there: a mysterious presence rushed to frighten and
envelop him, but he stood firm until it recoiled in defeat, and
allowed him to progress towards the light. This strange episode,
described in *A Small Boy and Others*, is vaguely intended to symbolize the awakening of his power over the mystery of Art, with
which Paris was already linked in his mind: his brother William
James was taking drawing lessons there at the time, and the
two youths were being conscientiously taken around the museums.
Besides, Henry's first memory of the city was of the Place
Vendôme seen at the age of two *as if it were a painting*:

I had been impressed with the view, framed by the clear window of the vehicle as we passed, of a great stately square surrounded with high-roofed houses and having in its centre a tall and glorious column.

Some twenty years later, while looking at pictures in the same *Galerie d'Apollon*, Christopher Newman meets Noémie Nioche and Valentin de Bellegarde and begins his adventure in Parisian society, which is the subject of *The American*. This encounter is far less successful than that of his creator with the ghost of Art: he and the other Jamesian heroes do not succeed in fathoming the French.

These two episodes in the Louvre sum up a general trend in James's approach to France. His study of Art leads him to analyse the taste the French are supposed to have acquired together with their artistic heritage; thence starts a central search after an understanding of French society. His first expatriate, Roderick Hudson, sets off to Europe as a pilgrim to the home of Art; his last traveller, Strether, returns to America in order to escape European artifice. Both Art and artifice seem to appear most clearly in France. James himself went to live in Paris in order to mix with a literary and artistic movement for which London and Boston had no equivalent, but returned to the Anglo-Saxon world because he was disgruntled and tired of French manners. In this he represents a general tendency of English men of letters, though he forestalls them by a few years: like Pater, he assesses France on her artistic merit, emptying his view of any political lumber. James contributed to this movement, and therefore has his place in it, even though it could be argued that it was because of the chance that led him to transfer his literary fortunes from Boston to Paris and then to London, and not for reasons germane to the spirit of English society.

At first his attitude is, indeed, typically American. The 'sense of Europe' that he shows being instilled into him by his family in *A Small Boy and Others* consists mainly in the overwhelming preoccupation with Art that to this day characterizes the various classes of American tourists. Mark Twain was soon after to satirize them in *Innocents Abroad*, while expressing in no uncertain terms his disapproval of the Europeans who exploit them. Though James's opinion of Europeans is very far removed from Mark

Twain's robust guffaws, his first letters home show a similar suspicion: that of a self-conscious puritan gingerly venturing into a notoriously wicked atmosphere. He confirmed in a letter to his mother in 1869 that Paris was an example of 'mankind's mad rush for pleasure'. But James stands apart from other Americans in that he is the first to be more than a mere tourist: as his interest in Art begins to centre less on the established architectural picturesque and more on contemporary workshops, as he begins to penetrate the French character and be fascinated by its moral standards instead of narrowly mistrusting them, his approach begins to resemble that of the English. Strether, the last of his heroes to venture to Paris, spends a considerable amount of time in England on his way there from Massachusetts. He is obviously meant to represent the Anglo-Saxon world in general.

The image of France forms an appreciable part of James's work: two main novels deal with it, and it appears in several of the 'international' stories, where French towns are given traits of their own and a certain influence over people's feelings, whereas German and Italian resorts are no more than varied settings for purely American adventures. As a child James had lived in Paris and Boulogne; he returned there twice for long periods in 1869 and 1875; later, his holidays on the other side of the Channel were the only events in an existence otherwise divided between Rye and London. He appears to have spoken fairly good French. His earliest attempts at writing were reports of Parisian life and travel essays intended for the gossip columns of the *New York Tribune*. Here the picturesque value of the country slowly acquires a symbolical meaning, and can thus be linked with what will be the main theme of the novels: a moral appraisal.

I. PORTRAITS OF PLACES

James's first journalistic attempts have been collected by his conscientious and scholarly editors, under the title *Parisian Sketches*. They hardly justify their rescue from oblivion. The fact that they were never read in England provides me with a welcome excuse to disregard them. The later essays, included in *Portraits of*

Places, are far more interesting though they still show the author's difficulty in reconciling good writing with the journalistic demand for European local colour. Occasionally he descends to the level of Baedeker, when he has no very personal impressions of a town but wants to finish his column: thus his descriptions of the local curiosities around Biarritz and the remarks about the racial characteristics of the Basques could well find their place in a rather musty guide-book. At other times he finds room for some reflections on French political life, as in the essay on Reims and Laon; there are also items of pure news value, such as his remarks on Paris just before the 1878 exhibition, or his accounts of new plays, some of them American. When filling up space with hasty generalizations on the French, James does not avoid the pitfalls of this practice: looking at a scene on the beach at Etretat he points out that most Frenchmen swim remarkably well! This is obviously for lack of anything else to say, since the same scene fits into the story called *Confidence*, and comes to life there the moment it is turned into the background to an acted drama.

There remain, nevertheless, interesting features in these ill-inspired essays. The main one is his constant preoccupation with Art. We have seen instances of this from his childhood in *A Small Boy and Others*: further on in the same book James describes vivid memories of wandering along the *quais* with his brother—the very words suggest that the mental picture has been changed by paintings seen later:

the long, black Rue de Seine—*such* a stretch of perspective, *such* an intensity of tone as it offered in those days; where every low-browed vitrine waylaid us and we moved in a world of which the dark message, expressed in we couldn't have said what sinister way too, might have been 'Art, art, art, don't you see? Learn, little gaping pilgrims, what *that* is.'

More or less consciously, James makes his essays about France similar to 'portraits' of French scenes, such as could be found in the nineteenth-century room of any picture gallery. The reader is taken on a journey divided into distinct scenes: the fishing harbour at Boulogne, with the colourful cafés and the fishwives and the varied crowd; some sketches of profiles seen in the train and a glimpse of the good fare and congenial atmosphere in French station buffets;[1] more profiles of typical faces drawn in the street, in 'Occasional Paris'—an *ouvrier*, 'with his democratic blouse', a *grisette* in the Latin quarter. Then more provincial subjects: the billowing vineyards of Champagne seen in a Seurat-like glimpse from the railway carriage, and a carefully detailed study of the cathedral façade at Reims, seen from the hotel window as from a proscenium—after Hugo's famous description of Notre Dame de Paris (which Strether remembers vividly in *The Ambassadors*), but more personal and alive than its model.

After a fresco of the old walled town of Laon and views of Coucy and Chartres, James takes us through the old streets of Rouen, then to the popular resorts of Normandy. Etretat is treated with a care similar to that taken by Sickert over Dieppe: James compares its old houses and picturesque bathing beach, where children are trying to climb on to a raft, with Delacroix's picture of Dante and Virgil on the Styx. He remarks that the countryside between Etretat and Fécamp has the rolling curves of a Daubigny. After a glimpse of a racecourse *à la* Manet, we end up in an inn at St. Jovin, where Renoir would have enjoyed painting the healthy gaiety of the proprietors. Further south, James compares the Gâtinais landscape with 'one of the familiar pictures on a dealer's wall'; when he stops for a meal the glimpses he has of the peasants and the local curé remind him of the novels of George Sand.

James is constantly looking at France through the frames of an imaginary picture gallery, or seeing it reflected in works of literature. He shows quite clearly and with a certain amount of insight that he came to France ready to be impressed by the kind of picturesque he had seen in the shops of Boston art-dealers or read about in novels. He is a typical instance of his time. Though we are free to believe, if we wish, that James actually did remem-

[1] Dickens noted the same feature in 'Mugby Junction' (1866) and so did Mark Twain in *Innocents Abroad* (1881) and Arnold Bennett in *Things that have interested me* (1921). The station buffet is naturally the first impression the traveller gets, both of French people and of French food, since the boat he takes is usually English. When *Punch* sends 'special correspondents' to Paris exhibitions during this period, they usually start off with a praise of French buffets. Trains used to stop there for half an hour and travellers could take a full *table d'hôte* meal.

ber the Place Vendôme as he saw it at the age of two, his description of the memory suggests that it was imagined, or at least
re-created, from pictures. The reverse can also be true: a real
scene may be valued because it reminds the traveller of pictures
or of scenes in novels. This frequently happens in the travel notes
of Englishmen of the time: France as a country had been isolated
intermittently by wars and political upheavals all through the
century,[2] but French novels had continued to be read and works
of art copied and sold abroad, so that the prospective traveller had
access to a whole set of pictorial or literary stereotypes. Art can
sometimes circulate more widely than tourists.

This kind of influence is a curious, and somewhat unusual one:
it appeared at that particular moment (the last twenty years of the
century) because the artistic influence of France was temporarily
greater than the Englishman's knowledge of the country through
his own men of letters. A similar state of affairs existed a few years
after the last war, when France was seen through the eyes of
Sartre and Camus. James illustrates it when he writes to his
parents of his delight at having met characters after Balzac in
provincial towns and villages.[3] When he ironically names
Strether, surely the least visionary of men, *Louis Lambert*, he is
using, not without affectation, the mythology of the *Comédie
Humaine* and following a literary fashion. Balzac had been consecrated by Anglo-Saxon readers as *the* French novelist of manners. George Moore, too, often refers to people as 'a provincial
Rastignac' or 'a replica of Goriot'. Balzac had been adopted and
approved of. One might disagree over the realism of Zola[4] and

2 Special passports were needed from 1850 to 1866 and again for a few years after 1870.
3 Louis Leverett does the same in *A Bundle of Letters*.
4 James only refers to Zola's France once, but the case is so clear that it is worth quoting.
He has said in *A Small Boy and Others* that his memories of walks around Paris centre on a
public holiday when the Prince Impérial was to be christened:

The sense of that interminable hot day, a day of hanging about and waiting and
shuffling in dust, in crowds, in fatigue, amid booths and pedlars and performers and
false alarms and expectations and renewed reactions and rushes, all transfigured at
the last, withal, by the biggest and brightest illumination up to that time offered even
the Parisians, the blinding glare of the new Empire effectually symbolised—the vision
of the whole, I say, comes back to me quite in the form of a chapter from the *Rougon
Macquart*, with its effect of something long and dense and heavy, without shades or
undertones, but immensely kept-up and done.

One thinks immediately of the afternoon of Gervaise's wedding-day in *L'Assommoir*.

Flaubert; Balzac, both fashionable and respectable, was a staple reference. The influence of French literature is, if anything, greater in our day, since it is now occasionally used to describe even the English. Balzac has given up his enviable place to Proust, but when contemporary novelists like C. P. Snow bring the Baron de Charlus or M. de Norpois out of the blue into comparisons with their own characters, they are doing the same as James, except that Proust is a slightly more sophisticated reference than Balzac was. If England were actively interested in exploring France today, Proust might be used as Balzac was, as a kind of catalogue of the personalities one was likely to meet in Parisian society. The novelist, interested in people rather than in monuments, might carry *A la recherche du temps perdu* around like a guide-book.

James may realize that his memories of the public holiday and of the Place Vendôme are the results of his reading Zola or seeing some forgotten print. His autobiographies leave a great deal to the reader's interpretation. But when we come to the novels, the way he uses his portraits of places shows that the re-creation of scenery through art is perfectly conscious.

This appears in two ways. The first can be illustrated by *The Tragic Muse*, set only partly in France and where there are no French characters. The book opens in what we already know to be a classic way for James: in the Salon, which his main characters are visiting. Only at one point does Paris really become part of the story: this is where the author paints the scene of an evening as if the city itself were a theatre, thus suggesting to the reader who is walking through the street with Nick and Peter Sherringham that the 'battle-ground' of Miriam Rooth is itself a stage:

there were people all over the broad expanse of the asphalt; there was a profusion of light and a pervasion of sound; and everywhere, though the establishment at which they had been dining was not in the thick of the fray, the tokens of a great traffic of pleasure, that high-aspect of Paris which represents it as a huge market for sensations. Beyond the Boulevard des Capucines it flared through the warm evening like a vast bazaar, and opposite the Café Durand the Madeleine rose theatrical, a high, artful *décor*, before the footlights of the Rue Royale. . . .

This is more than a backcloth to the story: Nick and Peter are fascinated by the 'market for sensations' that the world of the Paris theatre is—the description emphasizes how they are being dazzled by it. A similar image is used in *The Ambassadors*, with more irony: Strether, unable to decide how much sincerity there is in Chad's 'Parisian' passion for Mme. de Vionnet, leans over a balcony rail:

the far-spreading presence of Paris came up in coolness, dimness and invitation in the twinkle of gilt-tipped palings, the crunch of gravel, the click of hooves, the cracks of whips, things that suggested some parade of the circus.

Again, the comparison with a form of artistry takes its place in the novel of analysis.

More striking than this is the way in which James's characters discover France through pictures, exactly as he himself seemed to be doing in *Portraits of Places*. The opening scenes of the novels often have a picture postcard effect, and show us the central character of the story, usually an American, discovering in the French countryside something he has only seen on canvas before. Thus *Madame de Mauves* starts with the view of Paris from the terrace at Saint Germain before the attention focuses on to an admiring figure in the foreground that turns out to be the young Longmore:

Paris lies spread before you in dusky vastness, domed and fortified, glittering here and there through her light vapours and girdled with her silver Seine. Behind you is a park of stately symmetry, and behind that a forest where you may lounge through turfy avenues and light-chequered glades and quite forget that you are within half an hour of the boulevards.

The American begins in a similar way, with a description of the Louvre; and Paris is introduced by another piece out of the James museum in *The Siege of London*, where Mrs. Headway, the adventuress,

felt the force of the romantic associations of the Latin Quarter as perfectly as if she had enjoyed all the benefits of modern culture. The autumn sun was warm in the alleys and terraces of the Luxembourg;

the masses of foliage above them, clipped and squared, rusty with ruddy patches, shed a thick lacework over the white sky, . . . on the long green benches, a row of brown-cheeked nurses, in white caps and white aprons, sat offering nutrition to as many bundles of white drapery. There were other white caps wandering in the broad paths, attended by little brown French children.

As if she had enjoyed all the benefits of modern culture: this Europe which is so 'full of romantic associations', can only be appreciated if one has learnt about literature and Art: Mrs. Headway feels this wistfully. This scene in the Luxembourg gardens is one of James's favourites, since it is described again in almost the same words in *The American*. It includes an old lady in black, a priest reading, a young soldier standing around, in fact the stock characters of a French park, and Mrs. Headway remarks:

'I like this—it's even better than the pictures in the gallery. It's more of a picture.'

'Everything in France is a picture—even things that are ugly,' Waterville replied. 'Everything makes a subject.'

Though a newcomer to Paris, Mrs. Headway has already contracted what the narrator in *Four Meetings* describes to Caroline Spencer as the 'great American disease':

we have before us the beautiful old things we've never seen before, and when we do at last see them—if we're lucky!—we simply recognize them. What experience does is merely to confirm and consecrate our confident dream.

Having come at last to the land of their dreams, these Americans have to undergo a real convalescence before they can become critical of their surroundings once more. Even after this, French scenery still acts strongly on them: when it appears it has a strange purifying effect. Thus in *Madame de Mauves*, at the point where Longmore has to choose between giving up an impossible suit or becoming basely an 'approved' lover, the countryside through which he walks calms his emotions and helps him to a wise decision:

He thought he had never seen anything so characteristically French; all the French novels seemed to have described it, all the French landscapists to have painted it. The fields and trees were of a cool metallic green; the grass looked as if it might stain his trousers, and the foliage his hands. The clear light had a mild greyness; the sheen of silver, not of gold, was in the workaday sun. A great red-roofed high-stacked farmhouse, with whitewashed walls and a straggling yard, surveyed the high road on one side, from behind a transparent curtain of poplars.

There is a similar scene in *The American*: Newman retires into the architectural beauty of Notre Dame to meditate on the despicable trick played on him by the Bellegarde family, and on his opportunity for revenge. He decides to leave them alone. In *The Ambassadors* Strether visits the Luxembourg gardens and reflects amongst the inevitable 'white-capped women' on the impact his recent meeting with Maria Gostrey has had on his feelings. Another mental recapitulation takes place a little later, again in Notre Dame: the atmosphere in the cathedral helps him to set Chad's liaison in the correct perspective, and as if the building itself were the symbol of his mind he presently notices Mme. de Vionnet sitting there.

These portraits of French places suggest a correspondence between emotions and thoughts and the landscape around; of course, in times of great mental stress we do notice the outside world more than ever, and exceptional fears, sorrows, or joys remain forever linked in our mind with the setting in which they entered into our life. But in this case there is a great deal more to it. The previous knowledge that France is the country of art, and that everything there makes a subject, gives James's characters a heightened consciousness of beauty at these moments, which acts as a kind of catharsis to their emotions. These Americans, who have come to France with the sharpened eyes of the tourist and the mental preparation of the art-pilgrim, imagine that they have at last found the place of innocence.

There are, however, all sorts of reservations to their candid approach to France. The eyes of the fervent art-lover give things a gilt frame that is rarely deserved: there is an ominous ring about the sublime confidence of the new-worlders on their arrival, which suggests that it will not last long. Indeed, disappointment appears the moment people are added to the pictures of places. Nowhere are the illusions of pictorial art more vividly set out than in *Four Meetings*. Caroline Spencer, as she lands at Le Havre with the author, is impressed with the traditionally romantic picture of a French sea-port that she sees:

> We walked along the sunny noisy quays and then turned into a wide pleasant street which lay half in the sun and half in shade—a French provincial street which resembled an old water-colour drawing: tall grey steep-roofed, red-gabled many-storied houses; green shutters on windows and old scroll-work above them; flower pots in balconies and white-capped women in doorways ... under an awning, several tables and chairs were disposed upon the pavement. The windows were open behind; half a dozen plants in tubs were ranged beside the door; the pavement was besprinkled with clean bran. It was a dear little quiet old-world café.

With the confidence of one who has found the land of her dreams, the little New England teacher marvels over the beauty of everything while she recites the plans for her journey through France and Italy:

> I feel so much in a dream. I've been sitting here an hour, and I don't want to move. Everything's so delicious and romantic. I don't know whether the coffee has gone to my head—it's *so* unlike the coffee of my dead past.

The very imagery suggests an arrival in Paradise. But the narrator has to leave her to continue his journey; the next time they meet, back in New England, we discover that instead of the romantic landscape she was expecting, Caroline only managed to pick up a sordid realistic cartoon. The author meets the French pseudo-countess who is sponging off her, and reflects:

> To what quite other scene did the sight of her transport me? To some dusky landing before a shabby Parisian *quatrieme*—to an open door revealing a greasy ante-chamber and to Madame leaning over the banisters while she holds a faded wrapper together and bawls down to the portress to bring up her coffee.

France includes the sordid and the shabby, the pretentious and the false, as well as the picturesque. Strether, in *The Ambassadors*, is similarly disappointed. He has taken a train to the country to forget for a day the decision he has to make, and to give himself to

that French ruralism, with its cool special green, into which he had hitherto looked only through the little oblong window of the picture-frame. It had been as yet for the most part but a land of fancy for him—the background of fiction, the medium of art, the nursery of letters; practically as distant as Greece, but practically also well-nigh as consecrated.

In fact he is looking for a view that will remind him of a Lambinet he once saw in Boston at a Tremont Street dealer's, and, perhaps as in the case of Chad's liaison with Mme. de Vionnet, he is seeing only what he wishes to see. Presently his wish is fulfilled:

The oblong gilt frame disposed its enclosing lines; the poplars and willows, the reeds and river—a river of which he didn't know, and didn't want to know, the name—fell into a composition, full of felicity, within them; the sky was silver and turquoise and varnish; the village on the left was white and the church on the right was grey; it was all there, in short—it was what he wanted: it was Tremont Street, it was France, it was Lambinet.[5]

An inn and the prospect of a good meal complete the attraction of the scene; then the bubble bursts—into the picture sail Chad and Mme. de Vionnet, boating together miles from Paris, unescorted and obviously with no intention of returning there that night. Their relationship cannot be virtuous after all; the illusion of art is destroyed, its innocence tainted. Moral values flood in and lead the art-lover on to another quest.

II. ARTIFICE

James is not primarily a moralist: his search is for artistic rather than for ethical beauty. But when people appear they spoil the purity he had seen in French landscapes: turning to them, he has to attempt a moral appraisal. His last book about France, *The Ambassadors*, shows clearly the path he followed. France, the mysterious home of Art, had given her inhabitants something

[5] The elaborate use of the Lambinet theme here is surprisingly similar to the more prolonged one of the *sonate de Vinteuil* by Proust.

called Taste, which distinguished them from other people. To understand what it was, James tried to assess their behaviour in society. In *The Ambassadors* Mme. de Vionnet stands both for artistic Taste and for a different moral outlook. Retrospectively, we can also interpret Claire de Cintré, of *The American*, in this way: but James's Frenchmen only progressively disentangle themselves from their standard national characteristics or their melodramatic foreignness.

Portraits of Places develops at several points the traditional series of comparisons between the French and the English: they are especially clear to the New England observer, who is used to seeing such a family likeness over the whole of his huge continent, and has always connected the Old World with the oldness of Great Britain, so that he is surprised by the striking differences only twenty miles from Dover.

James makes a few searching remarks on political problems. In Reims cathedral, when a beadle asks him to move out of the choir, he reflects on the large part being played in the imperial régime by the Church, and the contrast between the former greatness of the catholic ideal and its present servitude to odious reactionary causes. He wonders whether an active radical can allow himself to be moved by architectural beauty when it is put to the service of such an authority. Later, when a young officer directs him to the battlements at Laon, he thinks on the value of compulsory military service, and adopts the unfortunately common view that five years spent in the 'military mill' teach a young man a great deal about life.

Otherwise we are still on a low level of perception. French cooking appears, as in all the notebooks of English travellers: Frenchmen order their meals solemnly, savour them with taste, and frequently indulge in full-length repasts. As if to apologize for this commonplace, James then describes the artless attitude of the two more blatantly newly arrived Englishmen he met in the railway carriage:

If the conductor, appearing at the carriage door to ask for our tickets, had had the leg of a frog sticking out of his pocket, I think their only very definite preconception would have been confirmed.

When he analyses the traits of the French, James comes to conclusions similar to those of Matthew Arnold. They seem to him smaller and less strong than their English counterparts, but this difference is balanced by an appearance of intelligence:

the good looks of the French working-people are to be found in their look of intelligence. These people, in Paris, strike me afresh as the cleverest, the most perceptive, and, intellectually speaking, the most human of their kind.

There is an intellectual stamp about everyone. On the other hand, they look less 'respectable' than the English: James explains at great length that the demands of French society are much less formal and more personal.

The Frenchman has always, comparatively speaking, a Bohemian, empirical look; the expression of his face, its colouring, its movement, have not been toned down to the neutral complexion of that breeding for which in English speech we reserve the epithet of 'good'.

Thus the Frenchman, meeting a friend in the street, is more spontaneous and natural in the way he bows; when he tucks his napkin under his collar he also shows that his table manners are more practical. By comparison, everything in England seems 'pressed upon from the rear by an immense body of private proprietors and comforts, of domestic conventions and theological observance'. With their sociable approach to everyone, the French are more personal.[6] Far from the 'incorruptible dumbness of the British domestic', you find 'Adolphe or Edouard, in his long white apron and his large patent-leather slippers', who remembers your favourite table and your favourite drink, and utters a friendly greeting out of instinct and not out of professional obligation.

[6] Also noted by J. S. Mill, who had visited France in 1820, in his *Autobiography* (1873):
I even then felt, though without stating it clearly to myself, the contrast between the frank sociability and amiability of French personal intercourse, and the English mode of existence, in which everybody acts as if everybody else was either an enemy or a bore. In France, it is true, the bad as well as the good points, both of individual and of national character, come more to the surface . . . but the general habit of the people is to show, as well as to expect, friendly feeling in every one towards every other, wherever there is not some positive cause for the opposite.
This feeling could well be an elucidation of Arnold's radical generalizations on the 'Spirit of Society'.

We are reminded of these remarks in *The Tragic Muse*: Nick
Dormer, the enthusiastic young artist discovering the world of
sensations, always puts in a few days in Paris when he goes to the
Continent, and feels its 'sharp contagion'. In the realm of art,
we find these traits in the Salon: 'There was youth in the air, and a
multitudinous newness, for ever reviving, and the diffusion of a
hundred talents, ingenuities, experiments.' Nick and his friend
Gabriel Nash, caught by this atmosphere, ramble along the *quais*
in search of old books and prints, and then through the city at
night, engaged in a passionate and brilliant discussion, a thing that
would seem out of place in London.

James makes exceptions, however, where Frenchmen in uniform are concerned: the French official becomes part of the impersonal and efficient machine known as the 'administration'.
He is no longer modest and amiable, but your superior or your
equal;[7] the heavy organization of officialdom surprises James: the
porters on the railway station have to hand their tips in to a general
fund, the Customs pens look like gaols, and the Customs officials
are formidable.

Finally, a series of observations compare the lot of the French
woman with that of her Anglo-Saxon equivalent. At French
watering places James notes that the *jeune fille* is much less free to
mix with the young men of her choice, and has to stay under the
watchful protection of her mother. However, things are well
ordered, for

if a 'jeune fille' is for three or four years tied with a very short rope
and compelled to browse exclusively upon the meagre herbage which
sprouts in the maternal shadow, she has at least the comfort of reflect-
ing that, according to the native phrase, *on s'occupe de la marier*—that
measures are being carefully taken[8] to promote her to a condition of
unbounded liberty.

Once she is married she commands more respect than in England,
because she has reached the status of *mère de famille*: this is 'not

[7] See George Gissing: 'the Frenchman in office is, for the most part, a detestable
creature' (*Letters to his Family*).

[8] *On prend soigneusement des mesures pour* . . .: one of James's gallicisms, frequent at that
time.

a sentimental but really an official position' and there are customs concerning it that are observed with a near-religious respect.[9] Consequently the Frenchwoman plays an altogether larger part in domestic affairs:

> Go about and look for furnished rooms, you always encounter a concierge and his wife. When you ask the price of the rooms, the woman takes the words out of her husband's mouth, if indeed he have not first turned to her with a questioning look.

These ideas are later illustrated in characters such as old Mme. de Bellegarde, and Mme. de Vionnet. But they are incidental, and play a smaller part than one might expect in the characterization of the novels. They are mostly true, except that of course Frenchmen do not appear to have a 'Bohemian look' unless one has read Murger before visiting Paris. But, as we have seen with Meredith, the stock character is often more influential on the mind of the novelist than the real one. This simplifies the image of the French considerably when we turn to the three early novels about France: *The Reverberator*, *Madame de Mauves* and *The American*. The conventions in the English novel demanded an attitude of suspicion towards the French: hence the melodramatic episodes in *Madame de Mauves* and *The American*, otherwise hard to understand, which would probably have been similar even if James had not decided to confront Americans, representing Good, with Frenchmen, of more problematic morality. Because of these 'necessary' patterns, the first novels are far less broad-minded than even the articles for the *Tribune*: James had to follow a long path before arriving at the liberal attitude of *The Ambassadors*.

The pattern in the four stories dealing with France is much the same as that of *Beauchamp's Career*: the aim is to compare the moral outlook of Frenchmen and Americans by finding out whether personal relationships between the two can be successful: these are symbolized by love and would be crowned by marriage. The story could be set on either side of the Atlantic; but, after

[9] *The Reverberator* makes this point too. There James remarks that the conception of the family amongst the French has improved, even on the 'Latin' idea. Meredith, we have seen, described this in *Beauchamp's Career*.

I

The Europeans, an early attempt that describes the misunder-
standings between a French and an American family living on
opposite sides of a road,[10] the pattern is combined with the traditional one in which the American makes an artistic pilgrimage to
Paris. The author is thus able to make better use of the symbolism
of scenery and architecture; this solution is also more natural,
since it is the French, and not the Americans, that are to be discovered.

So Francie, Longmore, Christopher Newman, and Strether
come to Paris one by one and encounter the French. Francie, the
first victim, is on holiday in Paris with her father when she meets
Gaston Probert in an art studio. Longmore, rather disappointed
by the artistic haunts of the boulevards where he had hoped to
have thrilling experiences, is struck by the beautiful Madame de
Mauves on the terrace at Saint Germain, and is given an introduction to her by an American, Mrs. Draper. Christopher
Newman, older, richer, and more experienced, has come to
Europe to enjoy his money and with vague plans to find a perfect
wife: another American, Mrs. Tristram, arranges for him to meet
Claire de Cintré. In *The Ambassadors* there are two exiles, Strether
and Chad, but the main pattern is the same: they too are members
of the set of Jamesian characters who are possible victims of the
Old World, the only difference being that with those we are
interested in the failure is due to an encounter with a 'national'
moral system, whilst Isabel Archer in *Portrait of a Lady*, or
Caroline Spencer in *Four Meetings*, fall into the clutches of
individual adventurers.

Like Meredith in *Beauchamp's Career*, James must have felt that
it was particularly daring to introduce foreign characters to play
important parts in his stories: so, at the beginning especially, he
muffles their foreignness by a touch of casuistry in their family
history. None of them are really French. Take Gaston Probert, in
The Reverberator:

Born in Paris, he had been brought up altogether on French lines,
in a family that French society had irrecoverably absorbed. His father,

[10] Any meaning *The Europeans* can have had is spoilt, in any case, by the fact that
James gave it a happy ending at the request of his editors.

a Carolinian and a Catholic, was a Gallomaniac of the old type. His three sisters had married Frenchmen . . .

but there remains the redeeming fact that his father, though a Gallomaniac, was still an American: so it is not quite so shocking that he should fall in love with an American girl. In the same way our contemporary literature, in spite of obvious facts, will still only admit any mention of a relationship between a white girl and a Negro if it is made clear beforehand that he is educated, or anglicized, or has saved an Englishman's life. Mme. de Mauves, we learn from Mrs. Draper, was an American girl sent over to be educated in a Paris convent and who married 'an unclean Frenchman'. Claire de Cintré's parents were a French marquis and the daughter of an English Catholic peer: 'she is really more English than French', says Mrs. Tristram. We even see her receiving in her drawing-room over five o'clock tea. Mme. de Vionnet too, though brought up in France, was 'the daughter of a French father and an English mother who, early left a widow, had married again—tried afresh with a foreigner', says Maria Gostrey, making it sound a slightly unnatural thing to do, almost an accident. Jeanne de Vionnet, the daughter, says to Strether: 'Oh, but I'm not a little foreign girl; I'm just as English as I can be.' The Americans do not forget themselves to the extent of falling in love with really French people: Newman and Longmore especially admire rather the Anglo-Saxon perfections, the virtuous restraint of well-brought-up puritan maids, of Mme. de Mauves and Claire de Cintré; these qualities stand out against the French vices of their families.

For if concessions are made for the heroes and heroines, their families, on the other hand, are the incarnation of national traits, and they are the main obstacle to the match. Here there is an interesting progression in the responsibilities of the two sides. In *The Reverberator* Francie Dresson inadvertently gives away Gaston's family secrets to an American journalist. Gaston's family decide to forbid the engagement: this is inexcusable, because he still loves her. The Mauves family and Claire de Cintré's parents play despicable tricks on Longmore and Newman, but are slightly less to blame. They appear at least to consider the suitor;

and in any case they are protecting a daughter and not a son. But in *The Ambassadors* it is Chad's family that comes over to Paris from New England to break the match; and so the blame can conceivably be shifted on to their side.[11]

The French families in all except the last novel are so 'foreign' that they appear at times to be a collection of strange wild beasts. Old Mme. de Mauves, Euphemia's mother-in-law, seems to Longmore 'a graciously venerable relic of a historic order of things'. Newman is introduced to the Bellegardes in this fashion:

> It's the skim of the milk of the old noblesse. Did you ever hear of such a prehistoric monster as a Legitimist or an Ultramontane? Go into Madame de Cintré's drawing-room some afternoon at five o'clock and you'll see the best preserved specimens.

They submit to the most formal aristocratic tradition: the women owe obeisance to the head of the family, who observes a feudal morality, precisely the one that would seem most 'foreign' to an American. The Bellegardes deny Newman the hand of their daughter, the Mauves suggest that Longmore become Euphemia's 'official' lover: the American and the perfect woman being virtuous in both cases, they are cut off from each other. In *The American* the point is repeated through the character of Valentin de Bellegarde, his sister's counterpart. Newman's friendship for him is as strong as his love for Claire. Valentin too has Anglo-Saxon traits: his friends say of him, '*C'est plus qu'un anglais, le cher homme, c'est un anglomane*', and they are separated by an equally mysterious convention: having to fight a duel for a woman in whom one is no longer interested.[12] Valentin's death and Claire's retreat deprive Newman of the two Parisians he was interested in, and symbolize the impossibility of agreement between their peoples.

[11] This scheme has been widely used since *Beauchamp's Career* (published three years before *The American*): James gives it a greater meaning than Meredith. In the nineties it is frequently found in short stories, where it has, however, returned to a mere variant of the 'boy meets girl but quarrels with in-laws' pattern. See for instance E. Dowson's *Countess Marie of the Angels* (*The Savoy*, No. 2).

[12] Again, an episode similar to the one in *Beauchamp's Career*—only more melodramatic here. The duel was a current excuse for mistrust of the French.

The reasons for this do not lie in a different attitude towards Love or Beauty, as one might think. The Bellegardes may accuse Newman of being 'a commercial man', and yet they themselves make him appear to be buying Claire from them. Besides, he may buy bad reproductions, but he is not completely fooled and the description of the rooms he takes in Paris later shows that he has learnt a little about taste; he is as capable as they are in society, apart from his inability 'to say *fadaises*'. The Americans and the French appear rather to be divided on a question of frankness: time and again Newman accuses the Bellegardes of never coming out into the open, and they act with terrible hypocrisy in offering Claire's hand to a cousin at the very reception supposed to be in honour of Newman as the official pretender. But this explanation is not quite satisfying, since the French can act sincerely and still be despicable: Euphemia's family tell Longmore quite plainly that there will be no objection to his 'amusing' her. Besides, James admits in a preface to *The American*, written after *The Ambassadors*, that the weak point of the novel was that it had tried consciously to make the Bellegardes almost too bad to be true. This leads us to suspect that the moral may not be in the reasons for their behaviour, but in its effect: cutting the hero and heroine off from any agreement.

The French characters are indeed weakly drawn: as if even James understands the difference between them and the Americans imperfectly as yet, and makes up with elements from tradition. *Madame de Mauves* shows an American puritan walking into the set of a *comédie de boulevard* and spoiling the story by being quite naturally shocked. Mrs. Draper tells him summarily that Euphemia is

an American girl, born neither to submit basely nor to rebel crookedly, marrying a shining sinful Frenchman, who believes that a woman must do one or the other of these things. The lightest of *us* has a ballast that they can't imagine, and the poorest a moral imagination that they don't require.

The author goes on to pour ridicule on the adepts of the damnable moral outlook of Euphemia's family: her husband is adorned with a picturesque moustache, which he twists pictur-esquely when angry. He is the perfect villain of the Victorian stage, superbly urbane, polite, and a debauchee of the first order. He will end up, in a characteristically melodramatic fashion, by shooting himself because of his wife's scorn, as indeed his brother-in-law has already done after losing all his money on the Stock Exchange. Meanwhile, with his many mistresses he is the pride of the family; his sister tells Longmore:

There has never been a de Mauves who has not given his wife the right to be jealous. We know our history for ages back, and the fact's established. It's a shame if you like, but it's something to have a shame with such a pedigree. Our men have been real Frenchmen, and their wives—I may say it—have been worthy of them.

In terms of realism, this is a gross exaggeration: the sister, in real life, might have smiled at her ancestors' vagaries, but she would not have been so proud of her brother's vice. Besides, she uses the word Frenchman in an English derogatory sense that does not exist in French.

There are still traces of this exaggeration in *The American*: the terrible secret that Valentin hints at on his death-bed, and that the faithful (English) Mrs. Bread reveals to Newman at midnight, is romantic and unconvincing. James descends even lower by trying self-consciously to water it down: it turns out that the old marquis was murdered by a look from his wife. The novel does, however, reach a higher level at other times. In spite of his sense of bitter injury and frustration Newman's frame of mind at the end has progressed far beyond that of Longmore, the hero of the pre-ceding book, who in any case had been courting a married woman:

The most unpleasant thing that had ever happened to him had reached its formal conclusion; he had learnt his lesson—not indeed that he the least understood it—and could put away the book. . . . Newman's last thought was that of course he would let the Belle-gardes go. If he had spoken it aloud he would have said he didn't want to hurt them. He quite failed, all of a sudden, to recognize the fact of his having cultivated any such link with them. It was a link for themselves, their having so hurt *him*; but that side of it was now not his affair.

He merely abandons the game, as if he had realized that he and the Bellegardes were playing under different rules. In spite of the wickedness of Claire's fate, there is a certain grandeur in the way in which her mother and brother refuse to go back upon their decision though they know of the weapon Newman holds against them: Valentin, too, sacrificed himself in the duel in a way even the American can understand to be honourable, though the reasons for it escape him. Newman may not recognize the ideals involved, but he sees a certain value in the beliefs. He and the Bellegardes simply cannot bridge the gap between the two societies, with their incompatible moral atmospheres. Newman thus sees clearly what Longmore did not quite realize: he must return home wounded and content with having acted well according to his own principles.

From a realistic point of view this bitter conclusion cannot be ascribed to international misunderstanding. James set his story amidst the rotting French aristocracy that had little or nothing to do with the new industrial society of the 1860's. The conflict between Newman and the Bellegardes is rather one between the old and the new ruling classes than between the French and the Americans. There is a certain amount of snobbism in the way Henry James so often reduces Europe to its traditional gentlefolk.

As if to answer this objection, however, he has added to *The American* minor characters with whom Newman also disagrees, although he is of their class. Noémie Nioche, who has 'a prompt French eye too protrusive for perfect beauty', represents the mercenary instincts of the French bourgeoisie. She exploits her rich patron with hard, unflinching directness: thus when she is persuading her father to offer him French lessons:

—And if he asks the price of the lessons?
—He won't ask it, said the girl.
—What he pleases, I may say?
—Never! That's bad style.
—But if he wants to know?
Mademoiselle Noémie had put on her bonnet, and was tying the

ribbons. She smoothed them out, her shell-like little chin thrust forward.

—Ten francs, she said quickly.

—Oh, my daughter! I shall never dare.

—Don't dare then! He won't ask till the end of the lessons and you'll let me make out the bill.

Yet these are traits Newman might well be prepared to admire, since he, too, is a self-made man. He says elsewhere that he likes 'the wondrous French thrift'. But these qualities are badly used. As the feudal pride of the Bellegardes, though admirable, was applied to an unacceptable moral system, so Noémie and her father disgrace themselves in Newman's eyes by looking for a rich patron rather than for a husband. When he meets them in London on his way back to America her father is so weak and she so self-confident in her new part of coquette, that there is obviously nothing intrinsically wrong with such a career for her: again, the conclusion is simply that she is best left alone.

There was a similar episode in *Madame de Mauves*. Longmore, has left Euphemia's house in disgust and come across the innocent French countryside we have seen described. He meets a young painter with a charming and happy companion, and thinks that perhaps pure, innocent love is possible, even here:

All Frenchwomen were not coquettes, he noted, as he kept pace with his companion. She uttered a word now and then, for politeness' sake, but she never looked at him and seemed not in the least to care that he was a well-favoured and well-dressed young man. She cared for nothing but the young artist in the shabby coat and the slouched hat.

But he is disappointed immediately: the inn-keeper reveals to the rather obtuse hero that this woman's happiness is not innocent:

'Don't trust to it, Monsieur! Those artists—*ça n'a pas de principes!* From one day to another he can plant her there. I know them, *allez*. I've had them here very often; one year with one, one year with another.' Longmore was at first puzzled. Then—'You mean she is not his wife?' he asked.

Though these books turn on a difference in moral values, they have no moral, for they prescribe neither one system nor the other. Longmore and Newman return home bewildered rather than angry. It merely seems unwise to try to bridge the gap. In *The Ambassadors*, written twenty years later, James's position has, however, progressed. Here too there is a clash between values: but there are three attempts, instead of only one, to appreciate the French. The American observer is split into Chad, Strether, and the Newsomes, and all will have different reactions. The Newsomes return home puzzled, as Newman and Longmore did; Chad is completely converted; and Strether, in many ways the touchstone, chooses the Anglo-Saxon way of life although he knows he could have been happy in Paris with Maria Gostrey.

Strether realizes the ambiguity of his position partly as a result of meeting Maria Gostrey in England: he is the middle-aged representative of a respectable puritanism, sent out to save Chad from a loose life and bring him back to the fold, and yet he finds himself reacting to Paris as he did when a young man, and thinking of visiting the *Gymnase* theatre. Even here, where one is 'relatively safe',

having his young friend at his side would have been an odd feature of the work of redemption; . . . . He clearly hadn't come out in the name of propriety but to visit unattended equivocal performances; yet still less had he done so to undermine his authority by sharing them with the graceless youth. Was he to renounce all amusement for the sweet sake of authority?

In this very Jamesian debate, between light possibilities just below the surface, Strether does not go to the roots of his own motives. He wants to visit the theatre anyway, and his hesitations spring from his not knowing which appearance he wants to keep up. Because of this conflict, which stretches through the book, he is an essentially comic character whereas Newman and Longmore were tragic or melodramatic. His dual allegiance makes him mildly ridiculous every time he meets Mme. de Vionnet and her set of friends. He is intelligent enough to understand the brilliance of their conversation, and to aspire after it: he mentions that he had always wanted to build himself a 'temple of taste' and that this is an opportunity for him. But the narrow principle he has been made to stand for leads him to inquire repeatedly whether Chad and Mme. de Vionnet are virtuous according to the values of Woollett, Massachusetts, when he knows with another part of himself that the problem is not really on that level at all: for the French it revolves around Chad's debt of gratitude towards Mme. de Vionnet for having developed his taste. Strether sticks to the object of his embassy, remarking to himself that he would rather appear stupid than fatuous. He is perfectly lucid over his own ineptitude; he is also able to observe the progressive effect of Paris on the other characters.

It is made clear that Strether's problem is not that of the common visitor. James writes in his preface:

There was the dreadful old tradition, one of the platitudes of the human comedy, that people's moral scheme *does* break down in Paris. . . . There was in fact the *trivial* association, one of the vulgarest in the world; but which gave me pause no longer, I think, simply because its vulgarity is so advertised. . . . [Strether's surroundings were] a minor matter, a mere symbol for more things than had been dreamt of in the philosophy of Woollett.

In other words, Strether is not going to Paris to have a good time, he is of a finer grain. But he watches Jim Pocock, who is; and who inquires as soon as he arrives what is on at the 'Varieties'. Jim is having the last fling of the middle-aged dog, 'sniffing up what he supposes to be Paris from morning to night'; indeed, such is the magic of the place, and the idea that it is the accepted centre for emancipation, that each member of the little group from Woollett starts on his own little adventure, under the ironic gaze of Strether, himself associated with Maria Gostrey. Jim, surprisingly enough, is impressed by Mme. de Vionnet, and goes to visit her on his own; Sarah, his wife, pairs off with Waymarsh and allows him to take her to intimate meals:

That's *her* tribute to the ideal—we each have our own. It's her romance . . . on this classic ground, in this charged infectious air. [Waymarsh is enjoying] the kindness of dining her, nose to nose, at the hour when all Paris is crowding to profane delights, and in the— well—in the great temple as one hears it, of pleasure.

Finally, Little Bilham attends on Mamie, and so everyone is satisfied. In Comedy, the manservant and maidservant consort in the kitchen while their master and mistress enjoy a more spiritual relationship in the drawing-room above, symbolizing the two levels of love while enhancing the value of the higher one.

For it is not the Paris of the 'Varieties' that tempts Strether; nor is it the Latin Quarter, which he visited before and where he returns with Little Bilham; nor indeed the archaic society of the Bellegardes, which Christopher Newman had met. It is a Paris of light, refined drawing-rooms, sociable and select restaurants, brilliant conversation, tasteful and discreet surroundings. It is the polished Paris of the Faubourg St. Germain a decade or so before Proust lived there, still gravitating around the nobility, but admitting distinguished foreigners, particularly Anglo-Saxons, to its tea parties and its Jockey-Club.[13] Strether was sensitive to Maria Gostrey's intuitive cleverness as soon as he met her, and he finds that she owes it to the atmosphere of Paris. As soon as she or Mme. de Vionnet are present, things are only half said but immediately understood (though not always by the reader), and the subtlety of the exchanges is rendered skilfully. When Strether happens to be with both Mme. de Vionnet and Mrs. Pocock, freshly arrived from Woollett, he feels 'quite as if he had been called upon to hint to Mrs. Pocock how Parisians could talk', and he endeavours to answer a suggestion of hers with equal refinement.

The sober elegance and manners that Chad displays when Strether meets him in the theatre come from Mme. de Vionnet: the word discreet recurs in descriptions of her—'something subdued and discreet', 'the charming discretion'. When they have an impromptu lunch together he is particularly sensitive to it: 'She was a woman who, between courses, could be graceful with her elbows on the table. It was a posture unknown to Mrs. Newsome, but it was easy for a *femme du monde*'. She brings

---

[13] During his first stays in France, James, like Strether on his first visit, only met an artistic and bohemian circle. It was only later that he discovered the fashionable Faubourg St. Germain. It seems probable that he merely misrepresented in *The American* what he had come to know and appreciate better by the time he wrote *The Ambassadors*—for he was only introduced into it properly after 1900.

Strether round to support her cause with perfect tact and intelligence, and this contrasts with the vulgar directness of Sarah Pocock
representing Woollett. This sense of a refined and elaborate art
was suggested in Claire de Cintré, though Newman never got
any further than realizing that she was 'a very expensive article'.
It was also hinted at in *The Tragic Muse*, where Peter Sherringham opposed the Parisian taste to the vulgar monstrosity of
London railway stations. It is apparent in all the enlightened
Parisians of *The Ambassadors*, and the beauty of the town itself
is made to quicken the appreciation of the higher morality based
on the power of the mind to reach, through beauty, a greater
spiritual fulfilment. Paris is present here, for the first time in
James's novels, not through 'portraits' but by a general atmosphere, by the sober whites in all the scenes. Chad's balcony over
the Boulevard Malesherbes is given a symbolic position, but even
more important are the sense of the past in Mme. de Vionnet's
house and the sense of the beautiful in Maria Gostrey's flat.

At one point Chad puts his future in Strether's hands, but
Strether is still divided. Even when he accepts an invitation from
Mme. de Vionnet to visit her in the evening, he is overcome by
feelings of guilt at the artifice necessary to visit a lady at that hour;
and he immediately projects them on to the people surrounding
him at the post office where he is answering her message:

the little prompt Parisian women, arranging, pretexting goodness
knew what, driving the dreadful needle-pointed pens at the dreadful
sand-strewn public table: implements that symbolized for Strether's
too interpretative innocence something more acute in manners,
more sinister in morals, more fierce in the national life. . . . He was
carrying on a correspondence across the great city, quite in the key
of the *Postes et Télégraphes* in general; and it was fairly as if the accept-
ance of that fact had come from something in his state that sorted with
the occupation of his neighbours. He was mixed up with the typical
tale of Paris, and so were they, poor things—how could they altogether
help being?

His puritan conscience realizes that by beguiling him into their
kinds of artifice, the Vionnets have dragged him into 'the dreadful old tradition' that James tried to deny in his preface. His

moral system is in danger of breaking down. He must therefore make a quick decision. He rather pathetically and half-humorously tries to redeem his and Chad's sins by suggesting to Little Bilham that he take Chad's place and marry Mamie:

I want, Strether went on, to have been at least to that extent constructive—even expiatory. I've been sacrificing so to strange gods that I feel I want to put on record, somehow, my fidelity—fundamentally unchanged after all—to our own. I feel as if my hands were imbrued with the blood of monstrous alien altars—of another faith altogether.

The decision, when it comes, is muffled in a typically Jamesian way: Chad should stay, because the Parisian ideal is worth while, but Strether leaves because it is fitting that someone who knows what is implied should remain faithful to the gods of Woollett.[14] The debate has been no less terrible, but more clear to the novelist, than that of *The American*. An open verdict is returned on the French.

III. THE REAL DIFFERENCE

On the surface, these novels show a fine appreciation of international relations: Newman and the Bellegardes, and to a lesser degree Strether and Mme. de Vionnet, continually watch the effect of their own attitudes towards the other, and bring into account suspicions of the other's motives and aims. This, the very mechanism of diplomacy, inevitably leads to misunderstanding between groups of people; where a foreigner is concerned it deprives personal relationships of an initial goodwill that can exist between people of the same background. *The Ambassadors* seems to point to the only way of avoiding this: to expose oneself to the complete influence of the other nation, as far as one's

[14] The pattern is the same in Miller's *Tropic of Cancer*: the author remains in Paris, but his friend Fillimore follows the same path as Strether, giving his similar reasons somewhat more bluntly:

I don't want to sit in a café and talk all day long. Jesus, we've got our faults, but we've got enthusiasm. It's better to make mistakes than not to do anything. I'd rather be a bum in America than to be sitting pretty here. Maybe it's because I'm a Yankee. I was born in New England and I belong there, I guess. You can't become a European overnight. There's something in your blood. . . . We can't make ourselves over, however much we admire the French. We're Americans and we've got to remain Americans. Sure, I hate those puritanical buggers back home—I hate 'em with all my guts. But I'm one of them myself. I don't belong here. I'm sick of it.

intellectual and not one's moral conscience will allow. The problem is of an eminently ethical order if we accept that morality, as James says in his essay on Turgenev, is an educated cosmopolitanism.[15]

Conflicts between two moral systems are not confined to the novels about France: there is one, for instance, in *The Spoils of Poynton*. But only with the French are the two systems allowed to subsist side by side: an idea of tolerance seems to be helping the author to grope for the essential difference between the French and the Anglo-Saxon world. Newman and Strether learn forbearance without yet realizing exactly what they must tolerate. To understand more one has to penetrate the superficial tension of the novels and try to explore beneath James's evasions.

His admiration for their art led him to explore the French more fully than Meredith: at the beginning he too had the traditional suspicions about frivolity, as his early letters to his family show. The French might be brilliant, but they did not appear to feel strongly for anything, as Anglo-Saxons could. This youthful point of view reappears much later in his life, when he complains of the long visits of Daudet and his family, who were not very welcome at Rye where James liked to be left alone. French feelings, he thinks, lack 'ballast': hence the callous Mauves family and the dry, quick little Noémie. There is no love in the four novels we have considered except between Anglo-Saxons or people with some English blood. And yet these French people seem to appreciate Art, and the new touchstone prolongs the quest. Mme. de Vionnet is the most French of them all; her liaison with Chad is built on a beautifully intellectual basis, and yet it is still marred in Strether's mind by plotting and calculating. Artistry seems to spoil affection.

Why this mistrust? James was not explicit about innermost thoughts. Perhaps the theme that runs through the maze of impressions is simply 'foreignness'. In spite of his wish to appreciate this splendid gallery of pictures as it deserves, James never

---

[15] He also writes: 'There comes a time when one set of customs, wherever it may be found, grows to seem to you about as provincial as another; and then I suppose it may be said of you that you have become a cosmopolite.'

really feels at home in France, as he does in England. The relationships between his Americans and his Frenchmen are all marked by a restlessness that suggests an essential difference somewhere in the realm of communication between people. Though Francie and her father, in *The Reverberator*, stay in Paris for the winter, they always remain a transplanted, lonely, and homeless group, and only their sense of duty as tourists prevents them from returning home. Even the most Parisian of the Americans still feel foreign. James could never fathom the French either and he was always an outsider in Paris.

At heart, he was fascinated by Europeans, and yet he always suspected them of possessing some secret that was out of his reach because they would never express it clearly: symbolized rather crudely by the younger Americans, Longmore and Newman, as the Bellegardes' or the Mauves' sense of honour, this secret is narrowed down further by Strether to Mme. de Vionnet's discreet, subtle taste. But even this is not sufficient. Furthermore, James's unrest increased as he travelled south, so that while England was very acceptable, France was doubtful and Italy unbearable. This is one of his main obsessions, perhaps the most important of all: his literary personality, with its endless self-qualifying speculation, reveals it. Europe, of which England was not really a part but France was the main representative, worried him because of its lack of frankness in rendering the key to its artistry. In America hearts are worn on sleeves; England it was perhaps possible for an American to penetrate by analogy; but the inner content of French life remained essentially foreign—the visitor was left outside the firelight to stare aimlessly as Newman does here during his visit to Claire:

This strange pretty woman seated at fireside talk with her brother in the grey depths of her inhospitable-looking house—what had he to say to her? She seemed enveloped in triple defences of privacy; by what encouragement had he presumed on his having effected a breach? It was for a moment as if he had plunged into some medium as deep as the ocean and must exert himself to keep from sinking.

The secret defences are symbolized here by the Bellegardes' house; in *The Ambassadors* Chad's balcony gives Strether a sense

of 'perched privacy': 'The balcony, the distinguished front, testi-
fied suddenly, for Strether's fancy, to something that was up and
up; they placed the whole case materially.' This inner life, which
Newman suspects and Strether tries to investigate, may be artistically superior to Anglo-Saxon frankness; but it may be the excuse
for a hypocrisy that really frightens James. His admiration is tempered by a moral fear that leads Strether to his quandary. Is the
mysterious veil that hides the feelings of the French one of amiable
courtesy, a superior form of politeness, or is it cunning falsehood?
Paris is made to symbolize this question in *The Ambassadors*:

the vast bright Babylon, like some huge iridescent object, a jewel
brilliant and hard, in which parts were not to be discriminated nor
differences comfortably marked. It twinkled and trembled and melted
together, and what seemed all surface one moment seemed all depth
the next.

In *Madame de Mauves*, Longmore's walk through the innocent-
looking countryside answers this question bluntly for him: the
seemingly modest girl and the becoming young painter were
living a life of sin under the cover of Art. The episode is as appo-
site as the conventional dream in solving the dilemma. In *The
American* the artistic symbols revolve around the same problem,
though they are not quite sufficient to solve it: Newman orders
copies of the best pictures with an unpretentious manner, but
realizes that they are for some reason bad, though he himself can
hardly distinguish them from the originals. The decoration of his
rooms in Paris, however, said by Valentin to be 'magnificent', is
really tinsel and will peel off soon after he leaves. The Bellegardes
are perhaps akin to false pictures and peeling walls: works of
artifice that pretend to be beautiful for mysterious reasons of their
own. Mme. de Bellegarde is compared with 'a painted perfume
bottle with a crack in it', her son gives Newman 'an impulse to
step backward, as you do to get a view of a great façade'. Social
poise can be wicked even though it be admirable: when Newman
tells Mme. de Bellegarde he knows she murdered her husband, she
merely coughs, 'a piece of dissimulation which struck Newman as
really heroic'. French is the language of Art: in *The Reverberator*
the Probert family always fall into French when they speak about

it, but, as Francie finds out, it can also hide a multitude of sins.

The Ambassadors hinges on the same clash between beauty and sincerity. Significantly enough, Strether's final decision is made after the scene in which he meets Chad and Mme. de Vionnet boating. It is not because this proves conclusively that they are concealing adultery—this has been dawning on Strether for a long time, though he has not admitted it to himself—but because of an agonizing pause, lasting for over a page, in which Strether on the bank and Mme. de Vionnet in the boat wonder whether to greet each other. During this extended instant Strether penetrates deeply into her thoughts, yet when she finally decides to wave to him he cannot quite understand her intention: he expected her to ignore him, and is obviously the victim of an apparent frankness covering multiple levels of insincerity.

Thus at the very last the American best equipped to deal with French hypocrisy suffers as much as the first one, Mr. Dresson, who had been so readily trustful of Gaston Probert: Frenchmen betray one's trust. This is the lesson of the novels. Although Henry James was widely received in Paris, he must have suffered some bitter disappointments, for the Parisians are no more readily open to foreigners than the inhabitants of any large city: we know that Flaubert for one argued with him violently and rudely over Mérimée, after having received James in his dressing-gown. After this, he professed to admire Flaubert's techniques, but always found substance wanting. Perhaps a few other experiences such as this one led him to generalize the criticism of French character.

There is, however, much more than personal vindictiveness in James's picture of France. Once he has risen above the level of the melodramatic, villainous Mauves and Bellegardes, his analysis of the 'foreignness' of France has a much wider value. There is in him a certain nostalgia for purity, perhaps for the sane moral atmosphere of his youth, that came to be embodied in his Americans in Paris even though they were more and more corrupted by Europe: were they to meet, Longmore would think Newman calculating and Newman would think Strether a hypocrite. Each represents for James a new stage of perplexity in the quest after the hidden private life of the French. He had conquered the dream of Art, but as he pursued Artifice it receded stubbornly, tempting him all the while to a kind of Evil that he hoped to belay by tasting more and more of insincerity, like a new Mithridates accustoming himself to the poison in order to resist it. But the secret of this 'real difference' never appears. As very often with James the fierce surface tension has only served to set the problem, without solving it. His Frenchmen are primarily foreigners: as he begins to understand them they grow more recognizably French, but their ultimate mystery remains.

This failure is open both to praise and to blame. Our first reaction is that of impatience with the author for not having finished the task. If James was trying to analyse the essence of the particular foreignness called French he surely set about it from the wrong end, since he recognized it first as an abstract value and then tried to put his finger on its content. In the process, it assumed the status of one of his ghosts: its spiritual significance had become too strong for it to be exorcised by factual proof against its existence.

But James was intent on psychological rather than on absolute truth: with the morality of the people exactly as with the image of the country through the portraits of places, he depicts the quest for France rather than France itself. And people do exactly what he describes, even if the novelist knows better. Some of them only see in France reproductions of the pictures or books they studied before they came; others set up a concept, 'French', extend it past its real limits which are political and legal, and then have difficulty in discovering its denotation. What is more, Anglo-Saxons are hampered, exactly as James's characters are, by two tenacious ideas: first that there is something morally wrong with the subtle and the courteous, secondly that the French possess some precious secret that endows them with artistry and taste. The first descends from the old Protestant tradition according to which France is a country of popish guile and luxurious manners, and the second from the rich literature and art that France has possessed over the last four centuries, and the fact that England has replenished her art regularly at that source. Both these ideas have been inherited and enlarged by the Americans.

· 7 ·

FROM CAFÉ TO STUDIO

George Moore and the Nineties

Paris may justly boast of being the most cosmopolitan city in Europe, where the artist, the scholar, the
merchant and the votary of pleasure alike find the
most abundant scope for their respective pursuits.
For its cosmopolitan character, however, the city
is chiefly indebted to its university to which students
of all nationalities flocked in order to be initiated
into the mysteries of scholasticism.

BAEDEKER

What exquisite indecency,
Select, supreme, severe, an art!
The art of knowing how to be
Part lewd, aesthetical in part,
And *fin de siècle* essentially.
ARTHUR SYMONS
(to Nini-patte-en-l'air)

I. MAIDS IN FRANCE TO KISS

THERE would seem at first sight to be a huge gap to bridge
between the elaborate symbolism of Henry James's novels
and the blunt artlessness of the *Confessions of a Young Man*.
The tension drops, we find facts and anecdotes, and by comparison
the new image of France may well appear trivial. Ideas first
introduced by James, Arnold, and Pater, reappear on a level more
reminiscent of Fitzboodle's sketches. Indeed, there are many
similarities between George Moore's approach and that of
Thackeray. The main difference is that Thackeray only happened
to be in Paris, whereas George Moore was carried there by the

main literary current of his time. His works are representative of
the large section of unsophisticated and apparently second-rate
literature that can be conveniently grouped under the heading of
the Nineties. In its view of France, as in most other things, it is
superficial. But this is a minor shortcoming, for its shallowness is
not barren: it is not imitating imperfectly, but creating con-
fusedly.

Though as a novelist George Moore should be rated little
higher than most of his contemporaries, his autobiographies
contributed a great deal to the background of this period. The
nineties tackled the same problems as the mid-Victorians, but in
a far more direct way. Two factors made for experiments in
unconventionality: on the one hand the reading public, and,
especially, the writing population, widened considerably as
Victorian England reached its richest point and books were produced more cheaply; on the other, Realism led to the gradual
breakdown of the accepted literary symbols and techniques. The
nineties thus ran the risk of rediscovering ingenuously what had
oft been thought but ne'er thought worth expressing—but they
occasionally came across fruitful ground.

The *Confessions of a Young Man* are an instance of such a
renewal. The underlying ideas are much the same as the ones
Henry James was still bringing to a head in *The Ambassadors*
fifteen years later: France has a genius for Art, and is the home of
a different morality. The two features run through the conscience
of the nineties. But James's analysis led to a dead end, since his
image of France was only an elaboration of two traditional trains
of thought. His symbols taken from Art are a nice link between
the moral and the artistic problem, but they do not provide a
definite answer to either. George Moore takes the bull by the
horns in two ways. First, he meets and describes artists rather than
Art: the link with morality no longer has to be symbolic.
Secondly, he sees France from the inside: whereas James was
always a tourist or a visitor, Moore could make some claim to
having a Frenchman's point of view.

This claim, however, was not very well founded. Moore
started out for France with the idea that he was predestined to

understand it as well as did his grandfather, who had begun a History of the French Revolution—never published—with this ambitious preface:

Though not a Frenchman, I am perfectly acquainted with the French language and there are few Frenchmen better informed with respect to the history, literature and what are called the statistics of France than I am . . .

After George Moore the English gentleman's custom of taking pride in speaking French badly was reversed. In *Avowals*, he tells us with a shade of satisfaction what Henry James had intended as a criticism of *A Mummer's Wife*: it was thought in French and inadequately translated. We see in Joyce's *Ulysses* that he liked his Dublin friends to call him '*notre ami* Moore'. But his knowledge is not perfect. His French is idiomatic, but not grammatical, his verse is poor. He writes *Les Goncourts* and *Georges Sand*. Walter Sickert, really and unpretentiously gallicized, had the laugh on him. He wrote in *The New Age* in 1914:

We knew that George Moore, though 'awfully Parisian', printed *Marchand de vins* with an s. We read in one of his articles his regret that the expression *l'addition* had ousted *la note*. 'I shall probably be the last man', he sighed, 'who will ask *pour la note*'. He was not only the last but the first.

Moore only once travelled further than Paris: in 1920 he went to Tours while writing *Héloïse and Abélard*. Of French literature he knows the fashionable poets and novelists of the nineteenth century and little else, and writes in 1919: 'French literature in the sixteenth century is represented by Descartes, Rabelais and Montaigne, all three Agnostics.' Descartes was obviously little more than a name to him. When he talks of Balzac, Flaubert, and the poets of the *Nouvelle Athènes*, he is as often as not content to repeat anecdotes and to show he was on the spot when literary history was being made. But, however unorthodox and personal his approach may be, though he often repeats commonplace opinions with the tiresome stubbornness of the self-taught man hardened still by provincial candour, he does look at France, to use his own expression, with a 'virgin mind'. He was exposed to real French culture during his most formative years.

At the beginning he makes out that France was for him, as for James and so many other pilgrims, the home of Art:

In London I made the acquaintance of a great blond man, who talked incessantly about beautiful women, and painted them, sometimes larger than life, in somnolent attitudes, and luxurious tints. . . . 'But if you want to be a painter you must go to France—France is the only school of Art.' I must again call attention to the phenomenon of echo-augury, that is to say, words heard in an unlooked-for quarter, that, without any appeal to our reason, impel belief. France, the word ran in my ears and gleamed in my eyes. France! All my senses sprang from sleep like a crew when the man on the look-out cries 'Land ahead!' Instantly I knew that I should, that I would live there, that I would become as a Frenchman.

At the time, Moore was a disciple of Walter Pater. This alone would have been sufficient to spur him to Paris had not his Irishism been genuinely fired by the idea of trying Art: the *Confessions* give us a pleasing impression of an enthusiastic youth taking up literature and horse-racing for equally slender reasons and showing in both an equal gift. Later on in his life, after he had lived in London for ten years, the outbreak of the Boer War brought his dislike of England to a head. In the account he gives of this in *Ave* his thoughts turn immediately to France and to Art: he walks about London discovering how ugly its monuments are.

Westminster was merely an echo of French genius, the church that a Norman king had built in a provincial city; and, going up Parliament Street, I shook my head over my past life, for there had been a time when the Horse Guards had seemed no mean structure. The National Gallery was compared to the Madeleine and to the Bourse; St. Martin's Church roused me to special anger, and I went down the Strand wondering how anyone who had seen the beautiful French churches could admire it. . . . The detestable race has produced nothing original: not one sculptor, nor a great painter, except, perhaps, John Millais. He came from one of the Channel Islands. A Frenchman!

Later still, in the *Conversations in Ebury Street*, he asks his friend Aubry to sketch out a little artistic tour of France for him. He will

visit Besançon because Balzac's provincial characters still live
there and the houses remind one of *Albert Savarus*, and the banks
of the Doubs bring Courbet to mind. He will miss Le Puy, which
is picturesque and no more; instead he will go on to Nimes
because the garden of La Fontaine there recalls Watteau and
Verlaine, then to Toulouse because Verdi and Halévy composed
there, and to Tarbes, where Gautier and Laforgue[1] were born,
and so on. The attitude here is the same, though a little more
pretentious, than that of James in his tour of the portraits of
France.

But these few cases are rather the exceptions, for Moore rarely
talks about Art in the abstract. In the *Confessions* he quickly
reaches his Paris days, and introduces us to the fervent artists in
the studios and the cafés: Ingres, Dujardin, Manet, Villiers de
l'Isle Adam, Catulle Mendès, Verlaine. We hear their talk about
technique and form and admire their enthusiasm and perhaps envy
them their vivid life. Meanwhile, the poetry of Gautier awakened
Moore to a new morality:

Shelley's teaching had been, while accepting the body, to dream of
the soul as a star, and so preserve our ideal; but now I saw suddenly,
with delightful clearness and with intoxicating conviction, that by
looking without shame and accepting with love the flesh, I might raise
it to as high a place within as divine a light as even the soul had been
set in.

In *A Modern Lover* this step is symbolized, again in a Jamesian
way, by the lights of Paris. Lewis and his protectress Mrs. Bentham are about to become lovers:

The beauty of the city acted on Mrs. Bentham and Lewis as a
narcotic; and in spirit they had already stepped into the pleasure
which Paris, in her capacity of fashionable courtesan, holds open to all
comers.

The measure of expectant waltzes beat in their feet, the fumes of
uncorked champagne arose to their heads, and the light wings of
unkissed kisses had already touched their lips. Lewis held Mrs. Bentham's hand, and, lying back, their thoughts and bodies swayed by the

---

1 Laforgue was born in Montevideo.

motion of the carriage, they watched deliciously the flashing and gleaming of the thousand lights that moved around them.[2]

But twenty years later, in the trilogy entitled *Hail and Farewell*, George Moore tells a very different story of his youth: here, it appears that Art was only an excuse to go to Paris in search of a wicked existence. He had been dazzled by a visiting French opera company from the *Folies Dramatiques*, and particularly by

Blanche d'Antigny, a tall fair woman who played the part of a young shepherd, She wore a white sheepskin about her loins, and looked as if she had walked out of Jim's pictures. I learnt from Dick that she was a great light-o'-love, sharing the Kingdom of Desire with Hortense Schneider and Léonide Leblanc.

It was well to sit in the stalls as Dick's guest, and it would have been wonderful to accompany him through the stage door on to the stage, and be introduced to the French actresses to whom he spoke in French every night. But I could not speak French, and I vowed to learn the language of these women, who disappeared suddenly like the swallows, leaving me meditating what lives they lived in Paris.

This version is confirmed by the fact that Moore hastened to take a room in the Passage des Panoramas, which used to run alongside the *Théâtre des Variétés*. He also wrote a book about the morals of actors soon afterwards. *A Mummer's Wife*, though inspired by Gautier's *Le Capitaine Fracasse*, does show an active interest in the life of players, whereas Moore never described an artist's studio at all convincingly.

On the other hand, there is a certain amount of retrospective boasting here: as he grew older Moore tried to suggest more and more that he had been a gay lad in his youth. He delighted in disappearing from London for a few days and hinting darkly at a *liaison* on the *rive gauche* on his return. Also, the story of Blanche d'Antigny is moulded on too common a pattern: Arnold too, as a young swell, had thought it fitting to follow an actress to Paris and then forget about her. This would not be the only time Moore idealized the story of his life. But it is clear,

[2] Zola's *La Curée*, which inspired *A Modern Lover*, depicts Paris in a similar way: indeed, this scene is taken from the first chapter of Zola's novel. But for Zola the 'incestuous' couple are part of the city, and so do not suddenly feel its influence.

at any rate, that Art was not the only enticement Paris had to offer. In an early article for *The Hawk* (1889) he describes with some relish how, in some of the smaller studios, the models have to undress in front of the students. Even in the *Confessions* he says that he visited the painter Surès, ostensibly to find a teacher of art, but in fact in the hope of seeing Surès's mistress, who had sat for one of his pictures. There is more enthusiasm for the loosening of social barriers than for Art. Thus:

A year passed; a year of art and dissipation—one part art, two parts dissipation. We mounted and descended at pleasure the rounds of society's ladder. One evening we would spend at Constant's, Rue de la Gaieté, in the company of thieves and house-breakers; on the following evening we were dining with a duchess or a princess in the Champs Elysées.[3]

In his literary allegiances, too, Moore was more attentive to morality than to art: he admired Baudelaire for what we would now call the wrong reasons—his satanism and personal revolt. Later, when he does talk of style and technique, Moore goes to the other extreme, and his later books all appear to be written for specialists. All that remains as a vivid picture of French life is the immorality of Paris: the excursions with Lewis Marshall and his mistress, the meetings with the famous 'lights-o'-love'. Moore's amorous successes are only obscurely suggested at this stage, but he at least enjoys the dissipated life vicariously through Lewis. This gradually becomes a pose with him. In *Conversations in Ebury Street*, in the middle of a serious discussion with the stiff-collared Edmund Gosse on the merits of French and English prose, he owes it to himself to take the wicked pleasure of interposing the story of a *divertissement* from some scurrilous book called *Les Arcanes de l'Amour*: several singing ladies who wanted to tempt a duke let him parade around the room in feathers which

[3] The reference to house-breakers is explained by the fact that Villon was the popular literary discovery of the time in Paris. The poets of the Nouvelle Athènes must have talked of him in front of Moore, and in 1882 R. L. Stevenson, who had been interested in the contrasts in Villon's life, had published an essay on him entitled 'François Villon, student, poet and house-breaker'. Moore no doubt had this title in mind when he wrote the *Confessions*, and I would say that this was the whole of the matter. It is difficult to imagine the young Moore venturing near the Rue de la Gaieté—in Paris, according to his French acquaintances, he was extremely careful whose hand he shook.

they pulled off one by one as he danced. Though for Moore himself the 'naughtiness' must often have consisted mainly in sitting up late smoking and talking about God,[4] all his stories suggest a France free from moral rules. Consider the titles in *Memoirs of My Dead Life*: 'A Waitress'; 'The End of Marie Pellegrin'; 'Spent Love'; 'Ninon's Table d'Hote'; 'The Lovers of Orelay'. The last story, one of the most charming he wrote, had merely a French setting, since Moore himself was the main protagonist and the heroine was masked; but this hardly mattered since by then everyone had realized that Moore was what the English call 'French'.

We find the same theme again in *Celibate Lives*; in 'Henrietta Marr' we see the life at the schools of painting around Barbizon where two of Henrietta's friends go with their painter lovers. The colourful gaiety there increases with the appearance of a French count who lives in a nearby castle built by Henri IV for his mistress, *la belle Gabrielle*. He organizes a ball which Moore intends as an illustration of the old-time French aristocratic gallantry, but which is in fact a swinging mixture of the *divertissements* at the court of Louis XV, and the floor-shows of the Paris cabarets in the 1880's. Meanwhile, Henrietta's friends indulge in the 'perennial discussion whether Madame Récamier [sic] had lived and died in strict singleness', a subject perhaps more plausible at the *Nouvelle Athènes* than amongst landscape painters. In another story, 'Emily Lofft', Emily discovers that the great sin of her sister's life was to have found an immoral French novel in a hotel room and to have kept it secretly. After her sister's death Emily feels free and sets off to France in a vague quest for happiness. In the same book, the case of Albert Nobbs, the transvestite, is explained by her disappointment: her master, Mr. Congreve, whom she loved in secret, took a mistress, who was of course French.

George Moore is trying to shock the English on the question of sexual morality: he advertises the French system more blatantly than James in his muffled suggestions, or Arnold in his high-

---

[4] '... we could continue our theological discussions till one in the morning, pulling all the while at our cigars' (*Salve*).

seated prophecies. The idea, however, is the same. Immorality is perhaps the main feature of the view of France during this period. It is high time we examined once and for all what kind of grounds there were for the accusation.

The nineties only revived long-standing suspicions in the English mind. Since the Restoration, France has always been known as the home of frivolous literature and amorous adventure. The vocabulary of shallow love in English is made up of French words: *affaire de cœur, liaison, petite amie, roué, demi-monde, risqué, épris.* The Frenchwoman is notoriously lewd and light: she will become your mistress in a trice. Yet the French think exactly the same of the Englishwoman. At the root of all this there must be a curious survival of tribal rivalry: the women of another clan are discredited, together with the rest of its belongings. There is also the fact that one meets foreign women in exceptional circumstances, and since everyday morality is the fruit of habit, the incidence of transgressions is relatively higher in these cases. Also, from the woman's point of view, an affair with a foreigner, if possible abroad, is less likely to be discovered at home and spoil her reputation. This, however, should apply to all foreign countries; yet France is particularly victimized, and not only in England. The greater part of northern Europe believes that French girls are easy to seduce and that the French air has an immoral taint.[5] There is another reason for this, stemming from literary traditions.

The main current of French literature since the seventeenth century has been devoted to psychological analysis as opposed to philosophy or adventure, and love is the favourite ground of literary psychology. A hasty impression gathered from French books thus leads foreigners to believe that Frenchmen are always either on their way to or from their mistresses. From there they fall into a whole series of blunders. First, they judge France from the example of Paris: in the nineties, few other towns but Dieppe and Rouen were known to the English, who went straight to the capital to seek the confirmation of what the yellow-wrapped

[5] In Germany for instance: see the French girl in the film *Westfront 1914*, or the opera *Lulu*.

novels had led them to anticipate seeing: a people interested
primarily in the mechanics of love. But a capital is not necessarily
the reflection of a nation, particularly where morality is concerned. There are always more idlers there, as well as a great deal
more freedom than in provinces, which are prone to small-town
gossip and have nothing to detain the class of people that spends
its money on pleasure.[6] During the last century this feature was
even more true of France than of England, since provincial society
there had not been uprooted and developed to the same extent by
the industrial revolution. The men of the nineties, since they all
professed to worship Balzac as Flaubert's or Zola's prophet, could
have taken more note of his accurate description of humdrum
provincial morals in *Scènes de la Vie de Province*.

The mistake is repeated on a smaller scale where Paris itself is
concerned. It is wrong to judge the city as a whole from the habits
of such circles of leisure as can, again, be found somewhere in
any cosmopolitan or artistic centre. Great capitals are characterized by the fact that you can be as moral or as immoral as you
please in them. George Moore and his friends did not meet one
real representative of Paris: how could they, on the *rive gauche* or
in Montmartre, districts frequented by foreigners, decadent
remnants of the aristocracy, and the ambiguous world of art and
entertainment? The real society of Paris is made up of a solid
bourgeoisie, perhaps a little more enlightened than its English
equivalent, but with strong family traditions and a similarly
respectable morality. These people occasionally amuse themselves
of an evening with the antics of the would-be duchesses and
phoney house-breakers that George Moore was so proud to
know. The English were probably half-conscious of their mistake,
but at this point the pleasure of freeing oneself from the buttoned-
up atmosphere at home came into play, and they did not investigate their models any further. For instance, one of the *midinettes*
in Henry Harland's *Yellow Book* stories settles down with an
English artist, not as his mistress, but to cure him of an addiction
to opium. She drops her stage name, P'tit Bleu, and becomes

---

[6] A privilege shared, since the beginning of this century, between capitals and international seaside resorts. But the latter were all French to begin with anyway.

Jeanne, a normal lower-middle-class Frenchwoman, parsimonious, practical, slightly domineering. At once she loses her appeal in the author's eyes:

Jeanne was certainly the most estimable of the two women, but shall I own that I found her far less exciting as a comrade than P'tit Bleu had been? She was good, but she wasn't very lively or very amusing.

She has even taken to going to church, apparently a very un-French habit.

The real trouble was that Paris willingly encouraged the illusion. Then, as now, it delighted in decking itself in immoral colours for the benefit of tourists. Most English visitors went straight to the cafés or theatres of which they had read, to confirm the rumours they had heard. Once the café and theatre managers had realized this, they did their best to satisfy them, offering what Leslie Stephen called 'Paris lowered to the comprehension of New-Yorkers'. Then, as now, it would have been relatively easy to look around and notice that most of the other spectators at the *Variétés* and the *Folies Bergère* were English or American or idlers too. Return to the haunts of Pigalle or Montmartre in the daytime, and you will see the staff of the nightclubs living a respectable life amongst perfectly ordinary, shabby, and moral surroundings.

In the nineties, however, this contrast was blurred by the overwhelming desire to find France spicily different from home; the resulting image, once established, was handed down with ever-increasing authority. There were several reasons for this. During the last two decades of the century French artists took to patronizing the world of light entertainment, a thing they had never dreamt of doing before and have not done since, except when they have wanted to live up to the pose created for them at that time. Painters especially were trying to destroy the conventions of academic vision, and cafés and theatres offered them a wealth of natural attitudes to take as subjects: Degas, Toulouse-Lautrec, Sickert, painted some of their best pictures in these surroundings and went to Pigalle to do so. But they still belonged to the Latin Quarter, where most schools of art, the *ateliers de poésie* and the intellectual circles of Paris had their home. The English visitors did not realize this, because their own status in Paris was ambiguous. Those who wrote of their impressions were all, like George Moore and unlike most of the French poets and painters of the time, men of some financial means. Though they had come to drink at the fountain of Art, they also had something of the tourist, and were not averse to sampling the more popular entertainment that the Paris of the boulevards offered them. When they found the French artists, too, appearing on both banks of the Seine, the distinction between Pigalle and Saint Germain grew confused in their minds, and they attributed to the Latin Quarter, which was what they took to be most representative of France, the immorality of the tourist traps on the other side of the city.

And yet, even at the *Variétés* and the boulevard theatres, it should have been evident that the French were not quite what is meant by 'immoral' in England. Nini-Patte-en-l'air, a famous cancan dancer, may have seemed

> Part lewd, aesthetical in part
> and *fin-de-siècle* essentially

to Arthur Symons, but was he not putting an English interpretation on her? If current entertainments in Paris can be taken as similar in spirit to those of the nineties, it is clear that the French and the English cannot have seen eye to eye on what exactly constituted immorality. To begin with, the puritanical idea that the theatre is immoral in itself was still alive in England. It was not entirely false, for in the London of the nineties theatres really were centres of vice, exactly as gambling clubs are now— prostitutes and various social parasites used them as dens. Parisians on the other hand had considered the theatre for centuries as a cultural and social entertainment. To see them visiting it quite openly and even taking their wives there set the English on the wrong foot for a start. They did not notice that the show itself was not immoral in the English sense. Even today Englishmen often feel slightly uneasy at the *Casino de Paris*, as if they had not had their money's worth: perhaps it was better in the good old days—but was it? French theatre managers still find it difficult to cater in immorality for Anglo-Saxon tourists, for they naturally tend to do it in a French way. The French idea of a 'wicked' show is one where love is viewed playfully or cynically and given a secondary part to play: sensation is not important, clever suggestion is more appreciated. This appeals less to Anglo-Saxons who, more prudish in everyday life, prefer, once they have decided to have a wicked evening, to watch the kind of striptease where the accent is on the most vulgar sensuality. The Paris night clubs that do cater for them have very few French customers. One could pick out similar traits in the literary tradition. Compare the reactions of the readers to the immorality of *Les Liaisons Dangereuses* and of *Lady Chatterley's Lover*.

A final point should be remembered when the French are criticized (or praised) as 'immoral' (or 'pagan'). When the word 'immoral' does not mean merely 'frivolous', an aspect we have already dealt with, it usually refers to sexual morality. The English were and still are obsessed by this question. When you talk of someone's morals you mean not their sense of ethics but their regard for the Commandment concerning other people's wives. France and French literature were usually judged on this score in the last century. Yet there were other moral precepts that the English disregarded and the French were acutely conscious of. Meredith has already shown us Everard Romfrey scoffing at Renée's family for being so silly over filial love. The Frenchman's respect for his mother was continually ridiculed. The English novels of the time frequently show heroes running into debt, a habit shrugged off as a harmless part of youth; in France it would have been a major sin. The degeneration of many of Balzac's characters (and of Frédéric in *L'Education Sentimentale*) is marked by the debts they get into: their amorous adventures are not judged in the same way. Pendennis on the other hand gets into several pickles, but his honour is not really at stake until it is suggested that he slept with a girl who was not his fiancée. When the French speak of the moral decadence of their Second Empire they are referring to the financial corruption under

Napoleon III. Today English girls may profess to be shocked (or thrilled) at the erotic sport of their French contemporaries, but French girls are equally scandalized by the performances of young Englishmen in getting bestially drunk at parties—a habit taken on their side of the Channel as a matter of course.

Given all these reservations, there was no doubt a good deal of truth in George Moore's impressions: there is a different approach to morality in France, but the difference is mainly one of appearance. There is no essence that makes France more immoral than any other country. Londoners in the nineteenth century saw France mainly through light plays and prostitutes, but these popular export products do not characterize it. It is only that, while England went through the puritan crisis and learnt to think immorality away, France continued to recognize the facts of life. Without falling into the French mistake of accusing the English of conscious hypocrisy, it is fair to say that because of the catholic background and the cultural tradition in France sexual love is considered with utter frankness there, whereas there is in England a huge amount of self-deceit on the matter. Both countries have evolved since the nineties, but the difference remains: what an Englishman may do furtively at week-ends a Frenchman will live with more openly. The French have never suffered from the romantic delusion that Man once married is for ever happy. In the street Anglo-Saxon lovers behave stiffly as long as they are in sight, whereas the French are less concerned about what the passers-by may think. This does not necessarily mean that the French are more pagan. One supposes that the basic concerns are similar. Until very recently the attitude of the two nations towards gambling was marked by the same difference. Victorian gentlemen also condemned the French for opening theatres and places of amusement on Sundays—but they themselves were beginning to read the Sunday newspapers in private. This is not the place to say which attitude is right: at any rate, most of the accusations that are flung to and fro across the Channel spring from these contrasting attitudes towards appearances. Taine, in his *Notes sur l'Angleterre*, complains that debauch is more sordid in England—he was struck by the scene on the evening of Derby day, when there was much dancing in music halls. A gentleman who wanted a woman would remain aside and direct a servant to go and fetch one. Matthew Arnold, or the respectable citizens George Moore wished to shock, would have been equally surprised to see young Parisians of the higher classes treating chance women with a familiar respect.

George Moore and his contemporaries were vaguely conscious of this, but the exact difference was never made clear. In order to spur Victorian England to a moral reform they used the French example, but as a bugbear rather than as a model. France for them was the land of release from English inhibitions.

II. BOHEMIA

George Moore's *Confessions*, his long hair, his python, and his Baudelairean cat set the fashion for the nineties. Whistler, Roger Fry, Sickert, and Rothenstein, returning from Paris at about the same time, described the life they had lived among the art schools of the Latin Quarter. They told artistic London in stage whispers that Paris was a city of artistic light, the home of revolutionary schools of thought, and, what was more, of a colourful way of life. These are in a certain sense truths. Since the nineteenth century had been a fruitful and self-centred age for English letters and Paris had been cut off politically for long periods, the Victorians had had time to forget that many of the literary and artistic movements in modern Europe have started in France. Paris, a catholic city, very young in spirit because of its large university, is indeed outwardly more gay, but the nineties were destined to be superficial in their view. Prepared by Arnold's warnings of their intellectual inferiority and by the instances of passionate lives led by Pater's Frenchmen, spurred on also by the 'obscure loss of self-confidence' that Cazamian notes, they were ready to swallow whatever was offered them. Chance, in the form of George Moore and some more unscrupulous poseurs, brought them a very strange dish—the image of the Bohemian Frenchman.

On the most popular level of all, the nineties are a turning-point for the reputation of the French. Until then every Englishman had secretly and immediately imagined them as moustachioed

cooks, dancing or fencing-masters. Since then, the white coat or
the rapier have made way for a stained smock and a brush: the
French have become painters—a promotion in the social ladder
for which they should not be ungrateful. Popular images are
rarely so kind. But together with this change of fortunes comes
the Bohemian way of life, a more mixed blessing since it pretends
to be exclusive, but is in fact equally flimsy.

It could be retorted that this view was chosen by the French
themselves, since Bohemia was drawn by Henri Murger and
Paul de Kock, partly from the Frenchman's idea of Paris, and
partly from Balzac's *La Peau de Chagrin* and *Illusions Perdues*.
But the French, apart from the first romantics, have never taken
this view quite seriously: it has always been a retrospective ideal.
A Frenchman, if pressed, may admit that he has glamorous
memories of his student days in Paris, but he will usually add
that thirty years before it must have been a really exciting place.
It always becomes a retrospective ideal of one's youth. Murger
himself, while pandering to a certain taste for colourful stories
about the '*vie galante et estudiante*' in the Latin Quarter, suggests
in the preface to his book that he wants to destroy its legend,
which attracts silly young provincials to Paris. The best way he
can do this will be to lower it to the level of romantic fiction.
He advises the reader not to take Bohemia as seriously as Musset
and Vigny did:

> *Ce sont des prédications dangereuses, ces inutiles exaltations posthumes*[7]
> *qui ont créé la race ridicule des incompris, des poètes pleurards dont la Muse*
> *a toujours les yeux rouges et les cheveux mal peignés, et toutes les médiocrités*
> *de l'impuissance qui, enfermées sous l'écran de l'inédit, appellent la Muse*
> *marâtre et l'art bourreau. . . . La Bohême ignorée n'est pas un chemin, c'est*
> *un cul-de-sac.*

He was trying to destroy a myth by focusing it into a colourful
image—later Anatole France did the same in his deliberately
amiable satire, *Le chat maigre*—but in England he created a myth.
Parisians wink at the vagaries of young bohemians, as Cambridge
tolerates the antics of roof-climbers, because they are usually no
more than youthful pranks. In the nineties, however, a certain

[7] Probably Vigny's *Chatterton* and similar works.

number of fully grown Londoners and New Yorkers visiting Paris imitated them studiously. Already in his short essay on Murger in *The Symbolist Movement in Literature*, Arthur Symons, usually a lucid critic, makes this blunder. He urges the reader to visit Bohemia because without it his grand tour would be incomplete, and adds that things have hardly changed since Murger's day.

Claude Washburn, an English expatriate of the time, wrote that Bohemia

stands vaguely for a radiant manner of life, the concomitants of which are poverty, ideals, ambitions, and an ignorance of money entailing a certain pleasant dishonesty in dealing with shopkeepers. The word has to the popular mind a kind of enchantment; it stands for what is left of romance.

We may add that in the nineties it is confused and merged with the artistic way of life suggested by Pater. The Bohemian Frenchman of the time is theatrical, he belongs to the stage or to the short story. It would be a mistake to look for him in Paris. Thackeray had noted his name, but had not met him in the flesh. Shabby relations of his could be seen on the left bank of the Seine, but his real home was by then alongside the impecunious novelists and relentless editors, the lost women and cruel husbands, that peopled English literary periodicals during the era of the short story. Never was he more picturesque; indeed, his appearance was his real value. Arnold, Pater, and James had described the French in terms too abstract for the popular mind. Arnold's 'culture' or 'popular intelligence', James's 'private life' are hard to picture, but the painter with the smock and the dissolute life is quickly sketched in one's mind and as easily remembered. For the Bohemian Frenchman had no soul, only a way of dressing. If one tried to scratch under the colourful varnish one found only a map of the Latin Quarter. In the studio he wore a smock and a béret; in the street he could be singled out by his velvet jacket and lace tie (loosely knotted), his soft felt hat, flannel shirt, and baggy corduroy trousers, his long hair and his dry, racking cough. A remote descendant of Hugo's Pierre Gringoire, and a son of Mimi Pinson and Lucien de Rubempré, he was born in a stage

set of Puccini's *La Bohême*. Though no one ever gave him a leading part in England he became a stock character in the most
fashionable periodicals. In his latter days he began to discriminate
less, took to accepting small parts in the popular novel, and ended
up a little later in the rather second-rate works of Leonard
Merrick and W. J. Locke.[8] By 1911 he had become so well-
known and widely travelled that Richard le Gallienne met him
in an American wood, of all places:

the Frenchiest-looking Frenchman you ever saw—with his dark,
smoke-dried skin, his fine, rather ferocious brown eyes, his long,
delicate French nose; his bristling black moustache and short, sting-
shaped imperial. He wore on his head a soft white felt hat, somewhat
of the shape affected by circus clowns, and too small for him. His coat
was of a green velveteen corduroy and he wore knickerbockers of an
eloquent plaid.

Indeed, like a circus clown, he always did his best little turn in
front of the same backcloth: this was a Latin Quarter café, a
slightly fantastic affair rather similar to an *impressionismus* set.
Le Gallienne goes on to reflect on it: 'the world smelled of absinthe, and picturesque madmen gesticulated in clouds of tobacco
smoke, and propounded fantastic philosophies amid the rattle of
dominoes.'

Together with a concern for the French artistic trends, the
many short-lived periodicals of the time developed a passion for
the left bank of the Seine. One of them, *The Quartier Latin*
(1896–99), dealt exclusively in Bohemian Frenchmen. Some of
the most characteristic descriptions are in *The Yellow Book* and
The Savoy. There are instances in Henry Harland's tales of
romantic reminiscence:

We used to spend two or three evenings a week together, at his
place or mine, or over the table of a café, talking till the small hours—
Elysian sessions, at which we smoked more cigarettes and emptied
more *bocks* than I should care to count. . . . I fancy the Boulevard St.
Michel, flooded with sunshine, broken here and there by long crisp
shadows; trams and omnibuses toiling up the hill, tooting their horns;
students and *étudiantes* sauntering gaily backwards and forwards on the

---

[8] See *The Beloved Vagabond*.

trottoir; an odour of asphalt, of caporal tobacco; myself one of the multitude on the terrace of a café. . . . I fancy this and it seems an adventure of the golden age. Then we would drink our *apéritifs*, our Turin bitter, perhaps our absinthe, and go off to dine together in the garden at Lavenue's.[9]

This passage is a good example of the invasion of French words for perfectly ordinary things, which is one of the affectations of the nineties: as if there were something mysteriously significant in drinking from a *bock* instead of a glass or in walking, not on a pavement, but on a *trottoir*.

Meanwhile, the Bohemian Frenchman spent most of his life sitting over coffee or absinthe, talking and gesticulating picturesquely. If you walk through Paris and glance at the pavement cafés, and do not stop to reflect, you might admittedly think this is what most Frenchmen do all the time. Later in the evening he would go to a *café-chantant* where he could admire new verse and music amongst a morally emancipated company that included women. Then he would walk home through the colourful streets at the head of a band of poets:

One seems to see a straggling company wandering down at night from the heights of Montmartre: the thin faces, long hair, flat-brimmed tall hats and wide-brimmed soft hats, the broken gestures, eager voices, desperate light-heartedness.[10]

These scenes recur endlessly, with the most amusing mistakes. Cafés where dominoes are rattled become in retrospect artistic *cénacles*. One might as well have imagined the customers of the *Cheshire Cheese* playing skittles. Harland's students and *étudiantes* (his favourite joke being that *étudiante* could also be the feminine of *étudiant*) are as often as not chronic painters or simply hangers-on. They mix the Latin Quarter and the dancing quarter, St. Michel and Montmartre. In 'P'tit Bleu' an Englishman who professes to know Paris remarks of his friend's mistress: 'There's only one sort of girl in the *precincts* of this University'—one imagines

9'When I am King', *The Yellow Book*, vol. iii. There are similar scenes by Harland in 'The Bohemian Girl', vol. iv, and 'P'tit Bleu', vol. viii: also in *Mlle Miss and Other Stories*.
10 Arthur Symons: *Colour Studies in Paris*. Does desperate lightheartedness equal pagan sadness?

the Sorbonne as a kind of Oxbridge laced with dancing girls.

But these mistakes did not matter much, because the Bohemian Frenchman and his paraphernalia were only the background to the adventures of Englishmen or Americans. George du Maurier's *Trilby*, a best selling novel in 1894 and a stage success the year after, is a typical instance. The main characters in the story are three British art-students, a German, an Indian, and an Irish girl. The only Frenchman is a vague cavalry officer who meets them at a drunken party and turns out to be the son of one of the most blue-blooded families in Paris—hence a reference to the Belle-garde stereotype. The students are a mixture of pure bohemians and eligible young London bachelors (see *Pendennis* or *Rhoda Fleming*): they have sing-songs in their studio, draw on the wall, fence together, eat garlic, hobnob with models, painters, students, *grisettes*, and workmen (all in the same café), then dance the *cancan* or see *La Dame aux Camélias* at the theatre. They search for bargains amongst the left bank dealers and talk of 'every-thing' in a jolly manner, 'with all Paris for a playground and its dear old unregenerate Latin Quarter for a workshop and a home'. When the author describes several students working in the same studio as Little Billee it appears that none of them are French; Paris, representing freedom from English stuffiness, fades away from the story after the first volume. Trilby herself is only a half-concession to Gay Paree: she sits in studios 'for the figure', but with a hasty reminder from the author that to the artist nudity only serves to bring a better appreciation of woman's beauty. She can dance the cancan and sing Béranger's songs, but she gives it all up as soon as Little Billee falls in love with her, and she can also on occasion behave like the daughter of an English deacon.

The other men of the nineties, like du Maurier, only introduced Paris to show they had been there. It was a feather in an artist's cap and a necessary prelude to a bohemian life. The pattern of Harland's short stories shows this clearly: something, a song, a name, a chance meeting, reminds the author of 'twenty years ago when I was a student in Paris'. Of course, this was before anyone else had been, and it was, as in the passage quoted above, the golden age. In another story he reminds the reader that he knew the

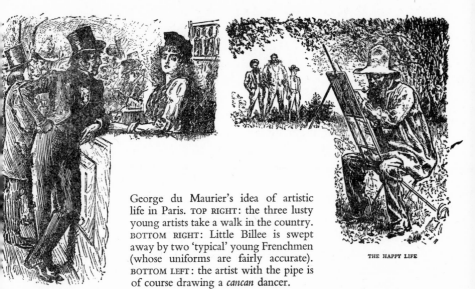

THE HAPPY LIFE

George du Maurier's idea of artistic
life in Paris. TOP RIGHT: the three lusty
young artists take a walk in the country.
BOTTOM RIGHT: Little Billee is swept
away by two 'typical' young Frenchmen
(whose uniforms are fairly accurate).
BOTTOM LEFT: the artist with the pipe is
of course drawing a *cancan* dancer.

TRILBY'S FORBEARS

CUISINE BOURGEOISE EN BOHÈME

"'I WILL NOT! I WILL NOT!'"

café Bleu, now 'the monster café of the Quartier', when it was:

> a single oblong room—with a sanded floor, a dozen tables, and two waiters, Eugène and Hippolyte—where Madame Chanve, the *patronne*, in lofty insulation behind her counter, reigned.

Here is how Max Beerbohm sets the scene for *James Pethel*:

> I had formed, in the dim past, the habit of spending August in Dieppe. The place was less popular than it is now. Some pleasant English people shared it with some pleasant French people. We used rather to resent the race-week—the third week of the month—as an intrusion on our privacy.

George du Maurier (who had been to a Belgian art school) was careful to set *Trilby* in the fifties, thus giving himself great precedence, whilst Arthur Symons pathetically contends in 1904 that he is one of the few to appreciate the bohemian part of Paris:

> To the English tourist Paris consists in the Champs Elysées and the Grands Boulevards, with, of course, the shops in the Rue de Rivoli. In other words, he selects out of all Paris precisely what is least Parisian.[11]

Baedeker, which catered for these inferior tourists, though it concentrated on the more famous monuments most of which are on the right bank, gave the best part of two days to the Latin Quarter in its fourteen-day tour of Paris.[12]

Now that any Englishman can go to Paris and back in a couple of hours or for less than a week's salary, it is difficult to appreciate fully the prestige of living or writing there in the nineties. For one thing, to visit France was still a gentleman's privilege: the period may have been decadent, but the arts were still gentlemanly, and Englishmen of leisure had always visited Paris first on their Grand Tour of Europe. A stay there still suggested an interest in good food and ideas, and the air of faint eccentricity

---

[11] *Colour Studies in Paris*. As for Symons, he selects out of all that is Parisian precisely what is least French.

[12] *Baedeker's Paris and its Environs* (1878 edition). Hotels on the left bank, described until 1900 (14th edition) as 'less convenient for sight-seeing, especially if the traveller's visit be short', become thereafter 'less frequented by the pleasure-visitor to Paris'. While on the subject it is worth noting that the *cafés-concerts* are until 1907 (16th edition) an entertainment 'never of a high class, while the audience is of a very mixed character'—but after this they are merely 'unsuitable for ladies'.

that the aristocracy has always cultivated together with its privilege of speaking French. There was also the novel feeling of a pilgrimage to the source of Art: the attitude of the English was similar to that of present-day Americans towards Europe as a whole. Their *et in Gallia ego* . . . was born of a social pose as well as of genuine artistic ambition. The nineties was an age of poseurs and this part suited them perfectly. It dies very hard. In spite of the massively developed tourist industries in the poorer countries of Europe, though schoolchildren and *Swift Tours* periodically invade Paris in their thousands, a stay there still has a glow of prestige which the literary atmosphere of the nineties helped to build up. A honeymoon or a dirty week-end there are still believed to have a distinctive flavour. Had some socialist government wanted to abolish class distinction in England with a few radical measures it could have done worse than to include a subsidy on cross-Channel travel.

Many of the anecdotes and literary pretences that make up the spirit of the nineties illustrate this attitude. The French names of some of the contributors to *The Yellow Book* (Renée de Coutans, Ella d'Arcy, Richard le Gallienne) undoubtedly helped to lend it some of its air of sophistication. Several other members of the yellow periodicals school were fortunate to be able to display, like George Moore, their French connexions: R. Stevenson and Harland had studied in Paris, and wrote 'we of the Quartier'; Whistler travelled back and forth across the Channel and grafted a French accent on to his natural American one; Dowson, who had spent his childhood in France, could even carry off the common pretension without being affected. The young British decadents envied these people who had trodden the sacred pavements of the *Boul' Mich'*, had met Verlaine and Manet and Bibi-la-Purée and Nini-patte-en-l'air and Aristide Bruant, and knew of their ideas and particular vices. Symons could cap many a story with the famous Nini's dancing lesson he had witnessed at her school, and he knew technical details about the *cancan*, the *quadrille*, and the *grand écart*. Beerbohm tells in 'Enoch Soames' how he was impressed by the Parisian mannerisms of Soames and his friend Rothenstein. The latter gives us the other side of the story:

No doubt I tried to impress them with my Parisian experiences as a 'dog' who had led the devil of a life, one who was on familiar terms with poets and painters whose names rang musically in the ears of young men of my age. I must have appeared a strange apparition in Oxford, with my longish hair, and spectacles, and my un-Oxonian ways and approach to things, and people. Moreover, I was supposed to be an Impressionist, a terrible reputation to have at the time.

In the story, Enoch Soames talks familiarly about the Café Groche and Puvis de Chavannes to the dazzled Beerbohm. He orders an absinthe, remarking casually '*Je me tiens toujours fidèle à la sorcière glauque*'. Sillier things were doubtless said in Paris at this time. Richard le Gallienne takes up the story in *The Romantic 90's*:

Absinthe! I had just heard of it, as a drink mysteriously sophisticated and even Satanic. To me it had the sound of hellebore, or mandragora. I had never tasted it then, nor has it ever been a favourite drink of mine. But in the nineties it was spoken of with a self-conscious sense of one's being desperately wicked, suggesting diabolism and nameless iniquity. Did not Paul Verlaine drink it all the time in Paris!—and Oscar Wilde and his cronies, it was darkly hinted, drank it nightly at the Café Royal.

This was typical of the current gallomania. Absinthe became so significant that there was a huge controversy in 1893 when a picture by Degas called '*L'absinthe*' was exhibited at the Grafton gallery. Absinthe is in fact a poison and its sale was later prohibited in France. It had, moreover, a symbolic meaning; its colour itself was evil, and it was connected with a school of art that had a heritage of satanism. The image of France in the nineties was somewhat similar to the conception of Italianate civilization in Shakespeare's time: as well as being a focal point of culture and manners, it possessed a spicy touch of evil which absinthe symbolized.

Absinthe was drunk at a café, and this really French, or at least Mediterranean, institution also served to crystallize latent ideas. It stood for free intellectual exchange and the 'spirit of society', both labelled on to France by Arnold. It represented a vague democratic freedom not to be found behind the closed doors and divided bars of an English drinking house. Moreover, it was a place of leisure, from which the English 'artists', who were trying to develop their sense of observation and had time on their hands, could watch the display of 'types' in the street. It symbolized the advantages of France. Meanwhile, wrote Arthur Symons,

how many ideas, of any particular importance to anybody, have come into existence in the London drawing-rooms and clubs of the period, where our men of letters meet one another, with a mutually comfortable resolve not to talk 'shop'.

Moore and the members of the Irish literary movement included it in their plans for an enlightened Dublin: 'A café was necessary too. A café was continental, and the new Dublin should model itself more upon continental than British ideas.' Besides, Verlaine was supposed to live in one. Arthur Symons prescribed it for London: he did not doubt

that Piccadilly (or is it to be the Strand) will some day more or less approximate to the continental idea of the necessary comforts of life, that it will have its cafés like every other civilized city, and so redeem England from the disgrace of being the only country where men have to drink like cattle, standing . . .

while le Gallienne half hoped that England would be conquered by France one day: 'we might hope for cafés in Regent St. and an emancipated literature.'

Had the management of the Café Royal in London been able to read these lines a few years before, it would have been less surprised to find its establishment somehow overrun by an army of young artist-bohemians, whose appearance must have caused the same sort of comment amongst contemporaries as that of present-day protest marchers. The hairy, velvet-jacketed young francophiles who took to drinking absinthe there made the Domino Room one of the centres of literary London for a considerable time after. It took years for the mistake to be discovered. Only when the artistic types, no longer content with distant echoes of Parisian jargon, really crossed the Channel to see for themselves, did they realize that they had thought the Café Royal was a café because it called itself one.

Beardsley's *Garçons de Café* from *The Yellow Book*

III. PERCEPTION AND MORALITY

In spite of all the trivial pretences, this gallomania really springs from a deeper trend of feeling. Like many features of the period, it now appears in an ambiguous light: it would seem at once superficial and significant. Montmartre was of course the fashionable resort, the pretext for the current literary snobbery, and yet further down it had a real value. Absinthe was a silly fad, but it stood for something insidious that was obscurely tending to change the face of society through a new art.

At the beginning, Matthew Arnold's ideas retain their currency. Arthur Symons, too, admires the intellectuals in his *Colour Studies in Paris*:

They have not more talent than people over here; they are much more likely to waste, as it is called, whatever talent they have; but these people . . . are after all the enthusiasts of ideas, and their follies bubble out of a drunkenness at least as much spiritual as material.

Few of the idealists I have known have been virtuous, that is to say, they have chosen their virtues after a somewhat haphazard plan of their own; some of them have loved absinthe, others dirt, all idleness; but why expect everything at once? Have we, who lack ideas and ideals, enough of the solid virtues to put into the balance against these weighty abstractions? I only ask the question; but I persist in thinking that we have still a great deal to learn from Paris, and especially on matters of the higher morality.

The praise was no doubt deserved: as I have already pointed out, the French literary scene readily assumes the appearance of an intellectual debate, while, even today, attempts at fresh criticism amidst the dull literary life of London often descend into mere highbrow slanging matches. The above quotation shows that Symons implicitly accepts the Arnoldian contrast between intellectualism and morality ('ideas and ideals' weighed against 'solid virtues'). He merely reverses Arnold's admonitions within the same frame of reference.[13] For when he speaks of 'the higher morality', he is not transcending the current system, but attempting to change its angle.

This reaction against Victorian morality is inseparable from the idea of the 'sensuous'. The men of the nineties felt, as Pater had whispered to them, that the English scene was made up of repressions and disincarnations and that it was their duty to bring back an appreciation of material beauty, even of fleshly pleasure. Graham Hough has shown why painting had appeared since Ruskin as the most obvious vehicle for such feelings:

It is perhaps not surprising that the dissatisfaction should be felt most clearly by those whose main concern was with the visual arts. Painting is less easy to harness to social and moral ends than letters, and painters are more clearly dependent on their direct sensuous apprehensions.

Watts may have protested that his pictures were only a means of struggling against crime and injustice: it was nevertheless through painting that a breach was conceivable. Accordingly, the visual arts were an important part of the scene, and they will serve to

---

[13] See above pages 23–25 and 40–43. Harland develops ideas similar to Symons's as the yellow dwarf in vol. vii of *The Yellow Book*.

explain some literary reactions of the time. Notice that the current gallomania had been spread by a group of critics who had all been to Paris as art students: McColl, Moore, and Fry, writing in the *Spectator*, the *Speaker*, and the *Athenaeum*. George Moore's progress in Paris is significant. He first attended an art school for a time, then left to investigate the schools of new poetry, because he was not talented as a draughtsman, but also because the art school was already crowded with Englishmen. Although Moore is familiar to critics as the bridge by which the realist novel crossed the Channel, in his own credo he was a link between painting and literature, at least until the Irish revival. There are surprisingly few references to the novel in his autobiographies. His anecdotes, for good or ill, are usually taken from painting.

Britain had been vaguely conscious of the existence of a French school of art since the time of the Revolution, when the French aristocracy had brought with them to England many works of art that would otherwise have remained unknown in private collections. In the general confusion, others were carried off as spoils by English travellers. Thackeray helped to make a reputation for Paris as a centre of art, but we have seen that his sketches use the studio mainly for its sentimental value; meanwhile, English painting was settled in a quiet academicism. The awakening came in 1859, with the arrival in London of Whistler, who told of the French changes in technique, and sent dozens of students back to Paris. The modern French school, remote offspring of the Romantic movement, had by then been flourishing long enough to appear congenital to France. It produced Manet, Monet, and Rodin, three obvious masters, at the very time when English artists were beginning to cross the Channel. In fact, even if Paris was, during this particular period, the undoubted centre of Art, it would have been as well to remember that while Paris is always more or less interested in painting, the rest of France is not. One of the first successful students, Walter Sickert, stands for the opinions of the New English Art Club when he writes in *The Art News* that France is 'the sacred soil whence the art of painting first came to England in 1236 in the entourage of a French princess.'[14] According to him a fair judge of art must have 'lived in Paris, mixed with the artists, or heard the talk of the studios', Paris, 'where ideas count, where the town is stirred by a man, by an article, by a question of style, of wit'. Sickert writes of Whistler that the American was lucky to have learnt from the school of Delacroix and Ingres and not to have forgotten it all in London. Some arts are at times at home in certain countries,

and in others grow unwillingly in the manner of religions that are not indigenous, but imported, and only languish in exotic chapels. Speaking under much correction, I imagine that certain developments in instrumental music are at home in Germany, that the genius of song may be said to be lodged in Italy. Certain things are perhaps better understood about carving marble within reach, either of Carrara or Pentelicus, than elsewhere. Those curious of the refinements of criticism in bull-fighting would, I suppose, go to Spain to study them; of football or cricket, to England or the English colonies. And so I believe that, for some reasons to me hidden and inscrutable, the genius of painting still hovers over Paris, and must be wooed on the banks of the Seine.

Since painting was the easiest vehicle for the moral reform obscurely sought after, and France was the home of painting, it is not surprising that the iconoclasts of the nineties should have looked in that direction for new standards. Again, Sickert, writing in *The English Review*, provides the most lucid expression:

Oddly enough, our insular decadence in painting can be traced back, I think quite surely, to puritan standards of propriety. If you may not treat pictorially the ways of men and women, and their resultant babies, as one enchained comedy or tragedy, human and *de mœurs*, the artists must needs draw inanimate objects—picturesque if possible. We must affect to be thrilled by scaffolding, or seduced by oranges. . . . I would not advise a British painter to depict a scene dealing with anyone lower in the social scale than, say, a University Extension Lecturer and his fiancée, or to set his scene in a *lokal*, as they say in Germany, less genteel than a parlour, or to costume it otherwise than in 'faultless evening dress'. National dispensation, on the other hand,

[14] Eleanor of Provence brought court painters with her when she married Henry III of England.

by a paradox worth noting, is gladly given to pictures representing Cleopatra or Messalina, possibly because these ladies' dossiers are not present to the minds of critics 'on this side of the Channel'—ominous, emphatic and almost threatening phrase.

Sickert speaks here as a painter, and so he blames bad morality for bad painting rather than the opposite, but the link between the two is made clear, and it is easy to infer that good painting might produce a better moral system. Sickert was connected with the post-impressionists rather than with the impressionists. His polemical career started after 1905. But he throws light on the debate between the artists and the last Victorians.[15]

In literature too, as a result, Paris began to symbolize the sensuous trend in art and life. A frequently recurring pattern in the fiction of the period involves a young artist connected with Paris and with a 'past', and a girl belonging to established society. Their difficulties symbolize the struggle against this 'imported' morality. It was a realistic story as far as it went,[16] but it was a mistake to suppose that all Frenchmen lived like the English expatriates in the Latin Quarter.

Impressions gathered from the French literary scene were to some extent parallel to those of the painters. In the steps of George Moore, the emancipated Englishmen found flourishing in the city of impressionism a literary movement that, though it does not appear to us as sensuous as the prejudiced painter-reformers made it out to be, claimed descent from the *Art pour l'art* theory, and so could be thought to oppose established morals since Gautier had professed to be anti-bourgeois. The French, however, knew better. The avant-garde circles in Paris since 1840 had demanded that art be pointedly separated from moral advice, to such an extent that artists were expected to appear outwardly unethical. But they too were unpopular amongst their countrymen: their position was not very different from

15 A debate depicted by Henry James in the first few chapters of *The Tragic Muse*, where Lady Agnes represents Victorianism. But James allowed his interest in the political novel of the time to draw him away from this theme, and the Parisian setting soon disappears.

16 See Lucas Malet's *The Wages of Sin*, or Moore's *A Modern Lover*, or *Trilby* (pattern reversed: the girl has the 'past').

SANCTA SIMPLICITAS!

Mamma. "Don't stand idling there, Tommy! Why don't you read *French* sometimes! Look at dear Papa, *he hasn't* much time for Reading ; but whenever he's got a spare moment or two, he takes a French Book out of his Pocket and reads it—*just to keep up his French, you know!*" [*Dear Papa is much tickled, but keeps his amusement to himself.*

that of the yellow periodical school in England. Zola had been persecuted in Paris not long before Vizetelly was martyred for him in London,[17] *Madame Bovary*, which perceptive readers even in the nineties must have realized was a very mild book, had been tried by a French jury. At best, the freedom of artists in Paris was a score of years ahead. The naturalists were of course revolutionary by comparison with the famous English three-volume circulating library novel, but in fact George Eliot is not far behind Flaubert, and in dealing for instance with sexual matters George Moore very quickly allowed himself more freedom than either Zola or Maupassant. He described somewhere his disappointment at discovering after a long friendship that the author of *Pot-Bouille* had a narrow mind after all.[18]

[17] The serial publication of *la Curée* was suspended in 1871 on the 'advice' of the public prosecutor. The newspaper *Le Bien Public*, presumably intent on living up to its name, did not dare finish publishing *L'Assommoir* (eventually continued in a parnassian magazine). *Germinal* was banned from the stage for political reasons.

[18] From the point of view of technique, Thomas Hardy points out (preface to *Desperate Remedies*, 2nd edition, 1896) that there were naturalist characters in the English novel 'before we had a French name to call them by'. French influence is surely exaggerated as a cause of 'naturalism' in England. It certainly provided a salutary shock, but it is

The final step was naturally to lend to French life the apparent traits of French art: it began to be thought more sensuous. This was encouraged by a simple psychological reaction. On arriving in a strange country, the organized circuits of perception, which normally cut out what we expect to see and hear and only let through to the conscious mind what will have a bearing on our planned course of action, break down. In familiar surroundings we are only *conscious* of crossing a street if a car is coming and we have to wait for it to pass. In a crowd, though we see everyone, we only fully notice someone we know or whose appearance is sufficiently unusual to penetrate the misty defences set up by the mind around its valuable moments of direct attention. In the country, Nature is only really seen at periods of sudden change, which we often perceive all at once though they have been going on for some time: suddenly, the leaves are out, or the trees are becoming bare. But at privileged moments, which can of course be consciously developed, the sifting mechanism is swamped and we perceive fully, for a time, everything around us. Lovers experience this: the first time they look 'through someone else's eyes' they have the impression that the world has been created anew for themselves. It is the same with travellers: in a strange country all the little details, the colour of the houses, the width of the streets, the cut of clothes, are sufficiently different for them all to pass the threshold of conscious perception. This is one of the main attractions of travelling for its own sake, a pastime that sometimes seems so irrational. It is no illusion that you can *see* more abroad than at home. The phenomenon is usually reproduced on a reflective level in published travel notes. These are always full of varied and excited impressions for the first day or two—then, as the mind reconstructs its filters to a new pattern, they become less interesting to read, because the author has to force himself to look for new material and falls back as often as not on commonplaces.

This reaction was particularly strong in travellers to France

seldom pointed out that England was ready for it—in London, too, Naturalism followed a general interest in scientific methods of research. Grant Allen was popular independently from French influence.

during the eighties and nineties, for two reasons. First, the geographical position of France favours it. Whereas land frontiers blur changes of atmosphere, a sea journey such as the Channel crossing emphasizes the breakdown of perceptive patterns because the new impressions are thrust suddenly upon the traveller. Today, an air voyage can have the same effect, except that it usually includes a long transition through an internationally uniform set of air terminals. Since, in the last century, the English went almost everywhere in Europe by way of France, this first foreign country was credited with most of the foreignness. By the time one arrived anywhere else, the first feast of perception had been dulled, and anyway to reach the second foreign country one had only crossed a land frontier. Secondly, many of the travellers to Paris were would-be painters or men of letters, and in artists the thresholds of this perceptive chain are brought forward, especially if the current fashion points to sensuous apprehensions rather than to classical problems of elaboration. Even those who were not artists knew before even setting foot in France that it was the happy hunting ground of a school that they were prepared, for the reasons we have seen, to consider unusually sensuous. French landscapes thus became in their eyes mysteriously more 'real' than others, and Frenchmen more sensitive—they projected on to the country and the people their own attitude as visitors.[19]

Little wonder then that they should appear superficial in their view of France. They combined the reactions of artless travellers with those of innocent-eyed artists. For in art the fatal predominance of subject over idea and technique rarely appears more clearly than in the identification of a style with the soil of the country that gave it birth. This has been particularly frequent since Romanticism convinced Europe that the political and sometimes linguistic entities we call nations were humanly and

[19] R. L. Stevenson contributed little to the image of France, but his attitude is similar if for different reasons (eccentricity, affected solitary wisdom). In *An Inland Voyage* and *Travels with a Donkey* France is a place of innocence and primitive delight: he stops to listen to church bells as if he had never heard them in Britain, and appreciates every friendly gesture of the natives. He meets less sophisticated people and more natural things, mainly because he has chosen to travel closer to Nature, in a canoe or on a donkey.

artistically different; but it existed before. It appeared in classical tragedy, which was content to seek in the history of the ancient world subjects that had not been exploited by the ancients. Between 1870 and 1930, when most new styles were spread through paintings made by Frenchmen of scenes from their own country, artists from all over Europe painted French landscapes in their turn: as if Cézanne had in some subtle way drawn his genius from provençal villages or Renoir his sense of colour from the cheeks of Parisian shopgirls on their day out. Painters may form a school: pupils, attracted to the artistic atmosphere surrounding the master and to the lessons he or his followers can give on the spot, will naturally go to Barbizon to learn the styles of Rousseau or Corot. If the technical progress of the moment is being made in Montmartre attics it will naturally be applied, by creators and imitators alike, to subjects drawn from Montmartre or the Paris around it. But if our attention is drawn to certain scenes of French life by works remarkable for their sensuous truth, this is because a particularly clever Frenchman named Manet, or Zola, brought up to a progressive movement, expressed his unusual powers of observation through a new technique of representation, and not because the material he used was more fertile in itself or Frenchmen in general were more perceptive.

The nineties generally made this mistake: they lent great importance to the magic qualities of French air. The reason the artists themselves usually gave was that French light was more favourable for painting, an idea attractive because of its admirable vagueness, which conveys a hint of mysteries beyond the reach of the layman. There is in fact in the south of France, though not in Paris, more ultra-violet light than in England. But this does not justify the feeling that France was more colourful, and hence more exotic, even though Pater may have suggested it. Turner's drawings and paintings of the rivers of France are misleading on this point. His picture of *Saumur*, for instance, might well be a representation of some Eastern country, if we are to notice the exotically clothed figure in the foreground. The banks of the Loire are really no more sensuous than those of the upper Thames on a sunny summer's day. Someone might have pointed out that

Turner had managed equally well in depicting exotically the infra-red gloom of London. The first French impressionists, who admired Turner, are said to have seriously considered visiting London to learn from the Thames mists the secrets of his palette.

The same illusion existed in literature. The artist, an important character in a decade passionately concerned with the future of art, is always associated with France. In one of Harland's novels an American who, to the great surprise of his friends, paints uncommonly well, has to admit in the end that his mother was French. There are fewer French characters than French land-scapes—because of the prejudice against foreign heroes in fiction, and the vogue of the short story, where there is no room for minor characters—but no one is an artist who has not been ex-posed to the Paris light. Also, exactly as impressionism seemed to ooze out of the French countryside, realism demanded for a time a French setting. The better writers realized that the technique mattered more than the scenery: thus Moore's *Esther Waters*, Arnold Bennett's *Clayhanger*, Somerset Maugham's *Liza of Lambeth*, all inspired by Zola, take place in England; John Davidson adapted Laforgue's poetry of Paris to London in poems such as 'Fleet Street Eclogue'; there were various adaptations, even at this late date, of *Mademoiselle de Maupin* to an English setting. But elsewhere France is seen as a 'naturalistic' country; a young author from the pages of *The Yellow Book* thinks that he must go there to be a success:

> I want some local colour. I thought I should be able to invent it, I find I can't. . . . If I were to go to France for—for six months or so—alone, that—in fact it would be the making of me.[20]

Harland's Edmund Pair ('When I am King') has picked his French mistress, Godelinette, straight out of *L'Assommoir*: she was the wife of a drunken tailor, who used to beat her. Even in *The Yellow Book* such a situation hardly arose in England, where the most daring suggestions about marital problems refer to mental cruelty or the temptations met by husbands in the street. Leila MacDonald's *Jeanne-Marie* describes a Balzacian passion in

---

[20] 'The Dedication' by F. M. Simpson, *The Yellow Book*, vol. i; one of the stories re-ferred to above in footnote 16 on page 168.

the country: peasants emit gruff ejaculations borrowed from *Les Paysans,* and one of the characters is the local *officier de santé—* a word very familiar to the readers of *Madame Bovary.*[21]

The link with painting is perhaps most obvious in the 'art transposition', a fashionable form inspired by Gautier and attempted by Hubert Crackanthorpe and Arthur Symons. The former, in *Vignettes,* presents France as a series of vivid, almost exotic scenes such as make up a painter's sketch book. Take, for example, this Normandy landscape:

A mauve sky, all subtle; a discreet rusticity, daintily modern, femininely delicate; a whole finikin arrangement of trim trees, of rectangular orchards, of tiny, spruce houses, with white shutters demurely closed. Here and there a prim farmyard; a squat church spire; and bloused peasants jogging behind rotund white horses, along a straight and gleaming road. In all the landscape no trace of the slovenly perfection of the picturesque; but rather a distinguished reticence of detail, fresh, coquettish, almost dapper.

'Subtle', 'discreet', 'daintily modern', 'finikin arrangement', 'picturesque', 'reticence of detail': all these epithets and phrases apply not to a natural landscape but to a painting of one, and an impressionist painting at that, since 'the slovenly perfection of the picturesque' presumably refers to Constable's style. Crackanthorpe has had to go to Normandy in order to discover what we, in our turn, would find no more than picturesque, in a scene surely quite common in Sussex or Kent. His *Vignettes* on England are by contrast colourless and over-sentimental.

The same feeling had prompted Henry James to see France as a series of portraits of places. It is not surprising, then, that he should have appreciated this feature in his critical introduction to Crackanthorpe's *Last Studies*:

to the appetite of the artist in him what, apparently, had most savour was the sweetness and the sadness, above all in France, of strong country aspects, of the sharp, homely, sunny foreignness of simple, local folk and out-of-the-way places.[22]

[21] *The Yellow Book,* vol. iii. See also Conrad's short story 'The Idiots' in *The Savoy,* vol. vi.

[22] In *The Ambassadors* Strether, too, is conscious of a sharpened perception in Paris.

James was obviously in sympathy, but the appreciation above has no value if the word 'French' has not previously been equated with 'artistic'.

Finally, the title of Arthur Symons's *Colour Studies in Paris* suggests that there are perhaps no colours worth studying in London. He too discovers perception in the land of painting. His scenes are sometimes directly inspired by French pictures, and in any case borrow their appeal from the reputation of Paris. In an essay on 'Montmartre and the Latin Quarter' the author says expressedly that the most characteristic scene of the district is drawn from Manet's painting of the Luxembourg gardens: because of this he always goes to spend his Sunday afternoons there. Since this enables him to imagine that he is on the canvas himself, the reader can presume that at such moments he feels life more intensely:

> Early in the afternoon groups begin to form; Marcelle and Suzanne bring their sewing, or a book of verse, for a pretence, and each has her little circle about her. The chairs around the band-stand fill gradually, the tables of the little green *buvette* spread further and further outwards, leaving just room for the promenade which will soon begin, that church-parade of such another sort from the London one . . . and the shimmery music, coming like sunshine into the sunlights of such an afternoon, just here and now, sounds almost beautiful, as things do always when they are beautifully in keeping. Marcelle and Suzanne, between two shouts of laughter, feel the poetry of the moment; they are even silent, biting meditatively the corner of a fanciful handkerchief.

Marcelle and Suzanne—we have for once escaped from the almost unavoidable 'Mimi'—are *midinettes*: career-girls, as we more politely call our shorthand typists nowadays. Being French, they are cultured enough to bring the right poetry with them, and perceptive enough to appreciate the harmony of the sensuous scene. The Manet original is still visible ('the promenade which will soon begin') and there is more than a hint of Paterian feeling ('biting meditatively . . .'). It is also suggested that there is something more than a mere human value in such a corner of privileged scenery, since it gives one a privileged sensitivity. Symons looks at the French through the mirror of their art. Further on, after describing Paris seen from Montmartre, he half-fancifully writes:

Aristide Bruant's heroes and heroines, the lady on her way to Saint-Lazare, the gentleman—who knows?—perhaps to La Roquette, they rest from their labours at times, and, leaning over the wooden paling, I am sure *enjoy Paris impressionistically*.[23]

An artistic technique, however, does not make a national feature: the nineties forgot that the current style in French art and literature had only appeared since 1850. From here they were led on to another mistake, perhaps more important since they were secretly and obscurely concerned with Victorian morality. They slipped from the *sensuous*, an artistic value, to the *sensual*, a moral value. We have seen Sickert equate the two; we have also seen with George Moore the external reasons there were for considering France more than ever immoral. Having decided, then, that France was by essence sensuous, it was easy to take the last step and say that it was sensual. In terms of a very restrictive morality such as the Victorian one, a reanimation of the senses through an art no longer didactic but perceptive can indeed seem immoral. But it is important to realize that once this transposition had been made the debate became a purely English one, in which Victorians and progressists used an imaginary France as a bugbear or an ideal.

As in most violent debates the two extremes appear in the foreground, where they give rise to two completely opposed images of France. The first derives directly from the literary paintings we have just examined. Since in France people perceive a more colourful world more completely, it follows that the sensual beauties of life must be appreciated more frankly there. Human realities more or less linked with sexual morality can thrive more openly, whereas they would cause stifled tragedies on this side of the Channel. We have seen that this is partly true. But it was developed much further. Frenchmen lived in a less inhibited atmosphere; their reactions were therefore more primitive and (here is the point of the debate) more innocent. As

[23] My italics. Saint-Lazare and La Roquette were two well-known prisons.

catholics of course they were able to accept sin almost as a natural thing, and after all perhaps it was. . . .

The theme of French innocence is remarkable in George Moore's *Héloïse and Abélard*, developed from a hint in Pater's *Renaissance Studies*. It includes side by side a picture of the intellectual life of Paris at the turn of the Middle Ages, and a story about the rediscovery of love of a kind closer to Nature. The first is a transposition of George Moore's Paris of the seventies. Discussions around the tables of the *Nouvelle Athènes* are cleverly dressed up to appear as mediaeval disputations. Moore also makes Paris the mediaeval birthplace of ideas, because the disputants are (already) morally emancipated: their most famous representative, Abélard, divides his time between the Sorbonne and the courts of love, which he visits as a wandering minstrel. He is perhaps the first person to realize that love for a distant object may not be religious: it may alight on a woman's face seen fleetingly at the window of a castle. This curious cross between a monk and a Bohemian Frenchman of the nineties indulges in a love affair reminiscent at the same time of one of Moore's surreptitious adventures in Paris, and of Pater's descriptions in the *Renaissance Studies*.[24] The twelfth century brings with it, as in Pater, part of the essence of France: an innocent joy taken in primitive pleasure. But Moore's Abélard is already very different from Pater's Frenchmen. These led passionate lives in the best romantic tradition and were destroyed by the inner tension between their melancholy and their strong sense of pleasure. Moore lays his emphasis on the fact that natural feelings do no harm. After their love affair and their quiet parting, because for Moore such is the fate of love, both Héloïse and Abélard return to their former lives and succeed in their work. There is a direct moral here; whereas Pater was only concerned with describing the full flowering of a single personality, Moore shows the innocence of love. When the lovers escape from the Church represented by Héloïse's uncle, and make their way

[24] 'the true child of light, the humanist, with reason and heart and senses quick' (see above, p. 93). During Abélard's stay in the courts of love, George Moore gives transpositions of *romans courtois* and of *fabliaux* where his debt to Pater's style of translation is obvious.

Two drawings by Beardsley from Wilde's *Salomé*. Beardsley tried to
include all the books he thought important: amongst them are *Fleurs
du Mal*, *La Terre*, *Nana*, *Les Fêtes Galantes*, *Marquis de Sade*, and
Manon Lescaut.

through the country to Brittany, the atmosphere, though unfortunately colourless, fits in with their simple attitude. Héloïse's
child is brought up in the convent, where it enriches the homely
life of the nuns: there are no furtive accusations or regrets.
Moore's plain, apparently artless style, is suited to this theme.

The nineties too had relished these ideas. Ernest Dowson's
'Apple Blossom in Brittany' tells of innocent emotions in a
French country setting that contrasts strongly with the warped
London society in the rest of that volume of *The Yellow Book*.
An Englishman who wants, and is advised, to marry his very
young ward is affected by the beauty of Nature and the sight of
her purity, which seems in keeping with it. He makes a simple
sacrifice and advises her to become a nun.[25] In 'Rideo', another
Yellow Book story, a provençal priest is tempted to a kind of
pure sin by a girl he has afterwards to marry to her lover. He then
goes mad, and tells his own story as if these elemental feelings
were in keeping with the countryside in which he lives. French
catholicism seems to stand for the frank and the sensual. Priests
get themselves into quite extraordinary situations in the yellow
periodicals; especially when they are bishops or cardinals, surrounded by sensuous ceremony. In Harland's light novel *The
Cardinal's Snuff-box* the prelate brings two shy lovers together,
thanks to his frank, experienced outlook.[26] In Lionel Johnson's
'The Lilies of France' the two colourful extremes of uncompromising French passion meet: Jean Dubois, the republican, free-
thinking, absinthe-drinking school-teacher clashes with a magnificent Cardinal, and ends up by murdering him.[27] Obviously, the
French live more sensually.

The fleshly details associated with the pomp of catholicism
point to the prurient preoccupations of puritans abroad. Trans-
pose the innocent, strong-feeling girl of Dowson's stories into the
sophisticated aesthetic atmosphere of Paris, develop simple
emotions into luxurious passions, and you find Salome. She
personifies the half-repressed longings of the nineties, and she

---

[25] See also Dowson's poems, such as 'Breton Afternoon' in *The Savoy*, No. 3, or
'Yvonne of Brittany' in his *Poetical Works*.
[26] See also his story entitled 'The house of Eulalie' in *Comedies and Errors*.
[27] *The Pageant*, vol. ii.

returns again and again. Besides Flaubert's short story, 'Hérodias', the original version, and the opera Strauss based on it, there are countless other instances. Oscar Wilde wrote a *Salomé* in fairly good French verse of the time, Beardsley drew a series of studies for the story in *The Yellow Book*, Symons wrote a verse tragedy and several poems on the theme of Salome and John. *Studies in Seven Arts*, which helped to establish him as a kind of literary conscience of the period, includes an article on Gustave Moreau largely given to a description of his painting of Salome, and an essay on Amiens Cathedral, written in deference to Ruskin but also because of a series of painted carvings there on the death of John the Baptist. Salome was associated with Flaubert and Mallarmé and the freedom of sophisticated Parisian art: her brief orgy of luxurious passion was felt to be French.

Arthur Symons is perhaps the best instance of the puritan on holiday in Paris. He thinks that moralists should not condemn the 'flaunting of vice' in the Latin Quarter:

> Is it not really less vicious, in a certain sense, than the corresponding thing in London, which takes itself so seriously as well as cautiously, is so self-convinced of evil-doing and has all the unhealthy excitement of an impotent but persistent Puritan conscience?

This lucid judgement could well be appended to an edition of his own poems as an ironic comment. He displays exactly that 'unhealthy excitement' over Paris. *Silhouettes* are studded with scenes to excite the envy of the poor repressed English: love amongst the chestnut trees of the Champs Elysées, love in the bleak Bohemian dawn, love on the bridges of the Seine (the song had not yet suggested that it was also possible underneath), love at the *Deux Magots*. The *London Nights* dated from Paris are in the same vein: the stage doors, the dazzling actresses, the *Moulin Rouge*, artists dying of consumption, a café in Montmartre painted in shades of green, the 'bright wickedness', the names of pleasure and fashion. Symons's *Studies in Seven Arts* dealing with Frenchmen are always erotically turned: the article on Rodin is a mere excuse for sensual descriptions of his statues; the mere mention of Degas in an essay on Watts reminds him of a story

A drawing for *Salomé* by Beardsley published in *The Studio*. He intended to tint this illustration green, the colour of absinthe, and include it in an edition of Wilde's *Salomé* that did not materialize.

on how the French painter drew a fleshly model in her bath. And
so what was originally a quest for innocent sensuality in France
ends up as sophisticated pleasure-seeking in the byways of the
new Babylon.

It is not surprising that there should have been a strong reaction
against such distorted, erotic enthusiasm. Other authors went to
Paris with Arnold's last essays in their pocket and a mind to
censure. One example should be sufficient: this is a bad story from
The Yellow Book called 'Wladislaw's Advent'. It is set, as so many
tales of the time, in the industrious atmosphere of an art academy.
A poor innocent Polish artist, already corrupted by wicked Paris
('it was the waitress of that café who initiated Wladislaw to
something I won't mention'), is chosen as a model for a picture of
Christ by the famous artist Dufour. Thus loaded with significance
—he is dressed up for the part—he arrives at the studio at the
appointed time and finds that Dufour has forgotten him and is in
the middle of a ghoulish orgy:

At a table heaped with the *débris* of a careless feast he saw Dufour,
his coat off, his waistcoat and shirt unbuttoned, his head rolled weakly
back upon the gilded wood-scroll of his Louis Quinze chair: his face
flushed and swollen, strangely broadened, coarsened and undone, . . .
in his hands an old lute, a studio property, from which he had been
picking poor detached, discordant notes.

There were other men, with wild arrested merriment in their
faces, the merriment of licence. Mixed among them, tangling like the
serpents and reptiles in an allegorical picture, were women of whom
the drapery or the bareness seemed indifferently lewd. . . .

Then Wladislaw drinks, for the first time of course, even though
he is supposed to be a Pole, and remembers nothing more of the
orgy. Unreal as such scenes obviously are, it is natural that they
should have been used to counter the boasting immoralism we
have seen. But they were used with such relish that one is inclined
to suspect the author of having enjoyed them as much in a more
perverted way.

In the English novel of this century, where the image of
France has once more become crystallized, the stock Frenchman
is a very open-minded and slightly bohemian character who

Title-page by Beardsley from *The Savoy*

makes no bones about his mistresses. A stay in Paris or in the innocent French countryside usually serves to make a match, bring about some sensual revelation, or excuse some vagary. All this stems from *A Modern Lover* and *Trilby* and the short-story writers of the nineties who wanted to shock England into a reform. But the 'philistines' could reply smugly that they were not describing human nature, but Gallic nature. The reputation of France had to suffer for England's scruples.

IV. PORTRAIT OF THE ARTIST AS A FRENCHMAN

One of the morals to be drawn from Meredith's *The Egoist* is that men of letters should be more respected. Vernon Whitford, the writer, has an inferior position in Patterne Hall, and Dr. Middleton is only honoured there because Sir Willoughby wishes to marry his daughter. Were society organized according to a better pattern, Whitford's merits, symbolized by the care he takes over young Crossjay's education and by his sleep under the flowering cherry, would be recognized. As it is, the only mark of real respect for Dr. Middleton on his visit comes from Armand Dehors, the French cook, and Sir Willoughby scorns this attitude:

> He took hommes d'esprit to denote men of letters. Frenchmen have destroyed their nobility, so, for the sake of excitement, they put up the literary man—not to worship him; that they can't do; it's to put themselves in a state of effervescence . . . the French only differ from us in wading through blood to discover that they are at their old trick once more: 'I am your equal, sir, your born equal. Oh! you are a man of letters? Allow me to be in a bubble about you.'

The idea was to be one of the dominant issues of the nineties, and here, in 1879, it is already clear that it will be connected with France. Paradoxically, the men of the nineties claimed descent from a French literary movement that denied any usefulness to art, but also felt that they should be given a better place in society on the strength of their art. It was difficult to put this ambiguous claim to an unsympathetic public. An easy solution, often chosen, was to be content with describing the closed world of art itself—

N

hence the many stories of the time that turn on literary success or the whims of audiences and publishers: they appear to give the artist a central position, but avoid the real issue.

Though the ultimate purpose of their art was to make for a social reform, men of letters cultivated this new interest in their own world, and here as in everything else they quoted the French example. They were acutely conscious of the French artistic scene: naturalism, symbolism, and impressionism all flaunted French pedigrees. In addition to this purely literary influence, attention was drawn to the status of French artists by two events. First, the trials of Baudelaire, Flaubert, and Zola brought these writers into the limelight and out of the privacy chosen by French men of letters since 1830. Secondly, the literary world became timidly cosmopolitan—Verlaine, Mallarmé, Daudet, and Zola were all invited to London and Oxford to return visits and speak to English audiences. They all wrote in their notes and correspondence of the pleasing stability of English literary life, but left behind them the impression, familiar to nervous hosts, that the welcome given had been shabby compared with what they must normally consider their due at home.

For a short period, Paris, the home of artists, was considered as the home of the most artistic of them all: the aesthetes. It seemed quite natural that Oscar Wilde should hurry there when he wanted to recapture his ecstatic languors. George Moore's *A Modern Lover* suggests that the dressmaker Worth is familiar with *A Rebours*: Mrs. Bentham goes to have a gown designed by him.

Liveried footmen announced them; and they were shown through the wide, square show-rooms, into the great man's private consulting-room. It was wainscotted in light oak, and Worth half rose from a dark green velvet divan, where he had been reclining, to receive them. . . . On the right was a high desk where a clerk stood waiting to take down the inspiration, as it came from the master's lips . . . after some moments of deep meditation, he murmured:

'Florentine, bronze-tinted, falling over a bouillonné pleating of pale moonlight blue . . .'.

But this image was short-lived. After the Wilde trial and the decline of the yellow periodicals, it was drummed out of literature, and made room once more for the Romantic Artist, who had enjoyed longer fame.

In the nineties he is called Pierrot and is a dream of ideal artistry, as Salome was a dream of lustful passion. He, too, appears everywhere: Banville, Verlaine, Laforgue, and in their wake Symons and Beardsley used him to symbolize the artist. In *Studies in Seven Arts* Symons gives an account of his romantic suffering:

> He has worn his heart on his sleeve so long, that it has hardened in the cold air. He knows that his face is powdered, and if he sobs, it is without tears; and it is hard to distinguish, under the chalk, if the grimace which twists his mouth awry is more laughter or mockery. He knows that he is condemned to be always in public, that emotion would be supremely out of keeping with his costume, that he must remember to be fantastic if he would not be merely ridiculous. And so he becomes exquisitely false, dreading above all things, that 'one touch of nature' which would ruffle his disguise, and leave him defenceless. Simplicity, in him, being the most laughable thing in the world, he becomes learned, perverse, intellectualizing his pleasure, brutalizing his intellect. . . .

Scratch the varnish of decadence from this aesthetic Pierrot, however, and you will find the grand-nephew of Byron and of Chatterton, the unhappy, scornful idol of a cruel and ignorant public. Behind his exquisite, intellectualized pleasure, there lie the lessons of Pater, and at the root of it all we can still distinguish Arnold's picture of the Guérins.

This appears mainly at a much lower level, in the Romantic Biographies of Artists, fashionable during the nineties and partly inspired by Pater's 'passionate' lives. The stereotype still exists in cartoon strips and historical novels. Certain figures fitted better than others into its mould: there were three such biographies of Watteau published in London between 1880 and 1925. But the pattern could be stretched to almost any life and, apparently, to any French life. Bizet,[28] Delacroix, Rousseau the painter, Puvis de Chavannes, were favourites. This type of 'passionate life' always has a faintly bohemian flavour: the artist is either struggling

[28] See the article by C. Willoughby in *The Yellow Book*, vol. ii.

against himself or against society. If his vocation comes from the artistic tradition in his family, he is made to resist this irresistible urge for a while, if not he has to fight against his family for his vocation. In both cases he is unhappy from the start, and this colours the childhood surroundings that will inspire his best works. He goes to Paris or to some big city (see Pater for the appearance of melancholy in cities) and tries to achieve recognition in a philistine setting. If he is not successful fairly rapidly a woman redeems his suffering. If he is recognized early, either his work goes out of fashion and he dies in poverty or his short period of success is spoilt by impending tuberculosis. The Romantic Biography is not of course only an English phenomenon: a series of popular biographies under the title *La Vie Passionnée de* . . . is currently selling well in France. The film about Modigliani entitled *Les Amants de Montparnasse* illustrates it perfectly. Romantic musings of the French about certain of their artists are not necessarily true, but as the stereotype crosses the Channel, history and romance melt into each other. It becomes difficult not to imagine that in some vague and picturesque way the French love and admire their artists more even when they are oppressing them for their good; that specially sordid attics are provided in Montmartre by an attentive nation that also possesses a ministry of Fine Arts to deal with their works when they appear. The distortion eventually grows into that of Hollywood Paris, where poverty assails the artist in a glossy setting and gives the unshaven but well-fed bohemian an excuse to lead a disorderly and passionate life amidst friendly tradesmen and gendarmes, who join in the chorus.

Arnold, it should be remembered, had been careful not to mix the Guérins with the Jouberts. On the one hand, some artists have a romantic value, and on the other, intellectuals can sway many people in France. His two lessons are true as long as they remain separate. Pierrot, though he leads a passionate life, does not share the respect inspired by Joubert. The nineties did not make a proper distinction between the dishevelled underworld of artistic poseurs, for whom they had a weakness, and the really active and responsible intellectuals of the left bank. There certainly is in

Paris a respect for the recognized or promising artist that still does not exist in England, where it is necessary to make one's name socially as well as writing books. The technique and ideas of a new novel or film can be the talk of Paris, and the more conscious the author is of the issues he has brought up, the more homage is paid him. But the Pierrots and the bohemians are no more than colourful figures. The example of the French symbolists could well have been heeded: Verlaine and Rimbaud, the romantic, passionate poets, were generally scorned until their poetry could be detached from their personalities. Rimbaud was 'safe' only when he had foundered into normal life, and Verlaine was never so well treated as on his literary visit to London. Mallarmé, the only one to achieve a great reputation outside the world of literary specialists while still at large, was a bourgeois secondary school teacher who was admired not so much for writing poetry as for writing about it first. Finally, respect for the artist comes from a larger section of society than in England, but still not from everyone: Arnold's 'idea-filled masses', we have seen, are illusions. But in London *The Yellow Book* often distorted facts wistfully: thus in 'The Death Mask' a young American meets the 'housekeeper' of the Master, who has just died in his top-floor Verlaine-type room:

Madame Germaine, as she was called in the Quarter, had loved the Master with that complete, self-abnegating, sublime love of which certain women are capable. . . . She adored him dumbly, closed her eyes to his vices, and magnified his gifts, without in the least comprehending them. She belonged to the *ouvrière* class, could not read, could not write her own name; but with a characteristic which is as French as it is un-British, she paid her homage to intellect where an Englishwoman only gives it to inches and muscle.

Here again, as with the image of the Bohemian Frenchman, there is a genuine trend of feeling underneath these superficial views of French artists. Again, Walter Sickert provides the most sensible view; perhaps it was because he was a genuine impressionist painter himself that he never felt the need to strike a pose. His ideas are direct and technical, and a relief after the flowery sentimentality of most of his contemporaries. It was the first time since Thackeray that anyone had come down to brass tacks on the question of French art. In his opinion the artist has a different status in Paris because he is prepared to admit a wider audience:

the best pictures in France have been at some time cheap. So that people of moderate means in France have always been able to collect. Artists in Paris wisely make no attempt to mingle in the life of the 'gens du monde'. . . . A painter in England is introduced to a peer. He sees, at last, in his mind, the patron who will enable him to realize a great life-work. Not a bit of it! The brute paints in water-colours himself! He knows just enough not to think very highly of the professional's work; but he is anxious for wrinkles in technique, and for the painter's vote and interest on the hanging committee of his gallery.[29]

Because there is at once less snobbishness and less of the amateurish approach to art, French families are able to afford a picture from time to time, bringing painting before a wider audience and putting bread into the professional artist's mouth during his lifetime. All this comes from the real artists forming a kind of recognized corporation of their own, with guarantees of seriousness.

There is also a more democratic attitude amongst artists. Rothenstein remarked on this in *Men and Memories*:

The distance between eminent French artists, and youngsters was much less in Paris, I fancy, than it was in London, where, forty years ago, Academicians were regarded as high Olympian figures.

Not obliged to live in false distinguished circles, the artist can act as he pleases: so we return to bohemianism, but once it is the mark of a corporation rather than a pose it appears to Sickert in a better light:

We were walking one morning down from Montmartre to go to Durand-Ruel's. Degas was dressed in a grey flannel shirt, a muffler and a suit that might almost have been ready-made. 'Ce n'est pas', I said, stopping as one does on the Continent, 'Sir John Millais qui se présenterait chez Monsieur Agnew fichu comme vous l'êtes.' He pulled up with mock indignation: 'Monsieur! Quand un Anglais veut écrire une lettre, il se met dans un costume spécial fait pour écrire une lettre, et après il se rechange. Etre foutu comme quatre sous, et être le Grand Condé! Voilà l'affaire.'[30]

If we translate *un Anglais* here to *un artiste Anglais*, then the observation is still true, and was probably even more so at the end of the last century. French critics use the expression *république des lettres*, which characterizes an atmosphere that must have struck the men of the nineties. A very old tradition, probably stemming from the enlightenment of the French kings and the identification of their court with their capital city, has given artists a semi-official position as a kind of corporation in French life. The main interest of the French Academy is not, as Arnold thought, that it is an arbiter of taste (it is notoriously not so), but that it symbolizes the status of the artist within the organized framework of public life. Hence the sense of democracy amongst artists and the respect for them as a group that were the ideals of the nineties in London. Sickert's observations can be applied with as much fitness to literature as to painting.

The men of the nineties were very much impressed by the *cabarets artistiques* after the model of the *Chat Noir*, which became popular in Paris at about that time. In a way they illustrated a similar feature: they were so to speak the inner temple of the corporation. On a lower level, the very music halls were more artistic. The following paragraph is taken from the article on Yvette Guilbert in *The Yellow Book*:

In England the text of the songs sung is written by illiterate people, the artistic part lies in the performer, and even then the performer is quite unconscious of his art. In France the songs written for the Cabaret are mostly written, as we shall see later on, by men of culture, of University education, and though there is perhaps less ability to be found in the ranks of the French than in those of the English performers, each performer in France knows that he is engaged in an artistic pursuit requiring talent of a special kind.

Even today a British artist mindful of his reputation would as little dream of decorating the walls of a coffee bar as a company director of picking up a hammer; nor is it easy to imagine a fashionable novelist writing the words of popular songs, as

[30] *Burlington Magazine*, 1917.

Françoise Sagan does, or collaborating with a producer in devis-
ing a film-script, as Robbe-Grillet did.

So Sickert points very lucidly to the reason why anything
'artistic' is faintly ridiculous in England: it is because of the pose
that goes with it and that in the end both isolates and belittles the
artist. If art is a technique that anyone with a certain training can
attain and a few transcend, it is more healthy and more respected
than what Sickert calls the 'lilies and languors of the Chelsea
amateurs'; these only really pander to the jaded interests of the
upper class, which buys expensive books and pictures. At one
time D. H. Lawrence was not considered a serious writer because
he did not attend tea-parties given by London hostesses. Henry
James remarks that in England 'art is pardonable only so long as
it's bad—so long as it's done at odd hours, for a little distraction,
like a game of tennis or of whist'. This was perhaps the heart of
the feeling that attracted the English artists to Paris. Impressionism was only a temporary feature: twenty years later Sickert
and Fry were helping to set up art schools and art councils in
London, too, but Paris was still the haven of artists. This was the
idea that prompted George Moore's enthusiastic investigation
of the *Nouvelle Athènes*, and all that followed. French artistic life
is the obvious ideal. In the nineties for the first and last time
English writers and painters tried consciously to group around
beliefs or styles—thus the Camden Town Group, or the New
English Art Club, run democratically since it elected the juries
for its exhibitions in close imitation of the *Salon des Indépendants*.
In literature these materialized in journals, such as *The Yellow
Book* and *The Athenaeum*.

This is the truest feature of the view of France formed in the
nineties. 'Immoral Paris' was on the whole a tourist trap; most
'bohemian Frenchmen' turned out to be Americans in disguise;
France as an 'impressionist' country was the result of misdirected
art criticism. But Paris is the home of artists everywhere. The
man in the paint-stained smock will be secretly flattered if you
say you took him for a Frenchman. He will make a mental note
to buy a beret.

· 8 ·

WATCH THE WOMEN

Arnold Bennett

ARNOLD BENNETT partly illustrates and partly destroys the romanticized view of France formed by the nineties. His *Journals* were written then, but the feelings that inspire them are those of a much later period of English thought. This is because, though Bennett was not poor, he crossed the Channel as a man of letters rather than a man of leisure. He went for the sake of his trade rather than with the desire to reform his country. He was attracted to Paris because he had read in George Moore and R. L. Stevenson that only the French novel mattered, and he appears all through his journals as a technician, without at first any preoccupation with art and artistry or with intelligence and morality. The only preconceived view he took with him was the one, quite usual for the time, that French scenes are somehow more realistic than their English equivalents: this was the only reason that made him stay there so long.

His lack of fixed aims causes at first a fresh appraisal of the glaring imperfections of French life, but it soon makes for superficiality. Here as in many other ways Bennett suffers from being a writer without a cause. His initial boredom led him to approach Paris from an angle only found again thirty years later, when the economic crises of the twenties and thirties cut off the cosmopolitan, semi-artistic community of the Latin Quarter from its funds in Britain and the United States, and forced young men like Henry Miller and George Orwell to discover the seamy side of the capital. Arnold Bennett did not follow this track for very long. Later in his life, in 1921, he attributed his knowledge of the country and its literature to mere circumstance; in his novels, France had rapidly become a series of colourful but dead images.

I. THE MERETRICIOUS

France for Bennett is still Paris. He travelled a great deal in the provinces but left them uncharted, except when he noted that a town was typically Balzacian.[1] He first went to Paris in 1897. By then intellectual and artistic Paris was becoming more Germanic than it had been in the seventies and eighties. Young men affected much more serious interests, went to listen to Wagner's music, and discussed German philosophy. 'Gay Paris' was becoming a tourist attraction rather than part of the artistic scene, for it was losing its novelty. Artists found that their chosen land was being visited by people like the Prince of Wales; English and American gentlemen, in search of Art or Ideas and with more money than the natives of the Latin Quarter, were beginning to move into the haunts of Saint Germain and drive the original bohemians elsewhere. Perhaps in part because of this, Bennett never found them, nor indeed any of the French artistic community. He led the life of a tourist, stayed in hotels, ate in famous restaurants, frequented the Anglo-American set he disliked, and went on visiting the 'catchpenny shows' he professed to scorn. As soon as he attempted to investigate the received ideas about the glamour of Paris, he naturally recorded little else than disappointment. His descriptions on this account are the exact reverse of George Moore's. Where Moore inflates the experiences he may not quite have enjoyed thoroughly, Bennett exaggerates his impressions of triviality and shabbiness.

The first entry in his journal on arrival is the most promising. Using an Arnoldian frame of reference—the contrast between the Latin and the Teutonic—he sets out to discover the difference between the two races. But it is soon obvious that he is only really

---

[1] In *Paris Nights* he merely says of Fontainebleau and Nemours: 'Everything was Balzacian; those who have read Balzac's provincial stories will realize what that means.'

using it as a problem on which to sharpen his powers of expression and observation:

Walking from the Trocadéro to the Bois de Boulogne, and so to the Arc de Triomphe and down the Champs Elysées, I search for the formula which should express Paris—in vain. The great central difference—the phrase which is to disclose the gulf between the Latin and the Teutonic, eludes and evades the effort of the mind to seize it; only the obvious, the palpable, the little discrepancies show forth: the grandeur of the streets, the large vision of the architects who made them, monopolize attention and thought and with the tail of the eye one notes slight peculiarities—ribboned costumes of nursemaids, coachmen's hats, toy balloons of children, cyclists' cowbells, and a thousand other trifles. One tries to get behind them, but without success.

Partly through a conscious effort to train his novelist's eye and partly out of discontent with glamorous Paris, he starts to probe behind it in the way many a lonely tourist will. Once his perceptive chains have re-formed (the above passage is a typical instance of the first feast of disorderly perception on arrival in France), he makes an effort to re-appraise things by examining their material aspect. He is impressed by the artistic value of a performance at a *café-concert* obviously intended for a lower-middle-class audience, but not before he has counted the number of spectators and reckoned that the artists must be very poorly paid. At another café there is a young woman singing, but he looks at her older colleague accompanying her on the piano: she is worn and finished. Disenchantment is a constant theme. In 1903, returning to Paris intent on settling there (his remarks make one wonder why), he visits the romantic site of the Sacré Cœur, which might have prompted a Le Gallienne to one of his rhymes, and from which we have seen Symons viewing Paris 'impressionistically'. The difference in approach is striking:

And it looked so small and square and ordinary. And I thought of the world-famed boulevards and resorts lying hidden round about there. And I thought: Is that all there is? For a moment it seemed impossible to me that, as the result of a series of complicated conventions merely, that collocation of stones, etc. (paving stones and building stones) could really be what it is—a synonym and symbol for all that is luxurious, frivolous, gay, vicious, and artistic. I thought: 'Really, Paris is not Paris after all; it is only a collocation of stones.'

Some other notes made in the same vein are developed in an essay on 'The *Variétés*' in *Paris Nights*. Stripped of all its initial glamour for the carping northerner, the famous theatre appears from the outside as it really is—dirty and rickety. Then—

We came to a very narrow, low, foul, semicircular tunnel which was occupied by hags and harpies with pink bows in their hair, and by marauding men, and by hats and cloaks and overcoats, and by a double odour of dirt and disinfectants. Along the convex side of the tunnel were a number of little doors like the doors of cells. We bought a programme from a man, yielded our wraps to two harpies, and were led away by another man. All these beings looked hungrily apprehensive, like dogs nosing along a gutter. The auditorium which was nearly full, had the same characteristics as the porch and the *couloir*. It was filthy, fetid, uncomfortable, and dangerous. It had the carpets of a lodging-house of the seventies, the seats of an old omnibus, the gilt and the decorated sculpture of a circus at a fair. And it was dingy! It was encrusted with dinginess!

To be fully appreciated, this passage should be placed opposite the corresponding description in the first few pages of Zola's *Nana*, where the same theatre seems brilliant, polished, and vast. Bennett notes that the management is slack and shabby and lives on its reputation. The director traditionally wears a dirty straw hat, and the public are attracted by this charlatanism. The play starts scandalously late, and is vulgar and hardly witty. People can only go there because they are snobbish or gullible: it gives a futile sense of waste.

A few artists and a financier or so at the core, wilful, corrupt, self-indulgent, spoiled, venal, enormously unbusinesslike, incredibly cynical, luxurious in the midst of a crowd of miserable parasites and menials; creating for themselves, out of electric globes, and newspapers, and posters, and photographs, and the inexhaustible simplicity and sexuality of the public, a legend of artistic greatness. They make a frame, and hang a curtain in front of it, and put footlights beneath; and lo! the capricious manœuvres of these mortals become the sacred, authoritative functioning of an institution!

The Old Wives' Tale, in which Bennett recorded many of his impressions, gives a similar image of dirtiness: for instance, in the course of a meal at a provincial inn, seen through the eyes of Sophia who has just left the scrupulous trading-class respectability of Bursley:

> The long, crowded table, with semicircular ends, in the oppressive and reeking dining-room lighted by oil-lamps! There must have been at least forty people at that table. Most of them ate disgustingly, as noisily as pigs, with the ends of the large coarse napkins tucked in at their necks. All the service was done by the fat woman whom she had seen at the window with Gerald, and a young girl whose demeanour was candidly brazen. Both these creatures were slatterns. Everything was dirty . . . all the faces, to the youngest, were brutalized, corrupt, and shameless. The juxtaposition of old men and young women was odious to her, especially when those pairs kissed, as they did frequently towards the end of the meal.

Sophia's disgust takes on a moral colour here. Later she explores the flat of the two courtesans who have sheltered and nursed her through her fever. She is impressed by the rich ornamentation, but when she discovers a hidden bathroom, the dirtiness of the French again disgusts her:

> She peeped behind the screen, and all the horrible welter of a *cabinet de toilette* met her gaze: a repulsive medley of foul waters, stained vessels and cloths, brushes, sponges, powders, and pastes. Clothes were hung up in disorder on rough nails; among them she recognized a dressing-gown of Madame Foucault's. . . . So this was Madame Foucault's room! This was the bower from which that elegance emerged, the filth from which had sprung the mature blossom!

Together with all the dirt and false beauty, Sophia scorns the flaccid life of the two women, their habit of rising late and idling in dressing-gowns until evening. (In *The Pretty Lady* there is a similar picture of Christine's flat: elegance emerges from sordid disorder.) Then moral squalor is added to the material squalor: Madame Foucault, who has lost her only remaining lover, collapses theatrically in front of Sophia who, like Bennett, refuses to be impressed by the pathos because she is sensitive to the ugliness.

Her face, especially as damaged by tears, could not support the ordeal of inspection; it was horrible; not a picture, but a palette; or like the coloured design of a pavement artist after a heavy shower. Her great, relaxed eyelids would have rendered any face absurd; and there were monstrous details far worse than the eyelids. Then she was amazingly fat; her flesh seemed to be escaping at all ends from a corset strained to the utmost limit. And above her boots—she was still wearing dainty, high-heeled, tightly-laced boots—the calves bulged suddenly out.

Thus moral corruption adds itself to physical corruption. The rest of the novel shows that Sophia is of a finer mettle, since she succeeds in business in Paris, even during the difficult period of the siege. After some hesitation Bennett himself noted in his *Journals* in 1909: 'My first vague impression was here at last defined, of Paris. Namely the perversity and corruption of the faces.'

Bennett's predecessors had advertised Paris and its art as immoral, and for a provincial, immorality is within a step of corruption. Bennett did not come to Paris prepared to see things in this light, but the stark, realistic, disenchanted approach he evolved while he was there made him turn to it. His journals show him hastening to observe the prostitutes in the cafés: impressions of one *cocotte* or another are recorded on every other page. He comments on prices and appearances, and with the morbid interest of the provincial come to town he sees them everywhere, in streets, theatres, restaurants. At the end of his life he still delights in describing those he sees gambling in a casino at Cannes.[2] This is, however, no flat condemnation. By a curious twist, Bennett records his impressions without quite identifying himself with them. An episode in the *Journals* is significant: he tells how he was shocked by the immorality of a play, then he describes the retrospective pleasure of understanding what it feels like to be a shocked Englishman. He savours and stores up the

---

[2] One of the few references to Paris in Yeats's *Autobiographies* mentions a chance meeting with a pretty girl in the Latin Quarter and an incident with 'painted ladies' in a café. Yeats might well have emulated Bennett's approach (though with undoubtedly greater talent) had he visited Paris in his early life, when he wanted to 'describe outward things as vividly as possible'. But by the time he went he was in fact more interested in mystics, Persians, Swedes, Symbolists, Parnassians, and Indians than in the French.

feeling without giving himself up to it. The novelist takes precedence over the man.

Most of these scenes are perfectly well rendered. The *Théâtre des Variétés* had been flattered by Zola, and was no doubt as sordid as Bennett says. Most Parisian theatres still are remarkably shabby and uncomfortable. French women, too, are unpleasantly shoddy and disorderly in their bathroom, though the finished effect may be more pleasant. But Bennett's approach is still distorted because he is all the time a self-conscious novelist in search of material. It is always felt that he is conscientiously doing his realist homework. This applies especially to the *Journals*. For instance, he goes for an early morning walk on a public holiday:

> Some persons were lying asleep on the pavement. I noticed many other early-morning items, and fête-day items: such as omnibuses passing, full of policemen in spotless white trousers; a cavalry officer in full splendour walking to his rendezvous; many people beginning the day's enjoyment on their way to railway stations, etc., the women dozing in the newspaper kiosks awaiting the morning papers; a youth walking along the middle of the road smoking a pipe a yard long; a drunken man trying to get up a fight with a barman concerning a small tricolour which he carried. . . .

These are things he could have recorded in England. It is easy to see that such an observer is uncommonly well armed for criticism the moment he feels bored or impatient with the people or the country or even the weather, since amongst the insignificant details he has accumulated some are bound to be open to censure. Also, he will be less inclined to forgive these small things abroad than at home.

A passage from *Paris Nights* shows clearly how this particular form of disparagement takes shape: Bennett carefully describes his mood as well as what he observes. He has just witnessed a charming scene between two dandies, a girl and her servant and a cabman in front of a café. He walks through the Chaussée d'Antin thinking that Paris is the city that is 'always forgiven' (he puts an immoral interpretation on the scene) and it immediately seems alluring to him. As in Moore and James it appears pervaded with light at moments like these:

The shops and *cafés* were all on fire, making two embankments of fire, above which rose high and mysterious *façades* masked by trees that looked like the impossible verdure of an opera. And between the summits of the trees a ribbon of rich, dark, soothing purple—the sky! This was the city. This was what the race had accomplished, after eighteen Louises and nearly as many revolutions, and when all was said that could be said it remained a prodigious and a comforting spectacle. Every doorway shone with invitation; every satisfaction and delight was offered, on terms ridiculously reasonable. And binding everything together were the refined, neighbourly and graceful, cynical gestures of the race: so different from the harsh and awkward timidity, the self-centred egotism and aristocratic hypocrisy of Piccadilly.[3]

But a few minutes later in the Tuileries a cold wind starts to blow and he cannot light his cigarette. Immediately, disgust appears:

The artfully arranged vista of the Champs Elysées, rising in flame against the silhouette of Cleopatra's needle, struck me as a meretricious device, designed to impress tourists and monarchs. Everything was meretricious. I could not even strike a match without being reminded that a contented and corrupt inefficiency was corroding this race like a disease. I could not light my cigarette because somebody, somewhere, had not done his job like a honest man. And thus it was throughout.

These reversals are frank but unsettling. The picture of meretricious Paris is a useful antidote to the illusions and pretences of the nineties, but Bennett can never quite decide even on the adjective meretricious. He is not quite sure whether to praise the organization of the commerce of pleasure, or to censure the shabbiness of the theatres. In the same way, Sophia does not know whether to condemn the corrupt Mme. Foucault, who has yet been so kind to her. Bennett quite rightly sets out to approach such a nebulous subject as the essence of France systematically, but in so doing he becomes less convincing. It seems at times that he is in France not because he is genuinely interested in it, but out of a sense of duty to his vocation. His comments are too methodical: when they appraise, it is for personal and not for national reasons. The editors of his *Journals* adopted the same

---

[3] See also the quotations on pp. 112 and 143.

frame of mind when they carefully indexed the most minute references to each of the cafés in Paris: obviously Bennett, a bluff northcountryman who can be trusted, is expected to supply future tourists with a list of the best haunts. His book must provide the definitive description of Paris: he is considered as a journalist. The result cannot fail to appear blunt and heavy-handed, especially compared with George Moore's charming if inaccurate accounts of evenings at the *Rat Mort* or the *Nouvelle Athènes*. The meretricious is a feature that appears mainly to the disappointed tourist who had expected too much.

II. THE 'SELF-UNCONSCIOUS'

The disillusionment is not, however, complete. Behind the disgruntled remarks and painstaking detail there is the suggestion of a coherent image. Bennett apparently felt a real sense of freedom in Paris, a city which can be partly forgiven for its pretensions on the strength of being the product of a very old civilization. This is what made him admire the scene in front of the café;[4] it also attracts him to French women, whose manners seem to be the ultimate achievement of centuries of effort.

Bennett tells in *Paris Nights* how he was invited to an artistic evening described on the card as *un peu de musique et d'agréables femmes*. He marvels at the scintillating conversation he heard, as Walpole must have done in the salon of Mme. du Deffand:

> Then the women joined in, and it was just as if they had all five learnt off by heart one of Landor's lighter imaginary conversations, and were performing it. Well convinced that they were all five absurdly wrong, fanciful, and sentimental either in optimism or pessimism, I nevertheless stood silent and barbaric. Could I cut across that lacework of shapely elegant sentences and apposite gestures with the jagged edge of what in England passes for a remark?

When they listen to music or poetry, Bennett admires them because they do not feel obliged to hide their feelings for either. A typical Parisian woman, bold and coquettish, arrives and holds the stage with an account of what a busy day she has had:

4 See above, p. 199.

It was the *journée* of a Parisienne who is also an amateur actress and
a dog-fancier. And undoubtedly all her days were the same: battles
waged against clocks and destiny. She had no sense of order or of
time. She had no exact knowledge of anything; she had no purpose in
life; she was perfectly futile and useless. But she was acquainted with
the secret nature of men and women; she could judge them shrewdly;
she was the very opposite of the *ingénue*.

Bennett met others like her. They are depicted as Christine in
The Pretty Lady, although Christine, as a courtesan, has some
purpose in life. Her simple shrewdness and natural common
sense combined with her utter uselessness attract Hoape, the
Englishman of fifty who is tired of the conventional falseness of
his West End circles. The same grace and distinction of movement, the same gentle delicacy characterize a prostitute who helps
to nurse the broken-down musician Diaz in *Sacred and Profane
Love*.

French women stand, in a way, for the social arts. In an essay
called 'French and English' (from *Things that have interested Me*),
Bennett links these with a lack of hypocrisy that he admires:

I would hold that the most important part of table manners is
conversation, and there the French are finished artists while we are
fumbling amateurs.

Further, the French can be urbane without cultivating make-believe.
Except when they want something very badly, they do not deny that
things are what they are. They admit and discuss the facts of life.
They have a proper intellectual contempt for hypocrisy, which is the
first and greatest curse of existence in Great Britain.

Freedom of expression, the greatest virtue of Paris, is evident in
social circles as well as in literature. During the course of the
artistic evening described in *Paris Nights* Bennett listens enthusi-
astically to a discussion on the hardships of prostitutes:

I then witnessed for the first time the spectacle of a fairly large mixed
company talking freely about scabrous facts. Then for the first time
was I eased from the strain of pretending in a mixed company that
things are not what they in fact are. To listen to those women, and to
watch them listening, was as staggering as it would have been to see
them pick up red-hot irons in their feverish delicate hands. Their

admission that they knew everything, that no corner of existence was dark enough to frighten them into speechlessness was the chief of their charms, then. It intensified their acute femininity.

Later he is struck by the same feature during an evening with a bourgeois family. A cousin who has just broken with his mistress calls in after dinner. The family all know about it, they sympathize with him and discuss the woman's faults and merits quite freely. To reassure his English readers, Bennett also shows the father going to say good night to his children in bed: in spite of the straightforward approach to love, family ties are strong.

Freedom is somehow even expressed in the street scenes. In the essay on 'French and English', Bennett points out that the French do not tolerate eccentricity and are always ready to say of something 'It isn't like anything else'.[5] He forgets this after a few pages, however, and goes on to say that the Frenchman prizes his individuality: he is not readily interested in public charities and movements, and does not form societies for meddling with other people's business and beliefs, such as one finds in Britain. At the times when Bennett is not at odds with Paris, it is the free openness of the people in the streets that he admires:

> There was everywhere a strange mixture of French industry (which is tremendous) and French nonchalance (which is charmingly awful). Virtue and wickedness were equally apparent and equally candid. Hypocrisy alone was absent. I could find more intellectual honesty within a mile of the Rue d'Aumale than in the whole of England.

This trait seems to encompass the faults and the qualities. In *Paris Nights* he finds a word to characterize it and that could easily have been 'the great central difference, the phrase which is to disclose the gulf': Paris is the 'self-unconscious'. Hence the candour and the blatant vice, the intellectual honesty and the impression that 'Paris is always forgiven'. The word is used in *The Old Wives' Tale* to characterize Sophia when she returns

---

[5] Bennett's translation of '*Cela ne ressemble à rien*'. He forgot that the English are quite ready to say, 'It looks like nothing on earth'. The idea comes from Arnold: the intellectual conscience, recognized standards.

from France and is seen out with her sister Constance, who is smaller: people notice the difference between them.

She ordered half a bottle of wine and drank two glasses. She stared about her quite self-unconsciously, whereas the little woman divided her glances between her companion and her plate.

The 'self-unconscious' could well solve many of the contradictions between the traditional merits and faults of France: it contrasts pleasingly with the covert self-indulgence so often felt in the English. It is also a step beyond the age-old image. In the eighteenth century, English visitors to France—Smollett, Walpole, Sterne—agreed that the French were not ashamed of their vices; but they were not frank, since they also suffered from an excess of politeness. This second trait, to a great extent superficial, was probably blotted out by the Revolution, but Bennett was the first to provide the correction. Such prejudice can easily live on in the national subconscious until someone contradicts it pointedly. As for the unashamed attitude of the French, it fits in with the old truism according to which in catholic countries sin is more readily shown and more easily forgiven, and also with Arnold's theory that the French have an intellectual, but no moral conscience. It is certainly the fairest way of expressing a truth about France that is often distorted and tainted, but it does not exhaust the 'great central difference'. Bennett himself could not have used it to explain the social virtues that he had also noted.

Bennett left Paris in 1909 and did not feel the need to explore the spirit of France any further. In four essays on France (in *Things that have interested me*) that form a sentimental autobiography of the francophile, he explains that he left because the permanent exile is a pathetic figure. In the remarks he makes, sentiment becomes all-important, at the expense of careful thought and of genuine feeling. Thus:

I definitely quitted the land where eating and love are understood, where art and learning are honoured, where women well-dressed and without illusions are not rare, where thrift flourishes, where politeness is practised, and where politics are shameful and grotesque; . . . I know why France is the darling of nations.

A good enough summary without the sentiment, but it is also a clean dismissal. Bennett regrets leaving Paris as he might regret moving from a well-heated flat to a more convenient but colder one, and that is all. In the same way, Sophia remembers France with affection on her return to Bursley which she finds so small and provincial and grimy, but later she does not give it a thought. The author sees that he has been an exile: as he had considered himself an apprentice realist before; as he had owed it to himself to go to Paris, he now owes it to himself to return. France does not stand for anything; he does not hate it, and he does not intend to draw on his experience to reform England. These are symptoms that reveal what I have called an 'ossified' image of France. In a way Bennett can be made to stand for the end of a quest.

From here onwards Bennett commits three blunders, which all derive from a lack of real interest. Even in *The Old Wives' Tale* the setting rarely reacts on the plot. Bennett went to some trouble to reconstitute the atmosphere of Paris in 1870, but Sophia might have gone through similar trials had she been exiled in Brussels or in Berlin, whereas in no other city but Paris could an American named Strether have become involved in quite the same way with a Mme. de Vionnet. The novel is about purely English feelings, and it uses a foreign setting. Scenes noted in *Paris Nights* or the *Journals* are 'used up' in it, and they have no further importance.

The first blunder is the misuse of French. This derives from an affectation of the nineties, when it became fashionable to flaunt one's knowledge of words and expressions. Harland and James illustrate it. Galsworthy sprinkles French colloquial phrases throughout his novels where three classes of people are concerned: aristocrats, artists, and lovers.[6] Bennett adds vanity to

---

[6] Thus Herr Paul (*Villa Rubein*): '*Allons! mon cher! c'est magnifique mais, vous savez, ce n'est guère la guerre.*' This is euphonically unlikely and irrelevant: a dog has just lapped up some soup.

Soames (*To Let*) is watching two prowlers in an art gallery: '*Epatant!*' he heard one say. 'Jargon!' growled Soames to himself.

A lover says in *The Dark Flower*: 'No, no, Oliver, *Dans l'amour il y en a toujours un qui aime et un qui se laisse aimer.*'

affectation and translates French speech literally into English. This does not succeed: it gives an impression of foreignness rather than conveying the feeling of the original. It can only lead to mistakes[7] or to the impression that the French are very queer birds, usually the view of hack novelists.

Secondly, he falls back into the insularity of Dickens and Carlyle concerning the childish passions of the French. The hysterical crowd watching the execution of Rivain, the elation in the Place de la Concorde at the false news of a victory against Germany, both in *The Old Wives' Tale*, are described on the supercilious level of *The French Revolution*.[8] In the second scene Bennett makes Chirac cry with emotion and shake hands with strangers after singing the *Marseillaise*. Meanwhile, Sophia feels that defeat is coming:

> She had no information, no wide theory, to justify her pessimism; nothing but the inward conviction that the race capable of behaving as she had seen it behave in the place de la Concorde, was bound to be defeated. She loved the French race; but all the practical Teutonic sagacity in her wanted to take care of it in its difficulty, and was rather angry with it for being so unfitted to take care of itself.

One would like to feel that Bennett is only describing Sophia's thoughts here.

Lastly, he propagates, on the most superficial level, the unfortunate view that the French air is pagan. Those English characters of his feel a lack of restraint as soon as they have crossed the Channel, even if they are only in transit on a train; and this impression is only confirmed if they come across the littered shards of the Bohemian Frenchman. Thus in *Sacred and Profane Love* Carlotta the novelist, trying to escape from an emotional tangle in London, tries a holiday at Torquay, but finds it is 'the chosen home of the proprieties, the respectabilities, and all the conventions' so she goes to France. Here she meets her lover by chance on the train. Under the effect of a French landscape, seen in the nick of time just before the train reaches Italy, they discover

---

[7] As above, see note on p. 203.

[8] In the first instance Bennett also follows the example set by Thackeray in 'Going to see a man hanged'.

their true feelings again. Later she returns to Paris and runs into Diaz, the concert pianist who had first seduced her in the Five Towns. He is of course on the terrace of a café. He is drinking himself to death with absinthe, but she cures him with the help of a kindly prostitute from the flat above.

This feature also appears in Galsworthy's *Forsyte Saga*. Paris is where Irene goes to free herself of her moral ties; it is there that she falls in love with young Jolyon, who is of course a painter. Galsworthy has at least the excuse that such a pattern is quite frequent in life. As Henry James put it, there is the dreadful old tradition that people's moral scheme does break down in Paris. Englishmen tend to travel there when they would like this to happen. But Bennett goes a great deal further, since his French women are always of loose morals. In *Whom God hath joined*, Renée, the governess, sins once with Charles Fearns and breaks up a family. Christine, the 'pretty lady', possesses innocent feminine grace, but her artless catholic faith leads her completely astray. We are reminded of Peregrine Pickle's godfather, who warned him as he set off for France to beware of priests, women, and false politeness.

· 9 ·

THE SALON

Bloomsbury

If London or Paris were to burn, if only for a fort-
night, literature and art would hurry back to the
study of princesses and to the language of the
Golden Age.

EDMUND GOSSE

This finest flower of social life refuses to bloom
where the English tongue is spoken. The explanation is usually that our women have not the skill
to cultivate it—the art to direct through a smiling
land, between suggestive shores, a sinuous stream of
talk.

HENRY JAMES

BLOOMSBURY is a legendary gathering whose existence is much discussed. The former inhabitants of Bloomsbury Square and members of the Society of Apostles who are still alive and within striking distance of literary historians usually hotly deny ever having had anything to do with such a group. Wild animals at the zoo are probably equally sure of being totally different from each other. In England, where introverted literary groups are rare, it is felt to be rather belittling to one's personality to be ascribed to one. Bloomsbury did not resemble the Rhymers' Club or the Camden Town Group in trying to build up a French *cénacle*. On the other hand, those scholars who are not concerned with debunking the debunkers of Victorianism set up Blooms-bury in a shrine, and some Americans amongst them find par-ticular satisfaction in proving who met whom where and when.

But we need not consider whether the Bloomsbury group existed or not. The problem is similar to the one of Shakespeare's 'identity': it is sufficient to say that there appears to the modern reader to be a remarkable phenomenon in a section of literature at the beginning of this century, and that Bloomsbury is a convenient name for it. The books make certain affinities clear: the image of France that we can evolve from the complementary remarks of Lytton Strachey, Clive Bell, Roger Fry, and their friends would on its own be sufficient proof of this. Though some of the books I am going to consider were published after 1918, I consider Bloomsbury as a pre-war phenomenon. The group was formed in the first ten years of the century, and one of its features is that it was influenced as little as possible by contemporary events. The Great War had if anything a negative influence on these writers: in trying to act as if what had happened between 1914 and 1918 could be forgotten, they emphasize all the more a state of mind really belonging to an age that had ended in 1918.

The prestige of France, increased amongst the less philistine sections of the reading public by the nineties, reached its peak in the first decade of the century for political as well as for literary reasons. The Entente Cordiale was not an important event in itself, dealing mainly with colonial matters. But certain sections of the press took it up with some enthusiasm two or three years later, as it became increasingly evident that the German Imperial Navy was being designed to challenge the British command of the seas. At the same time German trade began to compete strongly on the colonial markets. Faced with a common rival, England and France forgot most of their wariness. Only a few authors (Thomas Hardy for instance) retained the traditional view of France as a public nuisance. The Franco-Prussian War had not, after all, been a mere lesson to the French for their silliness. 'Splendid isolation' was forgotten; during the First World War England was to become violently 'continental' for four years. In the literary field, there was a huge boom in French books.[1] The popularity of the French symbolist poets was beginning to spread

1 See appendix.

beyond the few eccentrics who had introduced them into the country, and even realism had begun to gain a moderate currency. By 1918 Strachey was able to explain General Gordon's character with confident reference to Baudelaire's poems. French painting had also been recognized. The controversy around the post-impressionist exhibition of 1911 shows that Roger Fry's audience was larger than the men of the nineties had had for their eulogies: it proved that though the post-impressionists still appeared shocking, the impressionists had been accepted—hence the growing idea that France was a country of artistic pioneers.

But we have seen with Bennett that as the English adopted France, its literary image became less vivid. Bloomsbury moved away from Paris in a similar way. All the group, and Clive Bell in particular, made continual generalizations about France as if they were perfectly familiar with it, but in fact they were better acquainted with what had been written about it previously and what the French thought about themselves. Roger Fry spent years in Paris, but appears to have looked at little else but pictures. Clive Bell takes pride in having lived there in 1903 and made frequent visits later, for instance in 1921 to see the important *Salon d'Automne*: but no one could pretend to be a critic of art at that time who had not had such an experience. Besides, Bell also claims to speak French, but when he quotes the opinions of his Parisian friends and 'fellow artists' he does so in the ungrammatical French that he rather condescendingly attributes to Strachey in *Old Friends*.[2] Strachey himself, the high priest of Bloomsbury taste, never mentions anything more modern than Baudelaire. Writing to Virginia Woolf, who was staying in Paris, he said that he felt no urge to do the same: 'I think I should burst into tears if I woke up and found myself on the Pont Neuf.'

Unlike Bennett, Bloomsbury was genuinely interested in what it thought was France. The detachment of which we have just seen an instance is a general feature of its work. The exact opposite of the modern school that prides itself on being involved

[2] Bell says he has heard a phrase of Utrillo's so often he can repeat it: '*Sa peinture a une petite côté vicieuse qui est adorable.*' In the same essay Bell writes 'Beaudelaire' for Baudelaire, a mistake common enough among Cambridge students of French, but not perhaps among real francophiles.

in the contemporary scene, it had an ideal of cultivated leisure and preferred to show a wide knowledge of the 'grand tradition', of what Aldous Huxley described with reference to Strachey's criticism as 'the literary vintage of centuries'. This spirit partly explains the success of such works as *Eminent Victorians* amongst a public overwhelmed by the hardships of the decade. As a result, like the young Henry James, though for different reasons, Bloomsbury never thought of France separately from literature or art: and more particularly the works of the impressionist painters, the writings of Arnold and those of G. E. Moore.

I. THE GOLDEN AGE

It is always rather a shock to come across the photographs of the Bloomsbury group that have become the common property of literary historians: Strachey and Bertrand Russell sitting in comic positions in deckchairs, Desmond MacCarthy looking so like an Irish squire, Virginia Woolf in hats and dresses that cannot fail to suggest the comic films of the twenties. This is decidedly not how their writings make them out to be. In our century for the first time, the informal photograph has brought men of letters to life, and our illusions of them can no longer feed upon the studied and dignified frontispiece. They are both nearer and farther from us than before: they have become human beings, but their mere physical appearance empties the mental image drawn from their style and ideas. Also in this case the clothes are old-fashioned enough to look comic, but not ancient enough to look venerable: such was the impression they themselves must have had of the Victorians. Not only does each figure surprise us, but the setting itself seems wrong. We wonder what it is that is jarring. Then suddenly the deckchairs and suburban gardens and straw hats disappear, and everything falls into place. We are in an eighteenth-century *salon*, with Virginia Woolf reclining on a *bergère*; Strachey a thin wizened man, strangely reminiscent of a certain portrait of Voltaire, in an invalid chair by the fire; and Forster, Roger Fry, and Duncan Grant grouped around with powdered wigs and snuff-boxes. The scene is in France.

The works that spring to mind immediately are Strachey's

Landmarks in French Literature and his various essays, and Clive Bell's *Civilization*. In the first, Strachey insists on the continuity of the French spirit in literature and devotes most of his time to the *Grand Siècle*. For him the *fabliaux* for instance are no longer the first signs of sensual awakening, as they were for Pater: he sees them in a more sophisticated light.

The humanity, the dramatic skill, and the command of narrative power displayed in some of these pleasant satires, where the foibles and the cunning of men and women are thinly veiled under the disguise of animal life, give a foretaste of the charming art which was to blossom forth so wonderfully four centuries later in the Fables of La Fontaine.

Two-thirds of the book deal with the seventeenth and eighteenth centuries, and the author mentions repeatedly that these periods contain the essence of the French spirit. In *Books and Characters*, where the stress is laid on France, Stendhal is the only personality outside that age, but of course his ties with pre-revolutionary France were strong, and he used to speak of himself as a man of the eighteenth century:

sometimes, late at night, when the surroundings were really sympathetic, he could be very happy with his friends. 'Un salon de huit à dix personnes,' he said, 'dont toutes les femmes ont eu des amants, où la conversation est gaie, anecdotique, et où l'on prend du punch léger à minuit et demie,[3] est l'endroit du monde où je me trouve le mieux.'
And in such a Paradise of Frenchmen we may leave Henri Beyle.

Clive Bell suggests that the eighteenth century is the flowering of a national tradition: the salons are one of his 'paragons' of civilization, and are described at length. This French way of life, he says in *Civilization*, has been the most admirable in Europe 'for the last three hundred years'. Virginia Woolf recites the same creed as she speaks of the letters of Mme. de Sévigné:

Here is the garden that Europe has been digging for many centuries; into which so many generations have poured their blood; here it is at last fertilized, bearing flowers. And the flowers are not those rare

[3] Stendhal's spelling.

and solitary blossoms—great men, with their poems, and their conquests. The flowers in this garden are a whole society of full grown men and women from whom want and struggle have been removed.

Admiration or affectation? It is hard to see how they could decide that a given period was characteristic of France as a whole when they were not attracted by and knew little of modern Paris. The choice of the eighteenth century, too, seems strange at first sight: Pater had delved into the past of France, but had only mentioned Watteau because Watteau scorned the pleasures of his time; James had hinted that his Bellegardes were descended from something noble and ancient, but they are monsters of the Renaissance rather than eighteenth-century gallants. Since Canning's satires England had always considered the period frivolous. Historians and literary critics had mentioned it between 1900 and 1910 (most of the Bloomsbury essays are reviews of books), but there was considerably more interest in the seventeenth and nineteenth centuries.[4] It might seem that for Bloomsbury it was part of a general passion for that era. Strachey writes that the British spirit, too, was in its hey-day in the age of 'Walpole and Carteret, of Butler and Berkeley, of Swift and Pope'. We might think that France merely happened to be the country in which the eighteenth century had flowered best. All the works of Bloomsbury were about the past, but the nineteenth century did not really count as past: it was merely a recent lapse into darkness and Victorianism. Bloomsbury was therefore only adapting to its creed the general premiss that France was the home of art and of artistic living.

But this explanation is too neat to account fully for their attitude, which remains an affectation. The real test lies in a careful study of what was written: the glaring fact here is that though so much ink flowed over it, though to be admitted to the drawing-rooms of Bloomsbury Square one had to recognize it as the real age of enlightenment, no one really decided what was meant by 'the eighteenth-century salons'. There was no written dogma until 1928 and even that was muddled.

Strachey describes Mme. du Deffand as

4 See appendix.

perhaps the most typical representative of that phase of civilization which came into existence in Western Europe during the early years of the eighteenth century, and reached its most concentrated and characteristic form about the year 1750 in the drawing-rooms of Paris . . . it was the age of the Regent Orléans, Fontenelle, and the young Voltaire; not that of Rousseau, the 'Encyclopaedia', and the Patriarch of Ferney.

Mme. du Deffand's salon was indeed known to prefer the literature and habits of the seventeenth century. Though a few contributors to the *Encyclopédie* were to be seen there, Fontenelle, almost 100 years old, was an incarnation of the previous age; Voltaire, when young, admired classical tragedy and wrote a book on Louis XIV's time. But Mme. du Deffand's salon only became popular towards 1740 and went on until 1780, whereas the Regent Orléans had died in 1723. In the year 1750, the 'young' Voltaire was fifty-six and had been in Lunéville for the last three years. We can only conclude that the virtue of this salon, in Strachey's eyes, was that it looked back. This is confirmed when he excludes the second half of the century from his golden period, saying that Mlle. de Lespinasse and the emancipated Encyclopaedists were not congenial to Mme. du Deffand:

> Born at the close of the seventeenth century, she [Mlle. de Lespinasse] had come into the world in the brilliant days of the Regent, whose witty and licentious reign had suddenly dissipated the atmosphere of gloom and bigotry imposed upon society by the moribund Court of Louis XIV.

We should perhaps be lenient about dates, since Strachey is trying to define atmosphere more than anything else. Let us admit then that he admires the moral emancipation and yet the continued stress on the value of polite society in the first half of the century. Most authorities would agree on this. Lanson, whom Strachey had read, writes that after the middle of the century:

> *la vie mondaine devient plus intime, moins cérémonieuse, élimine la représentation au profit du plaisir. Le siècle tournera à l'idylle: notre beau monde traduira en sentiments et en pittoresque d'opéra-comique le goût de l'innocence rustique et de la belle nature que lui aura inoculé Rousseau.*

No sooner have we arrived at this plausible image, however, than Strachey contradicts it all in an essay on the Abbé Morellet in *Portraits in Miniature*. The theme is the *douceur de vivre* that only people who had lived in Paris just before the Revolution have known:

In Paris one's mornings passed in reading and writing—the quill dashing over the paper with a heavenly speed; and one's afternoons and evenings were spent in company. There were dinners at D'Holbach's; there were the nightly gatherings in the little rooms of Mademoiselle de Lespinasse; there were lunches with Mme. Geoffrin; and everywhere and always the conversation was copious and audacious to an intoxicating degree. . . . Then the more reckless spirits, headed by d'Alembert, would go out into the Tuileries Gardens, and, sitting under the trees, continue the discourse until the exploded ruins of religions, philosophies and conventions fell in showers about their ears.

This passage would suggest that, in spite of the moral inquiries of Rousseau, the second half of the century was interesting to Strachey for the very qualities that he had found in the first one: conversation, intellectual companionship, witty freedom of speech. There is a tone of incantation that suggests a search for something Strachey already knows or believes to exist. There is also a regrettable hint of boyish excitement at the thought of religions and conventions being exploded. Though Bloomsbury did no doubt talk audaciously, it was highly self-conscious. We are reminded of George Moore's pride at having sat up late smoking in Paris.

There are similar contradictions in *Civilization*. Clive Bell starts off by reviewing the most civilized periods in history:

From 1660 to 1789 is an age less glorious than that of Pericles, but hardly less renowned. It is the common opinion, and that it should be so is significant, that whereas the second half of the seventeenth century and the early part of the eighteenth is the greater, the second half of the eighteenth (which ends in 1789) is the more civilized.

This fits in with Lytton Strachey's second theory. But further on, Bell cites the *Hôtel de Rambouillet* as a near-perfect example of civilization. This salon was only active between 1620 and 1668 and it was eclipsed by others after Voiture's death in 1648: so it is outside even the 'wide' eighteenth century defined as 'from 1660 to 1789'. When Bell claims that it was a civilizing nucleus, he is being led too far back in his study of sources. In fact there were no salons of the sort he and Strachey describe until the turn of the century and the decline of Louix XIV's court, which had up to then been the main centre of society and the arts. The salons of the seventeenth century had been mostly given to political intrigue and refinements of language. Bloomsbury did not confess to admiring this, and yet there was a tendency not to make a clear enough distinction between Walpole's Mme. du Deffand and Molière's Philaminte.[5]

There are three reasons for this mistake. First, the men of the eighteenth century themselves confused the issue by claiming that their period was only a pale reflection of the one before, which—except in literature—was quite wrong. When Bell chooses his paragons of civilization it is evident that he is under the direct influence of Voltaire, who starts his *Siècle de Louis XIV* by a list that is identical, except that it does not include a period of Chinese history only discovered after his time. Secondly, most of these essays were written as book reviews, and in each case Bell and Strachey try to generalize from a limited topic they have not chosen themselves. Thirdly, their approach is too self-centred for them to bring themselves to admit they admire a general feature of French life and then show how the particular case illustrates, or partly illustrates it. The historian's ideal has to appear greater than the characters chosen for its incarnation.

All this points to the fact that Bloomsbury was transposing into the past ideals of its own: had it really discovered the salons in reading the literature of the eighteenth century, it would have known for sure which the golden period was. The salons were a

---

[5] In *Civilization* Clive Bell quotes Lanson as an authority:
'*L'hôtel de Rambouillet était avant tout un salon littéraire; on s'y communiquait des poésies, des lettres. . . . Ce public d'honnêtes gens et de femmes, connaisseurs en beau français—car on discutait avec passion des problèmes de grammaire, et l'on raffinait sur le style dans la chambre bleue—exerça indubitablement une influence sur la littérature et sur la langue.*' But Lanson goes on to make all sorts of reservations about the slide from '*rigueur*' into '*préciosité*'; he never suggests, as Bell does, that there was civilization here.

transposed ideal because of a feeling of exclusion from the present. Bloomsbury felt alien to its surroundings. Strachey's diatribes against the Victorians, amongst whom he had been brought up, are germane to this feeling. His reasons are those the reader will by now have become accustomed to—misplaced insularity (or admiration for national heroes), and the overtones of a conservative moral seriousness. In the nineties people had gone to Paris for much worse reasons. But the members of this group, though whigs, also belonged to patrician families descending directly from the eminent Victorians: they could not allow themselves the blatant originality of the aesthetes. Besides, as we have said, they already had an ideal of their own, handed down to them or acquired at Cambridge. They preferred to move away from modern England in time as well as in space. History is at once more secure and more amenable than reality.

The First World War emphasized this trend, crushing their hopes for a period of enlightenment after the burial of the Victorian age. 'It was no longer possible to believe that the world generally was becoming more civilized', writes Virginia Woolf in her life of Roger Fry. The love of the past became aggressive: significantly, the main articles of the faith were only set down in *Civilization* in 1928. Also, France had suffered enormously from the war. Had they wanted to return to the source of enlightenment in Paris they would probably have been disappointed. Even if there had ever been anything like it, it was clear in 1919 that the Paris of the 'gay nineties' no longer existed. We see George Moore, a francophile of the old school if there ever was one, and who looks rather out of place when he turns up again in the photographs of Bloomsbury, discovering this. On his return in 1919, he says everything has changed except perhaps the Latin Quarter, but even when he meets a student and a tramp in the Luxembourg gardens he talks to them of the Paris of the past:

how beautiful yon roofs, high pitched against the glitter. Our word castle evokes only images of moats and portcullises and rough life; but the French word château is evocative of the great kings of France; as we say it we see their curled wigs flowing over their shoulders, their gold-headed canes in their hands, and about them are many

P

beautiful women in hooped skirts that match the balustraded par-
terres.

He is obviously in the right frame of mind to turn towards the
past; indeed, he was writing *Héloïse and Abélard* at the time.
Though it is hardly necessary to prove that Moore's knowledge
of French literary history was poor, it is interesting that the
first reference of any note he made to the eighteenth century is
preposterous:

a century of feminine intrigue, subtle women devoted to the arts and
to the delightful abbés, who visited artists in their studios, drawing
attention to the points of their female models.[6]

An erratic picture, whether it was the subtle women or the abbés
who visited the artists. But George Moore was at least an authority
on the nineteenth century; yet in 1924 he completely changes
his outlook on it, such is the influence of Bloomsbury over
him. In a passage that savours of *Eminent Victorians* he notes that
fashion considers the eighteenth century mischievous and shameful, and goes on to attack realism, which is at the root of this:

We have always been under the domination of France, spiritually,
and having worshipped beauty must needs follow France into ugliness.
I would tell you who began the new cult if I could; there must have
been somebody before Courbet, who spoke about truth of effect and
local colour. Be this as it may, he was committed to it, and Troyon
still more so, and these were followed by Millet, who took it upon
himself to explain the miserable lot of the peasant. . . . Philanthropy
and realism entered into art arm in arm.[7]

Contemporary France no longer lent itself to idealized views,
but for Bloomsbury the eighteenth century was intact. The acute
sense of the past they drew from their familiarity with the byways
of literature helped them to build up a whole mystique around a
few brilliant figures such as Mme. du Deffand. They found in
retrospect, in the drawing-rooms of this most civilized period,
enlightenment and elegance, politeness and real friendship.

---

[6] Admittedly he was trying to shock his bigoted friend Edward Martyn.

[7] *Conversations in Ebury Street.* In a passage in *Confessions of a Young Man* the same
figures had been praised.

Sometimes the magic word 'France' provided a shell into which one could fit an eighteenth century of one's own. Roger Fry half admits this in an appreciation of Watteau where the painter is made to stand for an ideal dream world: Watteau's art, not the greatest, is of the kind that endeavours to 'gratify the imagined fulfilment of our egoistic wishes.' If we reflect on his paintings (perhaps, we may add, with Strachey's essays in mind)

we shall be endowed with a finer sense of the *nuances* of social life, a subtler apprehension of the meaning of a gesture, the implications of a smile. It is in that direction that Watteau gives to our earthly Paradise so distinctively French a quality, for it is only in France, perhaps only in eighteenth-century France, that the social temper was brought to so fine a point and so high a polish.[8]

The central expression of the ideal is in Strachey's essay on Mme. du Deffand. The passage is close to his heart, as we see from its position in *Books and Characters* and from the Bloomsbury-sounding adjectives such as 'consummate' and 'exquisite':

Never, certainly, before or since, have any set of persons lived so absolutely and unreservedly with and for their friends as these high ladies and gentlemen of the middle years of the eighteenth century. The circle of one's friends was, in those days, the framework of one's whole being; within which was to be found all that life had to offer, and outside of which no interest, however fruitful, no passion, however profound, no art, however soaring, was of the slightest account. . . Each individual was expected to practise, and did in fact practise to a consummate degree, those difficult arts which make the wheels of human intercourse run smoothly—the arts of tact and temper, of frankness and sympathy, of delicate compliment and exquisite self-abnegation—with the result that a condition of living was produced which, in all its superficial and obvious qualities, was one of unparalleled amenity.

Strachey is fairly lucid, even when indulging in this half-fanciful admiration. He admits that in these small circles there was a rigorous 'public opinion' and that they could be hives of jealousy. Though he smooths it all over with honeyed words, we can feel a harsh code underlying the brilliant surface:

8 Fry's dream of Watteau is at least more acceptable than Pater's.

Friendship might be allowed there, and flirtation disguised as love; but the overweening and devouring influence of love itself should never be admitted to destroy the calm of daily intercourse and absorb into a single channel attentions due to all. Politics were to be tolerated, so long as they remained a game; so soon as they grew serious and envisaged the public good, they became insufferable. As for literature and art, though they might be excellent as subjects for recreation and good talk, what could be more preposterous than to treat such trifles as if they had a value of their own? Only one thing, and that was to indulge in the day-dreams of religion or philosophy, the inward ardours of the soul. Indeed, the scepticism of that generation was the most uncompromising that the world has known; for it did not even trouble to deny: it simply ignored.

This correction is applied again to France in general in a letter from Strachey to Virginia Woolf:

The French seem to me a melancholy race—is it because they have no imagination, so that they have no outlets when they find themselves (as all intelligent people must) vis-à-vis with the horrors of the world? There's a sort of dry desperation about some of them which I don't believe exists with the English—even with Swift.

Strachey's own corrections of the picture are probably sufficient for us to put it back into perspective. The adjective 'decadent' might well be whispered of his idols. This view demands, however, a wider discussion, since Henry James has referred to it, and both Meredith and Bennett have praised the social and conversational virtues of the French. The salon is undoubtedly a French institution: as James remarked, it is unlikely that it will ever flourish in England, probably because women are given a different part to play in English society. They are taught to provide pleasant company rather than to tyrannize and provoke and sharpen the imagination and wit of the men who surround them; conversation with or before them is not a competition or a duel; they are not expected to bring a finer psychological insight as a leaven to brilliant social intercourse, and they are normally less sophisticated and demanding. Meredith's Diana Warwick is felt to be an exception in England. Her counterparts on the Restoration stage were imported from France, and Dickens's satire of the salon shows how alien their spirit was felt to be. Virginia Woolf herself, shy and unassuming in the company of her friends, when they used to meet with the Hôtel de Rambouillet in mind, must have been to them a living illustration of this difference.

The background to the Bloomsbury *montage* was thus well chosen. If they had to live retrospectively in the eighteenth century, then France was undoubtedly the centre of European culture at the time. Clive Bell points out that Newton had to be vulgarized by Voltaire, and Richardson passed on to the rest of the world through a French translation. Also, France had for some time deserved her reputation of being the home of refined conversation. A lively and subtle exchange in intelligent surroundings at the end of a meal is still preferred there to the English after-dinner speech, which usually lulls the mind instead of quickening it. The rough edges of romanticism hid this quality for a time; it is also most apparent during a rich and restful period such as the eighteenth century.

But on the other hand the Bloomsbury salons stand much correction. Apart from the fact that they need more historical precision, it is far from certain that they are, as Bell put it, 'a nucleus from which civilization spread outwards'. On the contrary, they seem to have concentrated civilization into small enclosed rooms and left depths of latent barbarity outside to remain forgotten, only to emerge during the Revolution. It is not even certain that they produced great works of art: the great men of letters of the time frequented them, but were not always inspired by them.[9] Voltaire, whose 'open house' at Ferney

---

[9] This point provides a perfect illustration of blindness in looking for what one expects to find. Bell quotes Voltaire to show that the philosophy of pleasure was dominant:

tout le monde avouait que les dieux n'avaient établi les rois que pour donner tous les jours des fêtes, pourvu qu'elles fussent diversifiées; que la vie est trop courte pour en user autrement; que les procès, les intrigues la guerre, les disputes des prêtres, qui consument la vie humaine, sont des choses absurdes et horribles; que l'homme n'est né que pour la joie; . . . Cette excellente morale n'a jamais été démentie que par les faits (Civilization, pp. 145–6).

Bell seems to miss the irony of the last sentence—indeed he may have misunderstood it, for he quotes it as if to prove that Voltaire agreed with the customs of the Orléans regency. In fact if Voltaire ever argued for luxury, it was for the many, not for the few. His youthful poem, in defence of hedonism, 'Le Mondain', was hastily corrected by its more utilitarian sequel, the 'Défense du Mondain'. The *Lettres Philosophiques* should dispel any doubt on Voltaire's opinion of most salons.

was really a relaxation from a huge literary production, despised
the easy kind of life they stood for. Finally, as Strachey himself
admitted, the salons were often literary academies or jealous
circles of a more petty sort. Writing at the same time, Proust was
vigorously exposing the salon of Mme. de Guermantes as a tangle
of snobbish rivalries. In his book on Proust, however, Clive Bell
does not mention this and leaves the reader with an image of a
gallant Marcel, with a flower in his button-hole, obsequiously
refined and polite, carrying on an exquisite conversation with a
duchess. Intimate friendship and artistic conversation were not
really to be found in Paris in 1660 or in 1750 or in 1910, so much
as in a certain book of highly tangled semantic philosophy, where,
towards the end, two sentences jar because of their clarity:

By far the most valuable things, which we can know or imagine,
are certain states of consciousness, which may be roughly described as
the pleasures of human intercourse and the enjoyment of beautiful
objects . . . the most valuable appreciation of persons appears to be that
which consists in the appreciation of their appreciation of other
persons.

At this point Bloomsbury, sheltered behind the parochial philosophy of *Principia Ethica* and a somewhat pretentious knowledge
of esoteric eighteenth-century literature, is three removes away
from France.

II. THE SENSE OF VALUES

Only the most ill-thinking critics of Bloomsbury would have
ventured to suggest to them that they were descended from
Matthew Arnold. Strachey's ironic essay on him sums up the
contempt it was fashionable to show for this would-be critic of
society who, being neither a born patrician nor a dedicated poet,
had neither the right nor the licence to preach with such authority. Seen from a distance, the truth appears very different. As
Strachey's literary criticism prolongs that of Leslie Stephen, so
Clive Bell's ideas on France derive clearly from those of Arnold.
At the end of the live period, Bloomsbury thus takes up and
confirms the foundations of the view of France. Scorn for the
nineteenth century did not change one's origins, nor could

Eminent Victorians exorcise the family ghosts. Arnold remained the Victorian Aunt Sally, a mildly ridiculous but close relation, whose early lessons had left their mark.

This is shown in a series of lengthy theories developed by Clive Bell and echoed in the works of his friends. I have already pointed out how *Civilization* begs the question by setting down an arbitrary series of paragons, and analysing them in order to recommend an ideal form of society that would have the same traits. It proves nothing, but reveals the ideals of its author. The periods Bell chooses are those that have left literary evidence of having practised G. E. Moore's ideal: friendship and refined conversation about the arts. The *Symposium*, the poetry of the decadent Roman empire, the correspondence of eighteenth-century Frenchmen are all interpreted as instances of salon culture. Bell then tries to discover more general reasons why such a perfect state of civilization should have occurred in France. His central passage is copied from another book of his, *Since Cézanne*, where he tries to explain why the French have a genius for painting,[10] so it would appear to be the mainspring of his thought upon France. In fact it is not clearly derived from either impressionist painting or the epistolary art of the salons, but from Arnold.

If we leave aside Arnold's moral condemnation of the French, his main points were that they had an 'intellectual conscience' and a 'social spirit of equality'. The second might well have been applied to the salons, but Bell concentrates on the first, showing that a respect for things of the mind gives the French an orderly consciousness of permanent values. In his terminology the idea is split under two labels: the 'sense of values', and 'reason enthroned'. For Bell they underly any civilization since the first steps that a savage takes are towards self-consciousness and critical reflection:

Self-consciousness, which leads to examination and comparison of states of mind, will give you the Sense of Values, while the Critical Spirit universally applied leads on to the enthronement of Reason as ultimate arbiter in questions of fact.

The first consists in

[10] *Civilization*, pp. 83–89, and *Since Cézanne*, pp. 130–3.

sacrificing obvious and immediate goods to the more subtle and remote. People who deliberately sacrificed comfort to beauty—with no practical or superstitious end in view—would appear to me to possess a sense of values. To prefer a liberal to a technical education, an education that teaches how to live rather than one that teaches how to gain. . . .

The second means that 'there is a prevalent opinion that everything requires, and must ultimately admit of, a rational explanation and justification.' The French eighteenth century surpassed all the earlier periods of civilization in that it combined the rational instinct and the sense of values. The Renaissance for instance had had the second but missed the first, except in the case of the 'airy Voltairianism' of Bonaventure des Périers and the 'dour, uncompromising atheism' of Etienne Dolet.[11] In the salons it was felt that Beauty was the utmost reason and Reason the supreme Beauty. Such was the harmony reached between the two norms that these people were able to enjoy pleasure rationally and to insist on reasoning being pleasant:

They believed so sincerely in pleasure that they thought even politics should be made agreeable. Economists were expected to present their theories in a form acceptable to fine ladies; but, remember, to be fine a lady was almost obliged to take an interest in theories. The serious discussion of fundamental questions, thought these amiable and courageous people, was not incompatible with good temper and humanity.[12]

Though Bell mainly describes the salons, he does suggest that these qualities are congenial to Frenchmen in every age. In an essay called 'Order and Authority' (the very title has an Arnoldian flavour) the two norms appear again, applied to modern France—the pleasure taken in Reason is what he calls 'order'; the desire for standards is 'authority'.

Since Arnold, the unfortunate expression 'Gallic logic' has gained currency:

---

[11] A 'subliminary' figure, like the Guérins, better known in England than in France. See the article by M. Pattison in *The Fortnightly Review*, 1881.

[12] These ideas are all borrowed from Lanson's *Histoire de la littérature Française*, vol. I, pp. 85–6, and his *Voltaire*, p. 85.

It is notorious that you may with impunity call a placable Frenchman *butor, scélérat, coquin fieffé, sale chameau, député* even, or *sénateur*, but two things you may not do: you may not call him *espèce d'individu*, and you may not say *vous n'êtes pas logique*. It is as unpardonable to call a Frenchman *illogique* as to shout after the Venetian who has almost capsized your gondola *mal educato*.

But as we have seen in the case of Bennett[13] such illustrations may give a pleasing impression of cosmopolitanism, yet reveal more of the author's ignorance than he would wish: *individu* has exactly the same derogatory meaning as 'individual' in its common misuse ('a rum-looking individual') and is not used as an insult. It might just as well be argued that because in the nineteenth century the English used the word *party* for a man in a derogatory sense, they were intense individualists. As for *illogique* why not translate it mildly as 'unreasonable'? Differences such as these, on an everyday level, are always exaggerated. True, Frenchmen appeal to 'logic' more often, and, to the Englishman's ear, more priggishly—it has been suggested that *logique* means what the English call 'cynical'—but when you hear two Frenchmen confronting their different versions of *logique* you realize that it is often only a manner of speaking.

Of course, as we have already noted in the case of Arnold, this trait applies most clearly in French literature, which claims the classical tradition of clear analysis as its directing force. For Strachey, Stendhal is an extreme instance of the French character. He can be compared with a brilliant talker in a salon, and thus illustrates the eighteenth-century ideal. On the other hand he idolizes what he calls '*la lo-gique*', for instance in the description of Julien Sorel:

we seem to be witnessing not so much the presentment of a fiction as the unfolding of some scientific fact. The procedure is almost mathematical: a proposition is established, the inference is drawn, the next proposition follows, and so on until the demonstration is complete.

The feature is due in this instance to the influence of Helvétius and Condillac, whom Stendhal admired. Here there are two

13 See footnote to p. 203 above.

obvious reservations to be made. First, national character has nothing to link it necessarily with stylistic tradition: if it had, why should the Puritans have objected to the very English traditions of the Elizabethan stage? At most, a particularly brilliant period may hand down a literary tradition that can be considered in some way to reflect the 'spirit of the age': thus, for instance, the French seventeenth century. When Strachey speaks, in summing up his *Landmarks in French Literature*, of the French clearness of mind he is taking a hasty step; up to then he has only spoken of 'psychological realism'. To illustrate this point, he makes a few remarks on the *fabliaux*, which reveal 'some of the most abiding qualities of the French genius', but the words he uses ('realism', 'cutting satire') still apply to style and not to character:

Its innate love of absolute realism and its peculiar capacity for cutting satire—these characteristics appear in the *Fabliaux* in all their completeness. In one or two of the stories, when the writer possesses a true vein of sensibility and taste, we find a surprising vigour of perception and a remarkable psychological power.

The other reservation is suggested by Strachey himself when he admits that there is also in Stendhal a man of passion and flourish:

in these rhapsodies he expresses in an exaggerated form a very different but an equally characteristic quality of his compatriots—their instinctive responsiveness to fine poses. It is a quality that Englishmen in particular find it hard to sympathize with. They remain stolidly unmoved when their neighbours are in ecstasies. They are repelled by the 'noble' rhetoric of the French Classical Drama; they find the tirades of Napoleon, which animated the armies of France to victory, pieces of nauseous claptrap.

Strachey mentions this almost reluctantly, as he only spares a few passing words for those French Romantics who were not faithful to the rational tradition. Yet it is a feature found in such very French people as Corneille and Victor Hugo, and could easily be generalized, as by Thackeray: but Bloomsbury was once again removed from reality, this time by the juxtaposition of a literary taste for the classical age and memories of Arnold's wavering racial psychology.

There is perhaps more truth and more direct experience of France in the second idea that Clive Bell develops from Arnold: the French submit to authority, and have standards. Critics of Arnold had complained, and he himself had not denied,[14] that there was too much conformity in France. It was a doubtful blessing that a minister of education should be able to say at a given time what all the schoolboys in the country were being taught. Clive Bell uses this apparently familiar debate, since he starts by describing the progress of a youth of probable genius in both countries. The English one meets philistinism, evoked by Bell in a way that would have warmed Arnold's heart, while his French compeer is

having rough corners gently obliterated by contact with a well-oiled whetstone, and is growing daily more conscious of his solidarity with his accomplices in a peculiar and gracious secret.[15]

This secret consists of the French conventions and rules. Unfortunately, it prevents many Frenchmen from becoming men of genius. They are taught standard accomplishments, whereas in England talent is given a free hand.

There are journeys a Frenchman dare not take because, before he reached their end he would be confronted by one of those bogeys before which the stoutest French heart quails—*C'est inadmissible, C'est convenu, La patrie en danger.* One day he may be called upon to break bounds, to renounce the national tradition, deny the pre-eminence of his country, question the sufficiency of Poussin and the perfection of Racine, or conceive it possible that some person or thing should be more noble, reverend, and touching than his mother. On that day the Frenchman will turn back. *C'est inadmissible.*

Bell points out that, for instance, the cartoonist Constantin Guys was considered eccentric in the Paris of the 1850's because he would not accept these two words. This feature has two results. On the one hand the conventions offer a comfortable partnership in civilization to a great many people: if they had to fight for themselves there would be few in the top class. Secondly, even in

14 See above, pp. 30-32.
15 This whetstone is linked with the idea that France could not produce poets: the nineteenth century believed that only an unpolished genius could write poetry.

the least fertile periods France has kept standards and has been an inspiration to the rest of Europe. A concrete example of this is to be found in French cooking:

you may dine at any of the half-dozen 'smartest' restaurants in London, pay a couple of pounds for your meal, and be sure that a French commercial traveller, bred to the old standards of the provincial ordinary, would have sent for the cook and given him a scolding. Consider, however, the cause: it is not that the most expensive English restaurants fail to engage the most expensive French *chefs*; they are engaged, but they soon fall below the mark because there is no one to keep them up to it.

Civilization, a book avowedly written to throw a clear light on to the values that 'Europe' has just undergone four years of chaos in order to preserve, thus justifies the important place it gives to France.

Another consequence of the French sense of conventions, developed in *Since Cézanne* and again inspired by Arnold, appears in a less favourable light: not only does France lack great men such as England's flamboyant Elizabethans[16] or original thinkers like Newton and Locke, but her culture is 'provincial' in that it is self-centred, and only admits the influence of foreign artist or philosopher if they are accepted by French authorities or translated. A French critic of Shakespeare would not be ashamed to admit that he had only read him in translation, whereas when Rupert Brooke mentioned that he had no French his comments on Racine were laughed at. Though French art, beset by convention, does not progress until fertilized by foreign influence, the French are too proud to admit this, and insist on placing their own culture at the core of everything.

A Frenchman discoursing on foreign peoples or on mankind in general—a favourite topic—suggests to me sometimes the fantastic vision of a dog-fancier criticizing a steer. Grant his premises—that whatever he admires in the one must be essential to the other—and nothing could be more just and luminous than his remarks. Undeniably the creature is a bit thick in the girth and, what is worse, bull-necked . . . there is not much more virtue in the objection to Shake-

---

[16] Strachey had two completely opposed sets of tastes in his explorations of esoteric literature: the French eighteenth century, and the Elizabethan dramatists.

speare's later tragedies that they are not written in rhymed verse. Blank verse, however, is not in the great tradition; and the French critic, with one eye fixed submissively on authority, doubts whether he would be justified in admiring it.

There is partial truth in these remarks. First of all, the suggestion that France has no men of genius is even less worthy of attention than the inference that she has no poets. But on the other hand French culture often is self-centred and does not recognize its benefactors. Few Frenchmen realize how much the 'physiocrat' philosophers of the eighteenth century owe to Locke and Hobbes, or that Newton's place in European culture is probably greater than that of Descartes. Though the French romantics knew of their debt to Byron and Shakespeare, it was only because these authors had been adapted and 'adopted' in Paris. In France more perhaps than elsewhere there are barriers around the national culture. Once these are passed, there can be excessive admiration: Bell mentions that Poe and Chesterton are overrated across the Channel, and we might add Charles Morgan and Lawrence Durrell, while pointing out, however, that these instances are all easy to explain by causes that have little to do with intrinsic literary judgement. Poe had been used as a platform by Baudelaire, Chesterton was a catholic, Morgan, known to be a francophile, had the good fortune to be admirably translated by René Lalou; and Durrell's experiments in fiction on a plane 'perpendicular' to that of Proust's, happen to coincide with an experimental phase in the French novel. The French do not make so much of English literature as the English of French literature; but we must remember that in the period immediately before Clive Bell the influence of England over France had been the exception for a very long time. When George Moore writes that Turner and Constable deserved more recognition from the impressionists than they received, he is making an adjustment in perspective, but should not be taken radically. In *Landmarks in French Painting* Bell exaggerates the 'continual coming and going between London and Paris': most of the traffic was outward-bound. As to the complaint that French authors do not read English, Bell forgets that French is professed to be understood in

London mainly as a literary pose. One wonders whether he himself read Racine perfectly, since he certainly misunderstood Voltaire and Renan.

The assessment of French standards is far more interesting. Bell, echoing Strachey's introduction to *Landmarks in French Literature*, is right in insisting on the permanence of values in France. The Michelin Guide to restaurants, with its elaborate system of rating, springs to mind. But a country can well stagnate because of this feature. Arnold set too much store by the French Academy, usually the backwater of French letters; the recent reform of the Comédie Française has attempted to change it from a place of traditions out of touch with modern acting as well as with modern writing. This is also evident outside the field of culture: the French army still trains its conscripts with rifles eighty years old and teaches its officers ground manoeuvres based on the blue-prints of 1915 campaigns. There is perhaps more willingness to change in England.

Clive Bell borrowed one last trait from Arnold: the particular kind of 'double-think' that praises France in such a way as to convince the English that all is well. The quotations above all have a semi-ironic note that is more damning than direct criticism. They lead the reader to think that French civilization is a curiosity rather than something to be seriously imitated. Arnold did this because his youthful enthusiasm had subsided, and he thought comparison in itself was profitable. It seems that Clive Bell did it because in the first place Bloomsbury was only trying to justify itself through France.

One instance should be sufficient to prove this. For Arnold, French intellectualism was democratic; Clive Bell and his friends make it aristocratic. For them France is no longer an idealized republic, but a society of leisure devoted to the arts and forming a civilizing nucleus. Clive Bell mentions 'an early essay of Renan's' in support of this point, but this is another of his blunders. Renan meant that the intellectual *élite* forms a kind of aristocracy: Forster understands him perfectly when he mentions 'the aristocracy of the intelligent and the sensitive'. But Bell seems to interpret this as 'the intelligence of the aristocracy': for him the leisured class is bound to be intelligent, for Renan the intelligent class must be given leisure.[17] A passage from *Civiliza-tion* makes this clear:

> The poor . . . are concerned actively with civilization only in so far as by their labours they make it possible, and, passively, in so far as their manners, habits, opinions and sentiments are coloured by it. For the positive and unmistakable characteristics of civilization it is useless to go to Athenian slaves or French peasants.

Arnold may have been blinded by nineteenth-century idealism in suggesting that all French peasants had received the sweetness and the light, but in return Bell is blinded by the myth of the eighteenth century in supposing that standards come from a leisured class whose business it is to maintain them. The French not living in salons are not equivalent to Athenian slaves, nor are they all educated, except for the purpose of an English argument.

III. SENSUALISM

In 1912 post-impressionism was becoming an artistic movement in England. After the second post-impressionist exhibition Roger Fry organized cultured meetings and French poetry readings for the 'masses'. The light that would finally defeat Victorianism had obviously come from France. Fry and Bell took up once again the idea that Paris was the traditional capital of the visual arts in Europe: it had been so for three centuries and its position was particularly high compared with that of London. Clive Bell wrote in *Since Cézanne*:

> In the old racing days—how matters stand now I know not—it used to be held that French form was about seven pounds below English: the winner of the Derby, that is to say, could generally give

---

[17] Bell does not give any reference, but it seems that he was thinking of *L'instruction supérieure en France*. Here Renan wrote:

> la haute culture est, à quelques égards, une chose tout à fait aristocratique. Pour y prendre part, il faut des études supérieures, une vie entièrement vouée à la recherche et à la méditation. . . . Pas plus dans l'ordre des choses de l'esprit que dans l'ordre politique et social, le peuple n'est capable d'analyser ce qu'il veut; mais il veut avec justesse. Ce que l'influence démocratique favorisera sera, j'imagine, très aristocratique.

the best French colt about that weight and a beating. In painting
English form is normally a stone below the French.

Fry, and Bell after him, undertook the artistic education of the
English public: they wrote histories of French painting,[18] and in
lengthy introductions they both made up catalogues of what the
word 'French' stood for. Nowhere is the artificiality of such
generalizations so obvious; nowhere do they appear so literary in
the worst sense of the word.

The sources of their ideas are literary in a slightly better sense.
Strachey had remarked that the wit of La Bruyère and Vauven-
argues was characteristic of their country:

> The greatest misfortune that can happen to a witty man is to be
> born out of France. The French tongue is the appointed vehicle of
> brilliant thought; an Englishman, if he would be polished, pregnant,
> and concise, must command, like Bacon or like Burke, not only a wit
> but an inspiration; and it is perhaps as difficult for him to translate a
> French epigram as to compose an English one.[19]

Translated somehow into the language of painting, wit is identi-
fied by Fry with a sharpened perception:

> the French are witty and that implies the power to see and express
> relations between things, so unexpected that the sudden revelation
> of them shocks us into laughter. It implies therefore, a peculiar alert-
> ness of observation and nimbleness of mind. In order to seize these
> unexpected relations, one must be able to turn very quickly this way
> and that, one must not be too much preoccupied with a single purpose,
> not too much set in one's track. Most people see only what they expect
> to see; anything that contradicts that escapes their notice, but the
> Frenchman tends to have more power to turn around and say to him-
> self 'How odd! that's like that, is it,' and he enjoys the fact that life
> is so full of queer and unexpected things. This implies of course a
> great interest in life as it is. We English are often so much absorbed in
> thinking how life ought to be. . . .

Fry compares two studies of the Virgin and Child, one by a
Burgundian artist and one by an Italian of the same period. The
Italian achieves greater rhythmic and plastic beauty, lending

---

[18] Clive Bell: *An Account of French Painting*, and Roger Fry: *Characteristics of French Art*.
[19] *Characters and Commentaries*. See Arnold's remarks on Joubert (above, p. 23).

meaning to his group, but the Frenchman is more interested in the natural pose of a mother with her child. He strolls around the town looking for his subject without any preconceived idea:

Suddenly he sees that young mother sitting with her baby, and in a flash of recognition he says to himself 'Tiens! voilà ma statue'. I have to say it in French because that word 'Tiens', for which we have no equivalent, exactly expresses that sudden alert turning of the mind in its tracks which is the special quality of French art.

We have somehow passed from wit to realism, and Fry is making of this modern style a feature of the whole French school. In *Since Cézanne*, Clive Bell calls this 'painting separate from literature' and uses almost the same words to describe the difference between Renoir and Piero di Cosimo as George Moore had chosen to explain why he dropped Shelley and took up Gautier.[20] He suggests that this 'down-to-earth' quality be called 'Frenchness', because it is to be seen in any French commercial traveller sitting at the Café Royal. He is making the mistake typical of the nineties: identifying the features of a particular style with the country that gave it birth. Thus in an appreciation of Renoir:

Here is the France of the young man's fancy and the old man's envious dreams. Here, if you please, you may smell again that friture that ate so well, one Sunday at Argenteuil, twenty years ago, in the company of a young poet who must have had genius and two models who were certainly divine. And that group with the fat, young mother suckling her baby—there is all French frankness and French tenderness and family feeling without a trace of its wonted grimness. . . .

And yet, turn over a few pages in Fry's *Characteristics of French Art*, and here he is saying the exact opposite. Literature (this time via Arnold) teaches us that the French are a logical race. Again translating this into the language of painting, Fry insists on the classical tradition in French art, on the desire for perfectly ordered and meaningful things. For instance:

When Poussin painted his picture of *The Israelites gathering Manna*, he did not, as Rembrandt would have done, project himself by an

[20] See *An Account of French Painting*, and above, p. 143.

effort of sympathetic imagination into the bodies of men and women dying of hunger; still less did he walk the streets to catch some stray hungry guttersnipe who had come upon a windfall, and note his gestures and expression. He began to think of what kind of gestures would be regarded by a rhetorical convention as appropriate to the theme.

This is illustrated by a good comparison of *The Massacre of the Innocents* with its preliminary sketch. In fact Fry now characterizes French art with the exact features that he had used to set it off in the work of the Italian artist. He is perfectly conscious of this: he makes the contrast the main theme of the book. French art is a perpetual dialogue between the rational and the realist principles. Poussin, David, Courbet belong to the first, Claude, Corot, Chardin to the second. But the argument is threadbare. When Fry discovers that the romantic school cannot fit into either group, he hastens to find another explanation:

It exemplifies neither the alert consciousness of actual life nor the passion for ordered construction.

It may be precisely because there is something exotic about the art of this time that the French seem to some of us to exaggerate its importance and to look upon Delacroix as one of their greatest artists.

Such criticism is dead. It would be as true to say that man is a perpetual dialogue between a piece of rock and a butterfly. Fry's analyses have of course a didactic value: to make the English public conscious of painting as something that could be explained and appreciated outside its traditional shrine. But as far as the view of France is concerned all this is devoid of meaning.

When writing about impressionists both Fry and Bell are far better inspired:[21] they choose the realist rather than the rationalist principle to characterize them. True, Fry proposes a compromise: impressionism is

typical of that French readiness to apprehend the unexpected aspects of actual life, but its data were explored with an almost scientific method and persistence which exemplifies French willingness to trust logical deductions.

[21] Fry: *Cézanne*, and Bell: *An Account of Nineteenth Century Painting*.

But this is hardly worth considering. On the whole, sensuous apprehension of the world is sought after, sometimes through vague, diaphanous shapes hitherto unexplored (Degas, Guys), sometimes through a new theory of light (Monet, Pissarro, Sisley). Fry's book on Cézanne tries to show how depths of purely plastic expression can achieve the weighty solemnity of the epic. Clive Bell then goes one step further, and says that French painters are interested in life: not life

with a capital L, but the good things of life, thought and feeling and sensation, bread and wine, sunshine and laughter, the pride of the eye and the lusts of the flesh, 'le vierge, le vivace et le bel aujourd'hui'.

Here he says that it is the essence of humanism. On another occasion he mentions 'paganism', and we are back once more at the idea that had haunted critics of art since Pater: 'French' means 'pagan', and perhaps 'immoral'. Bell shows that France in the nineteenth century needed a moral reform as badly as England.

Into this world came Edouard Manet, quite unconcernedly referring to the notorious fact that young ladies from Montmartre think nothing of bathing naked with young gentlemen who have often seen them without their clothes on, that *demi-mondaines*, lolling on *lits-de-repos*, receive nonchalantly bouquets from their 'kind keepers'. He called attention to it, by accident as it were, without one mitigating shudder or one palliating leer; he took it simply as the motive for a completely disinterested, a positively chaste, work of art. . . . No wonder the virtuous who gloried in their indignation at vicious scenes, and the vicious who revelled in their sense of naughtiness, were alike furious with the man who regarded such things merely as subjects.

This is exactly the view taken by the nineties, expressed perhaps more directly and eloquently. French art is sensual, close to paganism; it reacts against traditional morality; the opinions on artists naturally spill over on to French life in general. We have seen what these ideas are worth where immorality is concerned, but even from the point of view of art they stand considerable correction.

The struggle of the French school against middle-class prejudice has been exaggerated in England. They did not have to fight against a moral system, but only against the idea that literature and art should be moral. The Baudelaire and Flaubert trials achieved this, bringing France back to her tradition of artistic freedom, and henceforth they were not under any self-compulsion to be blatantly immoral—they were able to turn to problems of pure technique. Compare the paintings of Matisse to those D. H. Lawrence painted in a similar style; the first is a technician, the second a reformer. English observers, however, interpreted the movement according to their own intentions. They did not understand that the impressionists depicted scenes removed from ideal morality because painters tend to lead a more disorderly life than office clerks. What they wanted to crack was not traditional morality, but traditional perception.

Clive Bell and Roger Fry half understood the real aim. They called it, rather vaguely, 'significant form' and did not explain it any further: as with their myth of the eighteenth century and their remarks about the French sense of values, they were led off the track by their own preoccupations. This tempted them constantly back to the idea that the impressionists were sensual. In *Since Cézanne*, Bell made the unforgivable blunder of saying that Braque and Cubism were uncongenial to France: a mere glance at modern French painting as a whole shows that its aims are not sensual, but intellectual. Romantic art might conceivably be called sensuous, and yet even Delacroix had his pet theory about the relationship between painting and music. Pointillism, impressionism, cubism, orphism, futurism, vorticism, all these are intellectual attempts to reorganize perception in order to bring a created form to intelligibility. Ingres, Matisse, Cézanne, Juan Gris, Sérusier, were all speculators, half painters and half metaphysicians. They were imitating Nature, but not in the sense usually given to Aristotle's maxim and which makes him the apostle of realism; neither was it in the sense of a return to 'natural' morality, which was what Bloomsbury implied. They were imitating Nature in its creativeness and not in its shapes.[22]

Once more the Bloomsbury Group were seeing France at second

---

[22] Aquinas suggests this interpretation of Aristotle: '*ars imitatur naturam in operando, non in representando*'.

remove. In this they stand, in a different way from Bennett, for the gradual decrease of interest in France. They add little, except the myth of the eighteenth century, to the already formed image inherited from the previous fifty years. But they provide a pleasing end to the period, since they reach back through the nineties as far as Matthew Arnold, and help to show the unity of the live curiosity that sent three generations of English men of letters to Paris.

· 10 ·

THE USE OF FRANCE

Broke to every known mischance, lifted over all
By the light sane joy of life, the buckler of the Gaul;
Furious in luxury, merciless in toil,
Terrible with strength renewed from a tireless soil;
Strictest judge of her own worth, gentlest of man's mind,
First to face the Truth and last to leave old Truths behind—
France, beloved of every soul that loves or serves its kind!

THESE lines should ring familiarly in every Briton's ears,
since they were written by the most British of poets,
Kipling. They are the refrain to an ode to France published in 1913, and they sum up many of the more respectable
English feelings I have been trying to analyse. Since Fachoda,
Kipling had strongly advocated an Anglo-French alliance, and so
the Gaul turns up here, not frivolous, but with 'the light sane
joy of life'. The following line recalls the primitive strength of
emotions found in France by Pater. Then Kipling expresses
admiration for the quick recovery after the disasters of 1870
('strength renewed'), and alludes to the tradition of rational
humanism which had led Meredith, too, to see in France herself
her severest judge. France does indeed alternate between periods
of reactionary politics, during which old truths are given many
more chances than they deserve, and sudden radical changes.

By 1913 England was probably ripe anyway for the anti-
patriotism of certain men of letters during the previous sixty
years to bear fruit. The Appendix will show how the interest
in France had reached a really popular level. Even without the

war, the live period of interest would probably have faded away.

During the following four years the approach to France changed radically. Over five million Englishmen, not all gentlemen, were transported into Flanders and Picardy to dig trenches in the tireless soil and fire guns at members of a race their fathers had been convinced was closely related to theirs. The war produced a mass of literature, and one would expect much of it to relate to France. But this is not so, for a variety of reasons. The British and French armies kept to their own sections of the front, so there was little contact between them, except over a small area and at staff level. General Haig did not particularly encourage francophily at his headquarters. Also, the warfare was so devastating for the civilian population, that along most of the front fighting took place around abandoned villages. There were towns in the supporting area, but with the apparent exception of Armentières, contacts between troops and civilians were not widespread. Night clubs were forbidden, and some British commanders closed down the licensed brothels in their district. It should be remembered, too, that Picardy and Flanders are not among the most distinctively 'French' districts: many of the inhabitants speak Flemish, and the tourist usually hastens south through this rather desolate country. Sightseeing elsewhere was obviously out of the question. The few British officers who took leave in Paris 'saw the village', enjoyed cocktails, champagne, and women, but Paris was very subdued. Public entertainment was scarce, 'night life' prohibited. One meets First World War veterans who still speak of Paris with a sparkle in their eye, but I wonder how much they saw only because they went there with the preconceived views handed down from the nineties. London was undoubtedly a gayer place during the war years.

All this explains why the literature about France produced during the war is negligible. Of course, there were hymns of praise for the new ally, written by people who had not been the most active admirers before: Galsworthy, Gosse, Bennett, Maugham. But, with the exception of Henry James, they merely made slightly hysterical speeches of the sort people will listen to in wartime. Memoirs of life in the trenches did not include more than a few hints about the French. They were supposed to be cruel to prisoners: German soldiers were always relieved to fall into the hands of the British. They were said to be less paralysed by red tape at headquarters, and to be very brave in the trenches. There is very little else. The soldier poets rarely mention France, except when they conclude with a contrast between some hero's former life and his present fate. A few novels inspired by the war were written in the twenties, but they are influenced as much by previous literature as by direct experience. Though the war must have had some effect on the view of France held by the common soldier, it did not operate through literature, and therefore has little to do with this study. The literary content of the word 'France' remained more or less the same.

Like many adjectives of nationality, 'French' is ambiguous. It has a denotation and a connotation. Adjectives made from names of small, new, or distant countries only possess the former: no one in England would dream of saying of an event that it is typically *Belgian* or *Finnish*. Others, such as German or American, apply to something more than things and people made or born in, or belonging to, America or Germany. They extend to a connotation that is fortuitous and problematic. 'French' is the most important of these.

Its connotation varies in history. At times it is reduced to a few clichés; at others it swells and can reflect many real or imaginary aspects of English and French life. During the period between 1850 and 1918 it was very suggestive. This does not mean that all the men of letters contributed to it, or indeed showed any interest in it: Gissing, Wells, Shaw, and others are noticeably absent from this study. But by now three things should be sufficiently clear. First, 'French' meant a great deal more in 1918 than in 1850. It stood for a moral attitude, condemned or praised as 'sensualism' or 'paganism' by Victorians and by would-be reformers; it had become almost a synonym for 'artistic'; and it implied refinement both of manners and of ideas. Secondly, it had been emptied of some traditional meanings still to be found, for instance, in Thackeray and Meredith. Whereas in 1850 it was not after all inconceivable to those who had not travelled that

Frenchmen wore green ribbons and danced or fenced their way through barricaded streets, the young man we imagined visiting France in 1918 could think none of these things. Thirdly, its literary 'charge' has decreased appreciably since the twenties, and has passed down into the stereotype held by the man in the street. Current clichés such as 'logic', 'naughty', and images such as that of the painter or the brilliant conversation, stem from the literary debates we have explored.

Buckle's prophecy that the reputation of the French in England would improve has come true, but not because of the steam engine so much as through an obscure loss of confidence in purely English values at the end of the Victorian age. Admittedly, the economy of the twentieth century has tightened the links between countries. Europe has, between 1850 and 1918, become more cosmopolitan and the old national traits have been blurred. Many of the books we have considered were written at a time when the French were as 'foreign' as Russians are to us now. But if this were the only influence at work it would make for a denial of 'French' characteristics, whereas we have seen that in fact in 1918 the English merely hated or loved their neighbours for more subtle reasons than before. The active interest was literary, and died out in the thirties, when there was no further reason for it.

Perhaps the most noteworthy feature in this complex quest is that none of it was idle curiosity. A few figures such as Henry James were content to watch and describe the attitude of the others. But all these little stories have an English meaning. This alone is why, from a French standpoint which they did not share, I have found so much to criticize in their views. Less superciliously than Arnold, but with equal devotion to their task, all these writers explored France to find answers to their own problems. It is over two centuries since a Frenchman last did this in England. Perhaps, then, France is the source of light, as a certain tall statemonger would have it. Or perhaps Arnold was right after all and the English are a more earnest nation.

APPENDIX

France and the Book Trade

I HAVE shown, I hope, that the period of active interest in France culminated in the first decade of this century. One would expect it to have seeped down through the various levels of the book trade by then, and reached the popular levels of taste. My wife, who has examined the publishers' lists between 1900 and 1920, found this theory confirmed by the sheer number of books connected with France. There was a sharp rise in the selling appeal of France in 1903, a slight fall in 1910, and a slow decline beginning in 1913. At that time an average of 320 books a month was published, including reprints: roughly 4,000 a year. Of these, 160 a year were either translations from the French or concerned with some aspect of France: a total of 1,600 for the ten years from 1903 to 1913.

A closer look at the subjects the English were interested in revealed the following:

Books on Napoleon and his family   92 (i.e. 9 each year)
Books on the Revolution   70
Books on the rest of French history 120
    Mediaeval France   20 (Joan of Arc 7)
    Sixteenth century   10
    Seventeenth century   25
    Eighteenth century   16 (this shows that Bloomsbury were being
    Nineteenth century   39   somewhat original)
    Twentieth century   4
Travel and guide-books   107
French literature   61
French readers, grammars   59
French art   34

We then consulted the lists to find out exactly which books were deemed worthy of translation from the French:

Novels (including 2nd editions)   328
Theology   68
Technical scientific works   54
Poetry   37

Artistic theory	36
History (not including French history)	31
Medicine	29
Politics, economics, sociology	28
Geography and travel	25
England and English subjects	22
Philosophy	20
Children's books	9

Translations from the French outnumbered those from any other language by about eight to one. Of the French literary figures most popular in London the best seller was undoubtedly Dumas: each of his three books in the d'Artagnan series went through five editions in the ten years. He was followed by Hugo, Anatole France, Balzac, Molière, Daudet, and Montaigne, whose presence is perhaps more flattering to the English taste of the time.

In the following list titles that reached two editions or more are included in brackets:

	TRANSLATIONS	ORIGINAL BOOKS
Middle Ages:		
Aucassin et Nicolette	3	
Tristan et Iseult	3	
Héloïse et Abélard	2	
(the popularity of *Aucassin et Nicolette* was obviously due to Pater's study)		
Sixteenth century:		
Montaigne	11	2
Rabelais	6	
(no trace of the poetry of the Pléiade)		
Seventeenth century:		
Molière (mainly for schools)	14	3
Descartes	4	1
Pascal (*Pensées*)	4	2
La Rochefoucauld	4	
Mme. de Sévigné	3	
La Bruyère	3	
(no trace of Racine)		

	TRANSLATIONS	ORIGINAL BOOKS
Eighteenth century:		
Rousseau (*Confessions*)	4	5
Voltaire	3	4
Saint-Simon	3	
Bernardin de St. Pierre	2	
Beaumarchais (for schools)	2	
(no trace of Diderot)		
Nineteenth century:		
Dumas (*Monte Cristo, Tulipe Noire, Crimes*)	69	
Hugo (*Notre-Dame, 93, Légende des Siècles, Burgraves, Bug-Jargal*)	26	2
Anatole France (*Reine Pédauque, Jocaste*)	23	1
Balzac (*Père Goriot, Maximes, Eugénie Grandet*)	19	4
Daudet (*Tartarin, A Passion of the South*)	13	1
Bourget (*Divorce*)	8	
René Bazin	8	
Chateaubriand (*Mémoires d'Outre-Tombe*)	7	1
Flaubert (*Tentation de St. Antoine, Salammbô*)	7	
Pierre Loti	6	
Gautier (*Stories*)	6	
Renan (*Vie de Jésus*)	5	
Sainte Beuve	4	
George Sand (*François le Champi, La mare au diable*)	4	1
Musset	4	
Lamartine	3	
Maupassant	3	2
Comte	2	
Mme. de Stael	2	
Mérimée (*Colomba*)	2	
Baudelaire	2	
Stendhal (none of the novels)	2	

	TRANSLATIONS	ORIGINAL BOOKS
Tocqueville	2	
Zola	2	I

(no trace of Nerval or Rimbaud)

Amongst French artists, the most studied is Watteau, followed by Millet and Rodin, then Delacroix, Berlioz, and Puvis de Chavannes. There was a vague awareness of a 'Barbizon school', but there is nothing more recent.

Finally, in 1903 the *Book Monthly* interviewed booksellers in London to find out which were the foreign books sold. Statistics are of course impossible here, and it is extremely difficult to find out which books were imported; but the answers of the various dealers show that the authors the English read most in the original were Maupassant, Daudet, and Balzac, followed by George Sand, Anatole France, and Zola. The list contains no surprises. In poetry there was a market for Musset, Baudelaire, and Verlaine. Here again, the largest demand was for works on Napoleon and his period. The *Book Monthly* got similar answers from the second-hand dealers. One respectable shopkeeper replied: 'Which sell best? These, I am sorry to say [*indicating a pile of yellow-jacketed novels*]. We sell 'em as soon as they can be unpacked; we can't keep 'em.'

Another one, asked why people chose French books, said: 'Why French? To improve their knowledge, and because they expect something a little—a little—what could I call it—something a little *chic*.'

INDEX

MATTHEW ARNOLD

Early Poems (1849)

A French Eton (1864)

Essays in Criticism (1865)

On the Study of Celtic Literature
  (1867)

Literature and Dogma (1873)

Mixed Essays (1879)

Irish Essays (1882)

Essays in Criticism (second series)
  (1885)

Discourses in America (1885)

GEORGE MEREDITH

......nin (1865)

........ne : 'Ode to France' (1870)

*'Ode on the Proclamation of the
  French Republic'* (1871)

Up to Midnight (1873)

Beauchamp's Career (1874)

The Egoist (1879)

One of Our Conquerors (1891)

Swinburne : *Rondeaux Parisiens*
  (1894)

An Essay on Comedy (1897)

THE BLOOMSBURY GROUP

Strachey : *Landmarks in French
  Literature* (1912)

Strachey : *Books and Characters* (1922)

Bell : *Since Cézanne* (1923)

Bell : *Landmarks in Nineteenth-
  Century Painting* (1927)

Bell : *Civilization* (1928)

Strachey : *Portraits in Miniature* (1931)

Bell : *An Account of French Painting*
  (1931)

Fry : *Characteristics of French Art* (1932)

ARNOLD BENNETT

Whom God hath joined (1906)

The Old Wives' Tale (1910)

Paris Nights (1913)

The pretty lady (1918)

Sacred and profane love (1919)

Things that have interested me (1922)

Journals (1932)